The Wrongly Executed Airman

The Wrongly Executed Airman

The RAF's Darkest Hour

ALAN STRACHAN

Pen & Sword
MILITARY

AN IMPRINT OF PEN & SWORD BOOKS LTD.
YORKSHIRE – PHILADELPHIA

First published in Great Britain in 2023 by
PEN AND SWORD MILITARY
An imprint of
Pen & Sword Books Limited
Yorkshire – Philadelphia

Copyright © Alan Strachan, 2023

ISBN 978 1 39904 103 4

Typeset in Times New Roman 11/13.5 by
SJmagic DESIGN SERVICES, India.
Printed and bound in the UK by CPI Group (UK) Ltd.

Pen & Sword Books Limited incorporates the imprints of Atlas, Archaeology,
Aviation, Discovery, Family History, Fiction, History, Maritime, Military,
Military Classics, Politics, Select, Transport, True Crime, Air World, Frontline
Publishing, Leo Cooper, Remember When, Seaforth Publishing, The Praetorian
Press, Wharncliffe Local History, Wharncliffe Transport, Wharncliffe True Crime
and White Owl.

For a complete list of Pen & Sword titles please contact
PEN & SWORD BOOKS LIMITED
47 Church Street, Barnsley, South Yorkshire S70 2AS, United Kingdom
E-mail: enquiries@pen-and-sword.co.uk
Website: www.pen-and-sword.co.uk

Or
PEN AND SWORD BOOKS
1950 Lawrence Rd, Havertown, PA 19083, USA
E-mail: Uspen-and-sword@casematepublishers.com
Website: www.penandswordbooks.com

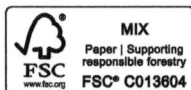

MIX
Paper | Supporting
responsible forestry
FSC
www.fsc.org   FSC® C013604

Contents

PART TWO

Author's preface to readers

I was introduced to the Tom Hutchings case when a wonderful man by the name of Bill Breuer, the driving force behind the amateur dramatics group in the small New Brunswick town of St Andrews where I lived, talked me into taking on the role of Crown in a courtroom drama he had written for local consumption.

We scheduled only four performances in the church hall due to an anticipated lack of interest, but as it turned out, not only was every seat sold, chairs had to be jammed into every accessible spot to double the amount of available seating in order to accommodate the overflow. We even sold seats in the jury box for an extra $5 each.

But as I stood up at the front of the room in my prosecutorial robe, haughtily challenging the defence's assertions, I kept thinking to myself, 'This man deserved a better defence. How was the original Crown allowed to get away with this?'

I was so intrigued by that question that I started looking into it.

The trial we were dramatizing had taken place in 1942 about 100 yards from the church hall, and still elicited an air of notoriety locally. I followed an extended response-chain of 'I don't know, but I can give you the name of a guy who might', and eventually learned that a man called Richard Blatchford had been similarly intrigued about fifteen years earlier and had done some proper research.

It took months to track him down, but when I did, he was incredibly gracious.

'I'm just an amateur historian,' he said over the phone. 'I'm looking into something else now. I did get some information on the Hutchings case a long time ago, but I'm not a writer. You're a writer and I'd love to see this story get told. You are welcome to use anything I have.'

It was about eight months after the play's run when we finally met, just outside Boston where he lives, and true to his word, he handed over a drawer full of paper. Much of it wasn't relevant. There was a lot of duplication.

But there were also items that were absolute gems. Once I saw them, I knew that I had to dig deeper. This is not meant to belittle Dick's work. The Canadian right-to-access laws have changed appreciably since Dick conducted his research. He requested certain documentation and was turned down. I asked for the same documentation and got it. And the government's tracking notes attached to those documents made it clear that no one, other than the civil servants who maintained the files, had ever seen it.

Without Dick's groundwork, this book would never have come about. Bill Breuer based his play on contemporary articles written for a local bi-weekly newspaper and he had no access to court records. Everyone I spoke to, even some government employees, insisted that the trial transcript had been sealed for 100 years. Not until I initiated the process of filing to have that embargo lifted did I learn that the proscribed period was fifty years, not 100.

Then, through a stroke of sheer luck, I was given an original copy of the transcript from the preliminary hearing. As far as I know, this is the only such document in existence and it provided a great deal of illumination, because even though testimony is given under oath, it might not be used in the trial itself or might not be admissible.

Nevertheless, there was still a lot of work to be done. As usual, I enlisted Marian Strachan to edit the manuscript as it evolved, and she did her typical excellent job. Gary Clewley, a Toronto defence lawyer, provided important advice regarding courtroom strategy. A retired New Brunswick judge, who shall remain nameless, was kind enough to read the finished product and assure that it was free of mistakes as far as trial procedure is concerned.

Barry Murray, an amateur, but dedicated, historian in St Andrews, not only set me on the right path again and again but also opened many doors that probably would have otherwise remained closed. Another St Andrews' resident, Sheryl Crighton, also pitched in with some crucial legwork and research.

And then, when it was time to put it all together, Lucie Leduc was invaluable in helping me to come out on top in the endless battles I wage with technology, especially computers.

I hasten to add that it is a work of non-fiction. Every piece of testimony comes from court documents. The sources of other quotes are made clear. Any speculation or conjecture is clearly identified as such.

Therefore, I have no excuses. The mistakes won't be in the documents; if there are any, they will be mine.

PART ONE

Chapter One

Had it been later in the year, Dennison Guptill probably would have tried to stall Royden Connors. He might have told him to phone again in the morning, using the excuse that it would soon be dark. Or he might have pointed out that it was after 6.45 p.m. on a Sunday, and in a Canadian fishing village in 1942, the only thing you were expected to do on a Sunday evening was go to church.

But the date was 7 June. The longest day of the year was less than two weeks away, so Guptill, the chief of police in tiny Black's Harbour, New Brunswick, acceded to Royden's request. He would use the remaining daylight to go out and look for Bernice – Royden's missing teenaged sister who hadn't been seen since she left a local dance late Friday night.

Since he was not only the chief of police but the entire Black's Harbour police force, there was little else Guptill could do. He would certainly have noticed that a large number of villagers were getting increasingly agitated about the lack of any official action on his part. Many of them had even gone out to look for some sign of Bernice as early as Saturday afternoon and now, around the same time that Royden made his phone call, Constable William Chahley of the Royal Canadian Mounted Police (RCMP) detachment in Saint John, the largest city in the province, had arrived in town.

Like most Canadian provinces, New Brunswick had no provincial police force, so scattered RCMP detachments got involved in matters that community forces and local marshals couldn't handle. A Mountie in town probably meant that someone had bypassed Guptill and requested the force's involvement in the search for Bernice Connors.

So, when Royden added his voice to the chorus, Guptill finally went to work.

It is understandable that Guptill would have had mixed feelings about taking part in a hunt for a missing 19-year-old girl. He had been a policeman for fifteen years, and if he had believed there was any possibility of foul play, he probably would have sprung into action quickly and taken the search very seriously. But he knew from experience that teenaged girls were much more likely to be involved in mischief than in foul play, especially in a village like Black's Harbour, where serious crime was rare. There was a certain amount of transience in the community, as is often the case with ports, especially wartime ports, but the population was no more than 1,500.

In any village, a commotion quickly creates interest, and interest creates a crowd. Already, three teenaged friends of Bernice, as well as her 25-year-old sister Etta, were nearby, letting it be known to anyone who would listen that they thought Guptill should comply with Royden's request.

In addition to the other factors, there is little doubt that Guptill ever forgot for a moment that Black's Harbour was a company town. His job was police chief, but his employer was Connors Brothers Ltd., the company that Bernice's grandfather and grand-uncle had founded in 1889. Originally, it was a canning firm handling several products, but the brothers soon realized that the millions of sardines brought into the port each year from the Bay of Fundy provided the most lucrative line. The company blossomed – so much so that even today, Connors Brothers, using the trade name Brunswick, is the largest sardine producer in the world. By 1942, the company had changed hands and was no longer owned by the Connors family, but nevertheless, the Connors name was still revered locally.

As soon as he stepped outside, Guptill met Thomas Gaudet, the caretaker of Forrister Hall, the community hall that had been the site of the Friday dance. The gaggle of girls, sensing what passes for excitement in a village, joined in. They too wanted to contribute to the search. Although they all had varying degrees of concern about Bernice, it is unlikely that any of them envisioned what had really happened.

Bernice was, after all, what the newspapers would describe in days to come as 'a flirt' or 'a tease'. She was also known to drink heavily for a 19-year-old. In fact, as far as the law was concerned, any drinking by a 19-year-old was too much. The minimum legal drinking age in New Brunswick in 1942 was 21.

It was not uncommon for her to spend a night away from home, especially after a dance, but by the time the search began, she had been gone for two nights, more than the norm. Sometimes she stayed with her sister in Pennfield, about 10 miles away, but Etta had gone to Pennfield and learned that Bernice hadn't been there. Another friend, Cavell Bradford, often provided a bed for the night, but she, like a number of other friends who were canvassed, had not seen Bernice since Friday night. Even though the

3

level of concern was simmering and had prompted the flurry of Saturday-afternoon activity, it had not reached boiling point.

The group headed towards Forrister Hall on Deadman's Harbour Road, and as they did so, Gaudet told Guptill that he and his friend Oscar Craig had been walking further down that very road a couple of hours earlier and had found some items that piqued their interest.

It was widely known that late Friday evening, Bernice had left the dance in the company of a serviceman, and that the pair had walked along Deadman's Harbour Road. Guptill and Gaudet headed in the same direction.

There were a few houses scattered alongside, but for the most part the land was open and treeless. It was covered with weeds, an occasional stunted spruce tree, low shrubs, wild grasses and some of the moss that is peculiar to the area.

They walked away from the hall, along the 712 feet of paved road, and then came to the unmade section. The electric streetlights ended with the paving, even though the transmission line continued. At night, only the light from the heavens would have prevented the area being pitch black.

At the side of the road, 30 yards along the unmade portion, Gaudet pointed out to Guptill some apparent signs of a scuffle that he and Craig had noticed that afternoon.

It was there, Gaudet said, that he had found a woman's shoe which he had picked up, and then put down again. The men had walked a little further before turning around to go back to town, and had noticed that the shoe was still there.

Nearby, Craig had spotted a green plastic ring, about an inch in diameter. When he picked it up, he realized that it was attached to a chain of similar rings and appeared to be a necklace. He passed one of the rings to Gaudet who put it in his pocket.

After Gaudet had gone home and discussed with his wife what he had seen, he had returned, retrieved the shoe and taken it home. Both the shoe and the ring, Gaudet explained, were now at his house and available for Guptill to examine.

As the men discussed the importance of those items, Constable Chahley arrived with yet another Mountie, Constable Duncan Dunn of the nearby St George Detachment. Chahley marked the spot with a stake, and the group moved on – this time without Gaudet, who, feeling that his participation was no longer needed, went home.

There is little doubt that had he known what was coming, he would have stayed.

The girls had moved ahead when the men stopped, but their mood had changed. Now, this appeared to be serious, no longer a light-hearted search for a friend who was possibly cuddling with a soldier somewhere. Now, there was no doubt about it. A Mountie in Black's Harbour was not a rare occurrence, but it was not terribly common either. To have Mounties from two different detachments showing up to look for a missing girl had the whole group fearing the worst.

It was a fear that would soon be justified.

As soon as the three men caught up with the girls, the search intensified. About 250 yards past the point where Gaudet had found the shoe, only 15 feet from the roadside, Constable Dunn discovered what appeared to be its mate.

At this point, the accounts differ slightly. Guptill later said he stood back and scanned the surroundings. Fifty feet away, there was a mound of moss that appeared to be slightly discoloured. 'I could see from that distance,' he said, 'two bright spots protruding from the moss which impressed me at that time as being light-coloured cloth.'

The four girls had already wandered near that pile of moss and had almost stepped on it without recognizing its significance. Moving closer, Guptill realized that what he had seen protruding from the moss was a human foot, and shouted, 'There she is!'

But contemporary reports say that it was one of the girls, Freda Wright, who first pointed out the body, and Dunn said it was a female who shouted, 'There she is.'

When asked about Guptill's reference to an exposed foot, Dunn said, 'I didn't see that.'

What he did see, he said, was a body, 'very well covered with the exception of part of the thighs'.

Either way, as the girls screamed and ran away from the mound, Guptill walked past the lower part of the body and removed some moss from the other end of the mound, exposing the blood-covered face of Bernice Connors.

The search and the presence of Mounties had not gone unnoticed in the village and already, even though Guptill and his entourage were more than a quarter of a mile from the dance hall, a crowd was beginning to gather on the road. Once the body had been discovered, curious onlookers started to move towards it.

Guptill announced that the area was a crime scene, ordered everyone to stay away, and designated a local resident, Winnie Bradford, as a guard, even though he himself remained in the area. He asked Constable Dunn to go back to town and phone the coroner and the undertaker. Also, since this appeared to be a serious crime, he asked him to inform the main RCMP detachment in the provincial capital of Fredericton.

A rope was procured from someone who lived nearby, and the area was cordoned off. Now it was just a matter of waiting for the RCMP support staff to arrive from Fredericton.

As soon as possible, RCMP headquarters responded to Dunn's call. Detective Staff Sergeant Frank W. Davis and Constable David Evans set out from Fredericton for Black's Harbour.

There were no four-lane highways in New Brunswick in 1942, just winding, narrow, mostly unpaved country roads – often in a state of advanced disrepair – passing through towns and villages, and even over covered bridges. The reason that Evans was selected to join Davis was that he, unlike others in the detachment, knew the way to Black's Harbour from Fredericton. And with New Brunswick being a largely unpopulated, rural province, Davis was probably occasionally slowed by horse-drawn wagons. By the time he arrived in Black's Harbour, it was just past midnight.

But Guptill had not been idle. He had arranged for one of the electricians employed by Connors Brothers Ltd. to tap into the overhead transmission line that ran along the road and provide temporary electrical power to the area. He had also acquired the services of a photographer who had used that power to activate his floodlights and had taken pictures of the mound containing Bernice's body and its surroundings.

Thomas Gaudet, meanwhile, had returned to Forrister Hall. When he had gone home and told his wife of the recent developments on Deadman's Harbour Road, she suggested that since he was the hall's caretaker, he ought to go and see if any of Bernice's effects were there.

Indeed they were. Bernice's coat and purse were still hanging in the cloakroom. It would appear that she had not been heading home when she left the dance. She had probably been in someone's company and had intended to return that night.

Gaudet took the coat and purse home and put them with the shoe and the plastic ring.

It didn't take Staff Sergeant Davis long to see all he needed to see at the crime scene. He removed the rest of the moss from Bernice's body and authorized further photographs. He then ordered the body removed to the Jackson's Undertaking Parlours in nearby St George for an autopsy.

By that time, the whole village of Black's Harbour, which would normally be asleep at that hour, was buzzing.

CHAPTER ONE

Gaudet took the items he had gathered during the day to the hotel where the RCMP had set up a command post. At 2.30 a.m., he handed them over to RCMP Constable Frank Tudor of the St Stephen detachment who took a statement from him.

Davis, meanwhile, continued to work through the night, talking to residents and making himself as familiar with the case as he could. By 3 a.m., he had selected two colleagues to join him and the three Mounties headed to what Davis felt was the best place to continue his investigation – the nearest military base.

Chapter Two

In October 1940, the war was not going well for the Allies. The British Expeditionary Force (BEF) had been pushed out of Europe and the Nazi advance appeared to be unstoppable.

The Germans had driven into Poland to precipitate the war in September 1939. Then, in May 1940, after eight months of relative inactivity, they unleashed their blitzkrieg, a tactic to which the Allies could find no answer. The supposedly impregnable Maginot Line was intended to protect France from invasion, but the Germans rolled across Belgium, thereby skirting the Maginot fortifications, and invaded France.

Being surrounded on three sides, the BEF had no choice but to evacuate, and when the British had to rely on tiny craft and fishing boats to get their soldiers off the French beaches at Dunkirk, it was one of the darkest moments of the war, even though the nation's media tried to build morale by calling it a disaster turned into a triumph.

Days later, France signed an armistice and pulled out of the war. The Germans tried to press their advantage with repeated air attacks on England, which became known as the Battle of Britain.

The Allies were down to a few fighter planes in their devastated Royal Air Force (RAF), and two unpleasant truths became apparent. First, any planes remaining in England were in danger. Second, a rejuvenation of the RAF was an urgent priority, but because of the repeated attacks and the need to use every available airfield for the war, England was not the best place to establish it.

It was in this climate in October 1940, that construction of a training base began at Pennfield Ridge in New Brunswick. The project, part of the British Commonwealth Air Training Plan, was too large and the need too urgent to give the contract to one company, so three were hired. One built the runways; one built the hangars and drill hall; and the third put up the rest of the almost forty buildings that formed the complex.

CHAPTER TWO

By January 1941, test flights were under way and the official opening took place that July, following the tried-and-true military practice of having an official opening long after a facility had in fact opened.

It was then known as No. 2 Air Navigational School, but being suited to many more aspects of training than just navigation, it became home to the RAF's No. 34 Operational Training Unit (OTU) in May 1942.

It was around this time that Sergeant Tom Roland Reginald Hutchings arrived from England. He and a number of other British servicemen had travelled by ship to Yarmouth, Nova Scotia in April. After a few weeks in the staging area there, they were transferred to the newly established 34 OTU at Pennfield, which was also in eastern Canada.

Tom Hutchings was an armourer-fitter and a good one, the best in his unit in fact. His commanding officer, under whom he had also served in England, would later say that he considered him to be an excellent soldier.

The usual practice would be to refer to him throughout this book as Hutchings, but in what is partly a coincidence and partly an example of the way the military does things, there were two men named Hutchings involved in this story and both played prominent roles.

There is Tom Hutchings who has already been identified and there is Edward (also known as Eddie) Hutchings. Both were RAF sergeants. Both were armourer-fitters. Both were married. Both had a child. Both were stationed at Pennfield. Both had been stationed at Blackpool in Lancashire, England.

In fact, because of the military propensity for alphabetical groupings, Tom and Edward had shared a cabin on the troop ship that took them from England to Yarmouth. At the staging camp, they shared a room. They also shared a room at Pennfield.

However, although they had the same surname, they were not related.

It is clear that at the time of the murder, neither Hutchings was familiar with either the region in which he was stationed or its inhabitants. In fact, they weren't really familiar with any part of Canada. They had been in the country a little more than a month and most of that time had been spent in a military camp in the company of members of the RAF.

On Monday morning, 8 June, while many of the airmen on the base were still at breakfast, Staff Sergeant Davis showed up at 34 OTU with two other Mounties – Corporal Charles Prime and Constable Evans. After producing identification at the gate, the trio went once again to see the acting commanding officer, Wing Commander W. Charles Coaker, the man Davis had consulted during his visit in the middle of the night.

The central administration officer of 34 OTU, Squadron Leader Barrington L. Musgrave, was also summoned, as was Flying Officer Sydney Saunders, one of the base's security officers. By 9 a.m. there were eight men squeezed into one small office – three Mounties, three RAF officers, an RAF clerk/stenographer and one other.

That was Tom Roland Hutchings (he rarely mentioned the Reginald when asked for his full name) whose presence Davis had requested. Coaker and Musgrave, acutely aware of their status as guests in Canada, had offered no objection to having Tom questioned. Saunders was there because as a security officer, he could make an RAF arrest if necessary.

Tom was the orderly sergeant for the day and as such, would normally have been on full-time duty. But Davis had convinced the RAF officers that this was a serious matter. Therefore, Tom had been temporarily relieved of his duties and brought to the room. Already, Davis was sure he had found his man.

Chapter Three

The wheels of justice turned swiftly in Canada in 1942, just as they did in most other parts of the civilized world. Even though Bernice Connors' body had not been found until Sunday evening, a coroner's inquest was convened on Monday morning at the same time Staff Sergeant Davis and two RCMP colleagues were at Pennfield Ridge.

Black's Harbour was too tiny to have its own courthouse, so the proceedings were scheduled to be held in Forrister Hall, the site of the Friday dance and the last building in which Bernice was known to have been seen alive.

The inquest did indeed start there, in that the jurors gathered, but it didn't get very far. There was a problem. One of the jurors, Bert Gallagher, had the mumps, a disease considered to be highly contagious, and under the rules of the day, he was proscribed from being in a public place.

The proceedings were, therefore, moved to Guptill's house. Being the local police chief, if Guptill wanted to allow the afflicted Gallagher to be a guest, he was free to do so. Members of the public, however, were excluded.

Guptill was a career policeman. He had served in the RCMP and had been the Chief of Police in the relatively large nearby city of Saint John before settling down into semi-retirement as Chief of Police in Black's Harbour.

He was the first witness called that Monday morning and he testified to what had by now become common knowledge in Black's Harbour.

He confirmed that the previous evening he had been part of the informal search party that had found Bernice's body.

Guptill had ushered away the girls who had been looking for their friend, removed enough moss from Bernice's face to identify her, performed his basic duties as a policeman, and turned the matter over to the RCMP.

At that point, the inquest technically should have progressed to the next step – the testimony of the person who examined the body after Guptill's identification.

But that person was Davis, and he was in Pennfield taking the investigation in a direction he considered to be more appropriate.

As a result, the coroner's inquest was adjourned after only one witness had testified, with the understanding that as soon as more evidence came forward, the hearing would be reconvened.

There is little doubt what Davis would have said had he been at the inquest. A few weeks later, he said it in court under oath.

He testified that he removed the sphagnum moss, a local springy variety not unlike escarole lettuce, from Bernice's body and found both her hands and her legs in a natural position.

To be precise, he said that 'the hands were lying on the abdomen in a natural position with the fingers half-clenched.' He added that 'the legs were in a natural position, approximately 8 inches apart at the feet.'

Areas of her face were swollen and it was clear that she had been bleeding from the nose and ears. She had a scratch about 8 inches long on the inside of her leg, starting at the crotch. She had a laceration on her forehead, another behind her ear and a clean 2-inch cut underneath her chin. Davis told the court that there was another clean cut inside her mouth where the lower lip meets the gums.

Except for her arms still being in the sleeves of her blouse, she was naked. Her brassiere had been knotted and lay on her throat. Her stained slip was under her skirt, which had been lain across her body. Her shoes and hosiery were not at the scene.

Even then, during his initial examination of the crime scene less than three hours after the discovery of Bernice's body, questions must have arisen in Davis's mind. He was a veteran policeman and certainly must have noticed a number of inconsistencies.

He must have wondered, for instance, why the murderer covered the body in such a makeshift fashion. First of all, if the perpetrator was an airman who was going back to his base within minutes of the murder, why would he bother to cover the body at all? As previously noted, there was no artificial light in that area. The body would not be found that night if left uncovered. But if the murderer was someone who wanted to hide the body for an extended period, there were far better methods than leaving it close to the road covered with light, springy moss that could easily blow away or be moved by scavenging birds or animals.

Davis's curiosity must also have been piqued by the arrangement of Bernice's clothing. The slip appeared to have been neatly rolled and placed under her skirt which lay across the middle of her body, but not around it. Why would a murderer who went to that trouble then leave a knotted brassiere on his victim's throat? Why wasn't the brassiere added to the pile? And why bother to knot it?

And what about the victim herself? Bernice was found in what Davis twice referred to as a 'natural position', with her hands crossed on her abdomen and her legs slightly apart, an unlikely posture for a girl who had just been raped and bludgeoned.

The murderer therefore must also have taken the time to arrange her body. Did this careful staging of the crime scene somehow suggest that the assailant was not flustered by the turn of events – unlikely in the case of a first-time murderer – but had in fact committed similar crimes before?

The state of the shoes and hosiery must have represented another dilemma for Davis. One shoe was found near the road adjacent to the scene; the other was about 250 yards away.

A reason for the latter circumstance may have come to light as recently as 2016. A local resident said his father, who was a 7-year-old boy in Black's Harbour in 1942, told him that he and some other youngsters had come across the shoe when they were out on their bikes the day after the dance.

His father had picked up the shoe, as a boy is likely to do, carried it for a while, then threw it away, but, because of a fear of recriminations, he never told anyone about his actions when he learned of the shoe's significance. That could explain why the shoes were so far apart but not why either shoe was near the road in the first place.

Again, Davis may have speculated on that point and come to a different conclusion. The area was boggy after all-day rain on Friday, and the uppers of Bernice's shoes were made of suede. If Bernice and a lover had been looking for a place to have sex, she might have removed her shoes and left them by the side of the road, intending to walk barefoot until they found some higher, and therefore drier, ground.

As for the hosiery, it was never found, but it may have been left with the shoes and blown away. Or it may have been taken by the killer, possibly as a souvenir of the crime. But the most likely option of all is that it never existed and that she wasn't wearing any hosiery because nylons were too expensive. That would fit with the idea of removing the shoes because of wet ground.

Whatever the case may have been, Davis was certainly not pursuing the thought that a local person was involved in the killing.

When Chief Guptill had talked to Davis at around midnight on Sunday, he had made it clear that a number of RAF men from the nearby Pennfield training facility had been at the Friday dance. In fact, the dance was sponsored by the Women's Institute and its primary purpose was to provide entertainment for foreign airmen. Therefore, Davis decided that the best place to begin his investigation was 34 OTU, where the airmen were based.

Which is why he was there early Monday morning, only hours after Bernice Connors' body had been found.

Chapter Four

In some later reports, it was implied that Tom's initial interrogation by Davis took place in his room, but that's unlikely. It would have been impractical to pack eight men into Tom's quarters – built to sleep four but not to hold meetings.

Instead, it was held in an office, almost certainly in the sergeants' quarters, and Tom's room would have been down the hall.

Davis began by delivering the usual police caution: that although he intended to ask some questions, Tom was under no obligation to answer them. Similarly, Tom was under no obligation to cooperate with any other aspect of the investigation.

If the staff sergeant had been expecting Tom to object to being questioned, or perhaps to exhibit some indication of nervousness or evasiveness, he would have been disappointed.

Tom appeared unconcerned and proceeded to cooperate willingly and fully with Davis. And why wouldn't he? He was as convinced of his innocence as Davis was of his guilt.

As an indication of the seriousness of the crime, the interview was transcribed by an RAF clerk and subsequently stored in the RCMP files. Usually, a police interview is reduced to its salient points which are scribbled in the questioner's notebook.

Tom was first asked to make a statement concerning his whereabouts on Friday night and was then questioned by Davis. Some minor editing changes have been made in what follows, but other than that, this is the transcript of that 8 June 1942 interview:

> Tom: I left camp about 7.30 Friday night with another Sergeant Hutchings (Regimental number 551949), LAC Morgan and another LAC. I went to Roy's taxi rank and got a taxi into Black's Harbour. Two more joined the taxi down the road who

went to St George and we all left St George and came on to Black's Harbour. We stopped at a gas station and went to a café in a block of buildings opposite the gas station at Black's Harbour. We left there and went to a bowling alley and I left Sergeant Hutchings and the LAC at the bowling alley and went with LAC Morgan for a walk, and went back to the bowling alley and met the others and all went to the dance about 10.30 or 10.40. We stopped there until the dance was over.

Q. Did you see anybody you know at the dance?

A. All the chaps I came in with and one or two aircrew, Sergeant Hutchings and the LAC.

Q. Who are those you know by sight? Do you know their names?

A. No. Some of the aircrew I only know by sight.

Q. Did you dance?

A. I had a few dances with some of the girls in there and watched for a while until the dance was over, and then went with Sergeant Hutchings for a taxi on the corner of the road. It came along and there were nine others in the taxi, and we came back.

Q. Can you name some of them?

A. Only Sergeant Hutchings.

Q. About what time?

A. I could not be sure about that time.

Q. Immediately right after the dance was over?

A. I should say about half an hour after the dance was over.

Q. Where did you go to wait for a taxi?

A. At the corner of the road.

Q. What road?

A. The main road at the corner of Black's Harbour.

Q. Just you and Sergeant Hutchings?

A. Yes, and we were joined later by some fellows.

Q. How long were you there with Sergeant Hutchings?
A. We were not there very long. I should say not more than ten minutes or a quarter of an hour.

Q. You state that you went to the dance at approximately 10.30?
A. Yes.

Q. Will you state the time you left there?
A. I left there when the dance closed.

Q. Did you have any particular girlfriend at the dance that night?
A. No sir. No one at all.

Q. Did you dance with many girls?
A. I danced with two.

Q. Did you leave the dance hall that night?
A. Once. I went out to go to the lavatory.

Q. How long would you be gone?
A. A couple of minutes.

Q. By yourself?
A. Yes.

Q. Where is the lavatory situated there?
A. I do not know. I went in the bushes.

Q. Then you would not be seen for the time you were absent from the dance?
A. No sir.

Q. You are quite sure of that.
A. Yes.

Q. That is, you did not leave the dance hall for any other purpose than to go to the toilet?
A. Yes.

Q. Are you a drinking man sergeant?
A. Yes. I drink like anybody else does.

Q. Did you drink that night?
A. A little.

Q. State what you meant by a little.
A. There is not a chance to drink a lot when there are no public houses about.

Q. About how much did you drink?
A. A bottle of beer and a drop of rum.

Q. Enough to make you intoxicated?
A. No.

Q. Where did you get the rum?
A. A friend got it for me. A fellow told me to see a fellow called Watson. We met him in the bowling alley and LAC Morgan and myself went out for a walk and got a drink.

Q. LAC Morgan and you went out to get a drink of rum?
A. Yes.

Q. Tell us what did you get?
A. We got a bottle of rum and a bottle of beer.

Q. What did you pay for it?
A. Four dollars for the rum. That was a pint.

Q. How much? About 26 ounces?
A. No answer.

Q. You are not quite sure about the size of the bottle?
A. No.
Q. At any rate, you and Morgan had a drink of rum?
A. We all four went and shared the drink.

Q. Did you finish the bottle?
A. Yes.

Q. So you finished the bottle of rum before you went to the dance?
A. Yes.

Q. Did you have anything to drink while you were at the dance?
A. Yes. One chap asked if I would like a drink and gave me a drink of whisky.

Q. Who was this?
A. I do not know his name.

Q. He is on the station?
A. Yes.

Q. Did you have any more rum to drink?
A. No.

Q. That is, you did not have any rum at the dance that night?
A. That's right.

Q. By this time, were you slightly intoxicated or not?
A. I was not feeling slightly intoxicated, just a bit merry.

Q. At any time did you leave the dance hall with a girl?
A. No. No one at all. No girl at all.

Q. I am asking if you did or not.
A. Definitely not.

Q. At no time in the evening before or after the dance did you associate with a girl in Black's Harbour?
A. Yes, one girl when I was with Sergeant Hutchings and the other two airmen.

Q. What time would that be?
A. That was just before the show started. Sometime before the dance.

Q. Way before the dance?
A. Yes.

Q. And that was the only time that whole evening that you associated with a girl inside the dance room? Is that right?
A. Yes.

Q. You never spoke to a girl?
A. No.

CHAPTER FOUR

Q. Where did you have your last drink of rum before you went to the dance?
A. Just outside the dance.

Q. Just before you went in?
A. Yes.

Q. You understand sergeant, that a very serious offence has been committed?
A. Yes.

Q. And that it is customary to ask people questions that I am asking you?
A. Yes.

Q. Have you ever been convicted of a criminal offence?
A. No.

Q. Do you feel you want to assist us in this matter?
A. Yes.

Q. And you are willing to help us?
A. Yes.

Q. And you are quite willing to let me search your kit voluntarily.
A. Yes.

Q. And let me do anything I want to do?
A. Yes.

Q. How many uniforms have you sergeant?
A. Two.

Q. Is that the uniform you were wearing on the night of 5 June?
A. Yes.

Q. And where is the other one?
A. Hanging up in my bunk in the sergeants' quarters.

Q. Would you mind taking off your hat please?
A. Certainly.

Q. Do you always wear glasses?
A. Not always. I can read and write without them.

Q. Do your wear them every day?
A. Yes. My eye gets strained if I don't.

Q. Do you wear them every night?
A. I think I do.

Q. Did you wear them to the dance?
A. No.

Q. Let me see your hands. Where did you get that cut?
A. I was unpacking cases and cut it on a nail.

Q. I see you have a scar on the right thumb. Correct?
A. Yes.

Q. And how did you get it?
A. On the nail. In the packing cases in the hangar.

Q. When did you get that?
A. Friday morning.

Q. Friday morning of this month?
A. Yes. A couple of days ago.

Q. You have some scratches on the hand too? Scratches on the ring finger.
A. Yes.

Q. How did you get that?
A. My ring.

Q. And how about this one on the back of your hand?
A. I got it the same way on the packing cases.

Q. You don't know?
A. Well, I should say it was definitely that.

CHAPTER FOUR

Q. And how about this one on your second finger?

A. I got that when I was using the tool for pulling nails and it slipped.

Q. When did you do these? (Three small scars across the nail of the second finger.)

A. Day before yesterday.

Q. Day before yesterday. Which would be?

A. Saturday.

Q. Have you any other scars?

A. No. No scars at all.

Q. Just take your coat off. You don't mind do you?

A. No.

Q. What have you got there?

A. Dirt.

Q. Have you cleaned this coat lately?

A. No. I pressed it yesterday.

Q. You have already told me that you don't mind assisting us?

A. Yes.

Q. Would you mind taking everything out of your pockets?

A. Certainly.

Q. You were wearing these trousers too?

A. Yes.

Q. Of course you don't mind me having these?

A. No.

Q. You have got a stain on the back. What's that?

A. I suppose where I sat down on the steps last night waiting for a taxi.

Q. What is your job?

A. Fitter-armourer.

Q. What do you fit?
A. Machine guns. I have been doing chalking on boxes.

Q. What kind of chalk did you use?
A. Red and white.

Q. I think that is about all now Sergeant. Sergeant, when you returned to camp last night, I believe you reported to Sergeant Wintle?
A. When I came in with Sergeant Hutchings, the guard on duty told us both to report to the guardroom where I saw Sergeant Wintle.

Q. Did you tell Sergeant Wintle that you had been in company with Sergeant Hutchings on that evening?
A. Yes.

Q. And had never left him?
A. I don't remember that.

Q. Did you in fact stay with Sergeant Hutchings from the time you went to the dance hall until the dance was over?
A. Yes, except when I went out to go to the lavatory.

Q. In other words, you were never away from Sergeant Hutchings for more than a number of minutes to go to the lavatory?
A. Yes.

Q. You are issued with two tunics, two pairs trousers and two pairs boots?
A. Only one pair of boots. We handed the other pair in at Blackpool.

Q. Two hats?
A. Only one hat. Sorry, two hats.

Q. Where is your other one?
A. Somebody took that at the dance last night.

Q. You lost that at the dance?
A. Yes. Somebody took it off the table just inside the door. Then I went out and when I came back, the hat was gone. I asked the girl at the table if she had seen it. She said, 'No.'

CHAPTER FOUR

Q. Then you came back from Black's Harbour that night without a hat?
A. Yes.

Q. Are you issued with a penknife?
A. Yes. They had to be handed in.

Q. Have you one now?
A. No.

Q. Not in your kit?
A. No.

Q. When did you hand yours in?
A. Sometime last year before we came here.

Q. Do you carry a sheath knife?
A. No, but I have one.

Q. Sergeant, you have given a statement absolutely voluntarily in the presence of W/C Coacker, S/L Musgrave and F/O Saunders?
A. Yes

* * *

To the best of his knowledge, Tom was, for the most part, totally forthcoming. His answers to the questions about the cuts – sometimes called scars by Davis – on his hands were logical and precise. It is interesting to note that the worst damage was to Tom's right hand even though he was left-handed. If Davis intended to show that the most severe cut was caused when Tom battered Bernice Connors, he was not off to a good start.

Tom readily handed over his uniform and explained the stain on the back of his pants which had caught Davis's attention. He admitted to having pressed his tunic, and had he wanted to make sure that he had removed all traces of any foreign matter, he had a perfect reason and every opportunity to do so. It had been his turn to act as orderly sergeant and it was not uncommon for those who pulled that duty to present themselves in a uniform more presentable than one that would be acceptable on a workday.

The only area in which Tom was somewhat disingenuous was the matter of the alcohol he consumed. This is not terribly surprising. There was still a stigma attached to drinking in 1942 and Tom was probably aware that whereas the pub was the accepted centre of activity in English life, Canadians had a much more Puritanical attitude with regard to their drinking laws, and tended to frown on those who frequented bars. He did not hide the fact that he had gone to a bootlegger, but he had drunk much more than he admitted and complained repeatedly on the way back to the base that he felt sick.

The liquor the RAF men had taken to Black's Harbour was consumed before the dance and they considered going back to the Pennfield base to buy more. They went to the café to discuss the matter and if necessary, to use the payphone there to call a taxi, but as they were going in, Tom lagged behind and asked a passing civilian if he knew where they could get more liquor.

Only government-operated stores could legally sell liquor, so bootlegging was common in small towns like Black's Harbour. The civilian suggested that Tom go to a house just outside the town limits and ask for Earl.

The RAF men made the trek only to be told by Earl's wife that he was not home but probably at the bowling alley.

Back they went, and by checking the score sheets, Leading Aircraftman Morgan determined which of the bowlers was the elusive Earl. As soon as Earl finished his game, Tom and Morgan left with him while Eddie Hutchings and Blakely, the other leading aircraftman in their original group, took over the now-vacant lane and bowled.

Earl took them to a house near his own and they bought a quart of illicit rum. While the two RAF men shared some drinks – some of the rum and some bottles of beer – with the hospitable host and his wife, Earl went to another house to procure a pint bottle of rum for the RAF men.

Adequately stocked, the airmen then went back to town and at 10.45 p.m., met up with their two colleagues.

After the Monday interview, presumably acting out of a concern that Tom may have been wearing clothes other than those he identified, Davis asked for and received a number of other articles. In total, he took a tunic, a pair of trousers, two pairs of socks, a set of underwear, a belt, two handkerchiefs, two collars, a tie and a pair of shoes.

In those days, most men wore shirts with detachable collars. Davis took two collars but only one shirt which had been washed and was hanging to dry in Tom's room. All these items were passed to Corporal Prime who marked them for identification.

At that point, having apparently been satisfied on every front, the entourage dismissed Tom. It is interesting to note that at this stage of the investigation, he was being accorded the full protection of the law. He had been apprised of his rights, as he should have been, and had been treated as if he were innocent until proven guilty. Both Squadron Leader Musgrave and Wing Commander Coaker had been in attendance primarily to make sure that the Canadian police took no liberties.

That level of concern for his rights was never seen again. After that, he was treated as guilty by almost everyone involved with the case, especially Davis who had clearly made up his mind.

Two days later, on Wednesday afternoon, the Mounties returned to the Pennfield Ridge base. Without further explanation, Tom was told that he faced a number of charges, the most significant being based on Sections 259 and 260 of the Canadian Criminal Code which involved the offences of murder and rape, both capital crimes in 1942.

In accordance with the information provided by Davis, Thomas Roy Hutchings was taken before a magistrate and formally charged with the murder and rape of Bernice Connors.

Tom objected. 'The name is not Thomas,' he said. 'It is Tom. And the name is not Roy, it is Roland. Roy is a nickname.'

Tom Roland Hutchings was then taken to the building known locally as St Andrews Gaol.

Chapter Five

The swing boat was always a popular attraction at the many travelling fairs in England in the 1920s. Essentially, it was nothing more than a glorified version of the backyard swing set. But instead of individual seats, it featured gaily painted gondolas which held at least four people on two facing benches.

Today, swing boats can hold thirty or more people and are electrically powered, but in the 1920s, the riders pulled on ropes to get the gondola to swing higher and higher.

Since the travelling fairs took a notoriously lackadaisical view towards safety, there were no restraining barriers and it was not unknown for someone to get hit by a swinging boat – especially a child who was wandering about or running while playing with friends.

In 1927, Tom Roland Hutchings was such a child. The swing boat struck the 7-year-old boy in the head.

The precise details of the injury he suffered are not available. The attending physician, Dr G. Eric W. Lacey of Woolwich, a suburb of London, confirmed in 1942 that the injury had occurred and that he had treated Tom at the time, but said that 'all records previous to 1933 were sent to augment the war effort.' Paper had to be recycled and old medical records were not considered to be of any importance.

Tom's father, however, testified in a 1942 letter to the British Air Ministry that his son was 'ill from August to Xmas', with acute rheumatism and chorea.

Both are serious afflictions and the chorea had a significant impact on Tom's development. According to the International Parkinson and Movement Disorder Society:

> Chorea is an abnormal involuntary movement derived from the Greek word meaning 'dance'. It is characterized

26

by brief, abrupt, irregular, unpredictable, non-stereotyped movements. In milder cases, they may appear purposeful; the patient often appears fidgety and clumsy. They can affect various body parts, and interfere with speech, swallowing, posture and gait. Chorea may worsen with anxiety and voluntary movements.

Even today, there is no known cure for chorea but it is largely controllable with modern drugs. The United States Department of Health and Human Services, a branch of the federal government, says that chorea can be caused by a head injury. Tom almost certainly acquired it in 1927 as a result of being hit by the swing boat.

Prior to that, he had suffered the usual childhood afflictions – measles, whooping cough and so on – but nothing serious, and certainly no chorea. After being hit by the swing boat, he was never fully healthy again.

On 11 September 1931, he was admitted to Banstead Surgical Home for Boys, probably to receive further treatment for chorea. Again, the detailed records were recycled, but it is known that he wasn't released until 4 October.

In June the following year, he suffered a laceration on his wrist, probably, although not certainly, attributable to the chorea.

In July, the rheumatism returned, and he was housebound until September. After a brief respite, his health again worsened and on 3 November he was admitted to Queen Mary's Hospital for Children in Carshalton, Surrey, not far from London.

For the next ten months, the rheumatism and chorea affected him to various degrees, and he was either in the hospital or housebound. It was not until 29 August 1933, that he was deemed healthy enough to go back to school. By that time, he had endured an uninterrupted stretch of roughly fourteen months of serious illness.

Tom must also have suffered a serious concussion from the incident at the fair, but in those days, the brain damage caused by concussions had not been recognized. A person knocked unconscious was deemed to be fully recovered as soon as consciousness returned.

On 6 October 1936, Tom, now 16 years old, left for school on his bicycle. He never got there and didn't return home until the next morning. He had fallen off his bike – again, an occurrence that was probably attributable to chorea. Whatever the reason, he had no memory of how he had spent the day, and in the evening, he found himself wandering near a police station far from his house. The local policeman would have had only a bicycle for transportation, not a car, and therefore would have been unable to take Tom home. Tom spent the night at the police station and was given a ride home by a truck driver the following morning.

Before the year ended, Tom left school. This would have been common in England in that era because he had turned 16, the standard school-leaving age. Only those in the upper classes attended university and although Tom's family was comfortable, it by no means qualified as upper class. All others would end their formal schooling in their mid-teens and either find a menial job or become an apprentice.

Tom joined Comyn Ching & Co., a well-established London firm that was involved primarily in heating and lighting. As an apprentice, he would have been expected to spend at least five years – or perhaps even seven – learning his trade as a fitter before becoming a qualified craftsman. But in May 1939, less than three years into his commitment, he was released from his apprenticeship to join the RAF.

Even though trouble was clearly brewing in Europe as a result of the rise of Nazi Germany, the United Kingdom was not at war, and many, if not most, Britons believed war could be avoided. At this point, enlistment was not the expected course of action that it was to become four months later.

Like all branches of the military in 1939, the RAF saw what it wanted to see with regard to recruitment. If a young man who appeared to be physically healthy offered to enrol, he was not likely to be turned away. An intensive medical examination – or even a close examination of his medical history – would certainly have found Tom to be unsuitable for military service, but neither type of evaluation took place.

To all appearances, he was a fine, healthy young man, a little under 6ft tall. He wasn't overly handsome, but there was nothing seriously unattractive about his appearance, although his ears did protrude a little. He sported a modest moustache and again, like other aspects of his appearance, it was nothing out of the ordinary, merely the width of his mouth and neatly trimmed.

During his time in the RAF, Tom proved to be a first-rate armourer-fitter and was promoted accordingly. He also got married to Joyce Emily Pearson in Peterborough, Cambridgeshire on 11 September 1940. The couple's daughter, Valerie, was born on 22 September 1941.

But although Tom's life seemed to be progressing in a fairly normal fashion, his acquaintances in the RAF noticed his peculiarities. Sergeant D.C. Huggett met Tom – who was invariably known by his nickname of Roy in RAF circles – in the staging camp at Yarmouth, Nova Scotia in May 1942. The two started drinking and when Tom acted strangely, Huggett initially attributed it to drunkenness. However, he soon changed his mind.

In a later submission to the Canadian court, Huggett noted that Tom's state,

> whilst queer, was not due to drunkenness, although he had been drinking.
>
> He had a blank in his memory, i.e. he did not know where he had been nor knew what he had been doing for some time before meeting me. On the other hand, his gait was reasonably steady and he did not require much assistance from me. I considered this condition queer at the time because he had the appearance of a man who, through drink, had become insensible to what was happening and after a period of insensibility had sobered up enough to take an interest in his whereabouts. To the best of my knowledge, this could not be so in the case of Sergeant Roy Hutchings as he had no period of rest in which to sober up. He appeared as though the drink which he had taken, whilst not making him drunk had very definitely affected his mental powers. He had blood on his head above the left ear which had run down the side of his face from a cut, but he did not know how he got it.

This sort of occurrence was nothing new to Eddie Hutchings who had seen it during his time as Tom's roommate in Yarmouth, Pennfield and Blackpool.

Referring to himself as Tom's 'closest friend', he confirmed Huggett's account. He told of a time he had arranged with Tom to go to a party, 'but after a few drinks, he suddenly disappeared and was next seen outside the gate of the camp by Sergeant Huggett in a dazed condition.'

Leading Aircraftman Samuel Blakely had seen Tom behave oddly on a number of occasions. He too had been stationed with him in Blackpool and had travelled with him to Canada. 'After a few drinks, he acted in a strange way,' he wrote in his submission to the court. 'He was forgetful and often wandered away by himself, and had no knowledge of his actions during such periods. Around the end of April, after a few drinks about 11 o'clock, he walked fully clothed into a lake.'

There was further confirmation from Eddie Hutchings who also recalled their time in Blackpool.

> On many occasions after a few drinks he was in the habit of suddenly going away by himself,' he wrote. 'We made arrangements to visit a place of amusement one night, but after drinking, he just left me and appeared to have forgotten entirely the date. After such periods, he could never account for any of his movements.

The fateful 5 June night in Black's Harbour started out like just another in a long series of similar occurrences in the life of Tom Hutchings. But this one was to have a dramatically different conclusion.

Chapter Six

The St Andrews Gaol in which Tom found himself three days after the discovery of the body of Bernice Connors was not built with the idea of rehabilitation in mind. Essentially, it had two purposes. The first was to be an escape-proof place of detention; the second was to provide punishment so memorable that lawbreakers would be discouraged from finding themselves imprisoned there again.

After the American Revolutionary War (1775–1783), British North America felt the need to fortify its borders. Since St Andrews is right across the St Croix River from what is now the American state of Maine, the British military forces moved in, surveyed the land, divided it into lots, granted those lots to men who had shown their loyalty to the Crown, and built the structures necessary for a fortified town.

One such structure was what its builders called a gaol. (In North America, it would normally have become known as a jail, but in many documents pertaining to this case, it was still referred to as a gaol.)

An area considered to be suitable was allocated, consisting of two large, damp, smelly ground-floor rooms in the same building as the courthouse.

Eventually, a need for modernization was recognized, so in 1831, at a cost of £3,393, a new jail was built with interior walls of solid granite at least 18 inches thick throughout. The outer walls were also granite, but 30 inches thick. Originally, there were ten ground-floor cells, but by the time Tom was incarcerated in 1942, some had been converted into living quarters for the jailer, so only four remained, all on the same side of a single corridor. There were another four upstairs for women and children. Children were rarely convicted of a crime but if such a fate befell their mother, they could not be left at home. The father, if one were present, would have inescapable work commitments, so the children went to jail.

Each of the cells measured 6 feet by 8 feet and contained a single metal bed, 36 inches wide with metal springs. The bedding consisted of a tick filled with straw; one pillow, also filled with straw; and two blankets. Every thirty days, the tick, pillow and blankets were washed and the straw was replaced.

The 'window' in each cell was 4 inches wide and 1 foot high, but it was merely an open, glassless vertical slit in the granite wall, reminiscent of those in a medieval castle. In the winter, which was known to come early and stay late in St Andrews, prisoners could petition for an extra blanket. Wooden blocks, which were available to put in the window, tended to be ill-fitting so the extra blanket was often crammed into the window to keep out the wind, rather than placed on the bed.

The cells had neither heat nor light, but there was a pot-bellied stove in the corridor. When the weather turned unduly cold, the stove was put into operation and most prisoners were occasionally allowed to move into the corridor at night. But Tom, because he was facing a capital crime, had to remain in his cell behind a solid iron door.

To accommodate personal hygiene, each cell had a bedpan. Occasionally, during the daytime, a prisoner was allowed to visit the 'washroom' on the other side of the corridor. There, he could use his bedpan in privacy and wash himself using water that dribbled out of a pipe in the wall. Although records are not clear on this point, it is believed by local historians that although Tom was allowed to use this room, he was accorded far fewer visits than other prisoners.

Once a prisoner was in his cell, four doors separated him from the town of St Andrews. The first, his cell door, was made of solid iron and was fastened with an iron draw bar. Near the bottom was an opening, roughly 5 inches square, through which a mug or a small bowl could be passed. It was not wide enough to admit a standard-sized dinner plate. At the end of the corridor were two more iron doors. The inner one was a grate of 2-inch-wide flat bars; the outer was solid except for a small rectangular hole near the top to facilitate viewing.

To leave the building, a prisoner had to pass the building's main door – also iron. Once locked, this door could be opened only from the outside, so even if the jailer was overpowered or otherwise incapacitated, there was still no access to the outdoors.

It was in these conditions that Tom was kept for six weeks while the judicial machinery went into action. Forms had to be filled out and filed. Witnesses had to be interviewed. The coroner's inquest had to be completed. Schedules had to be established. Hearings had to be convened.

He must have been terribly depressed. He was in a strange land while his young daughter, whom he hadn't seen for months, was on the other side of an ocean with her mother. He was out of touch with his friends. His brother, a squadron leader in the RAF, was a hero and had been awarded the Distinguished Flying Cross for bravery. Tom, meanwhile, was charged with rape and murder and was being held in solitary confinement in near-barbaric conditions.

Still, he continued to be polite and cooperative. He was jailed on a Wednesday and on the following Saturday, he got a visit from Staff Sergeant Davis who, depending on one's point of view, came either to tie up some loose ends or to cover up his oversights.

There was a development involving the cap that Tom had said he thought he had lost at the dance.

Thomas Gaudet, the caretaker who had found Bernice's coat and purse still hanging in the cloakroom at Forrister Hall after her body had been discovered, had been cleaning the hall the next day and had found an airman's cap on a windowsill behind some curtains. As expected, it belonged to Tom, and on Saturday, Davis went to the St Andrews Gaol to get samples of Tom's hair, presumably to match them to those in the cap.

Forensic testing was rudimentary at best in 1942, but at least Davis would be able to see if Tom's hair matched the colour and texture of hairs in the cap. Accordingly, he asked Tom for a hair sample, and once again, Tom submitted willingly.

During his visit, Davis was told by jailer George Goodeill that Tom had been wearing a signet ring which he had confiscated. Later, he handed Davis an envelope containing the ring. In his report, Davis simply said that he had acquired the ring without mentioning Goodeill's involvement.

Chapter Seven

Tom had been in St Andrews Gaol for six days when the coroner's inquest reconvened. It had met briefly the day after Bernice Connors' body was found, but with Staff Sergeant Davis still busy collecting evidence, it was adjourned before it managed to do anything of substance.

Two days after that, on 18 June, the preliminary hearing – the normal precursor to a capital trial – was supposed to begin. But like the coroner's inquest, it too had to be adjourned.

If possible, the circumstances of the death should be determined before the preliminary hearing begins, but without a verdict from the coroner's jury, that was not possible. The inquest finally got under way on 19 June.

Once again, Black's Harbour Police Chief Dennison P. Guptill was the first to testify. He repeated his account of the Sunday evening search for Bernice Connors and the subsequent discovery of her body. He also told of establishing a cordon around the scene and having the RCMP detachment in Fredericton called for assistance.

RCMP Corporal William Prime testified briefly, providing what was little more than a repetition of Guptill's evidence, apart from confirming that the body upon which the autopsy was performed was that of Bernice Connors.

The final, and most important, witness was Dr Arnold Branch of Rothesay, a suburb of Saint John.

After Staff Sergeant Davis completed his examination of the crime scene in the wee hours of Monday morning, Bernice Connors' body was taken to St George, the town in which Hutchings and his friends had made a brief stop on their way to the dance in Black's Harbour.

It was there that Dr Branch conducted his post-mortem examination. Branch was a qualified medical doctor, but he hadn't practised as such since 1920, preferring instead to concentrate on pathology.

Despite his decision to specialize, there is no evidence that he was among the leaders in his field, even in 1942. By today's standards, his methods would be deemed prehistoric.

No one challenged any of Dr Branch's testimony at the inquest. Tom Hutchings was still languishing in his cell in St Andrews 30 miles away and still had not been provided with a defence attorney, so he was unrepresented.

If he had been provided with competent legal counsel, that counsel would have attended the inquest in order to familiarize himself with evidence that might become a part of a trial. He would have been able to hear the testimony, especially the medical testimony, and research its validity, thereby putting himself in a better position to challenge it at the trial. Had he established himself as acting for an accused, a mere formality, he would even have had the right to question any witness.

But with Tom being left to fend for himself, unrepresented and not in attendance, none of that happened.

Instead, the Clerk of the Peace, Harry M. Groom of St Stephen, followed the same standard format that he would have used had the inquest been looking into the death from a heart attack of someone who collapsed in the street. He asked the doctor some basic questions and listened politely. After giving equally basic answers, the doctor sat down. The jurors, who had the right to ask questions of the witnesses, did not exercise that option.

In theory, the inquest wasn't terribly important to the chain of events. After all, it was evident to all concerned that Bernice had been beaten and had died. And Tom had already been charged with murder and rape, so unless Dr Branch offered an opinion that she had been neither murdered nor raped, Tom was going to face at least a preliminary hearing and probably, a trial.

But the inquest was crucial because at that upcoming trial Dr Branch would be on the stand again, and if he offered the same evidence, the Crown would have to deal with some significant inconsistencies.

He testified, for instance, that Bernice's hair was 'matted and wet', even though the body was found on dry land about half a mile from water almost two full days after the murder. There had been no rain in the interim.

He testified that with the exception of a scratch near her genitalia and a bruise on her thigh, all the injuries were to her head and face. On two separate occasions, he referred to her face's bluish colour.

He determined that there were no abnormalities that would account for death in either her abdomen or thorax. There was no evidence of a fractured skull. So he decided that the cause of death was shock.

He also said that there was evidence of sexual assault, namely a small laceration near the vagina that was 'quite recent', and spermatozoa. While those might be evidence of a sexual encounter, they were hardly proof of a sexual assault.

Only ninety minutes after the inquest was convened, the six men of the coroner's jury had heard the evidence, deliberated on it and issued a verdict:

> We unanimously agree that the deceased Bernice Connors came to her death on the Deadman's Harbour Road, Black's Harbour in the County of Charlotte, Province of New Brunswick, between the hour of 9 o'clock p.m. 5 June 1942 and 9:30 o'clock p.m., 7 June 1942.
>
> We also agree that her death was caused by injuries received as a result of a brutal attack inflicted upon her by a person or persons undisclosed.

In fact, not a shred of evidence had been presented to support the jurors' conclusion that Bernice was killed on Deadman's Harbour Road. It was certain that her body had been found there, but not that she had died there.

It now fell to the New Brunswick Supreme Court to prove that Tom Hutchings was the 'undisclosed' person to whom the jurors referred – if that was possible.

Chapter Eight

Throughout the delays in proceedings, Tom had been corresponding regularly by mail with his father, Tom Senior, in England. It must be kept in mind though, that this 'regular' exchange was subject to transatlantic shipping. The letters did not go by air mail.

Although the letters have been lost, it is known from other sources that the father was, as anyone would expect, distraught over the situation in which his son found himself.

Naturally, a father's statement regarding his son has to be seen as highly subjective, but as he was known to be an honourable man, some weight has to be given to his assertion that 'my son has always been a very affectionate, obedient and lovable boy, causing no anxiety apart from illness.'

Tom Sr was no stranger to the military. He had served in India and had been a captain in the Royal Artillery in the First World War. His other son, William Cyril, a wing commander in 149 Squadron of the RAF, had logged more than 1,300 hours piloting Stirling bombers and had been awarded the Distinguished Flying Cross.

Convinced that Tom could not have committed the acts of which he was accused, Tom Sr wanted to hire a private detective to look into the matter properly, something he had good reason to believe the RCMP had not done.

But England had currency restrictions in place at the time, and despite his best attempts to get an exemption for what was literally a matter of life or death, his request to send funds abroad was denied.

Tom, meanwhile, could do nothing to help his cause. He was stuck in solitary confinement in St Andrews Gaol, reading his Bible when there was sufficient light and counting the days to his preliminary hearing which, after being delayed while the inquest concluded, had been rescheduled to begin on 2 July.

In Canada, a preliminary hearing is held in a serious case to determine whether there is sufficient evidence to proceed to trial. It is roughly akin to a grand-jury hearing in the United States, although there are significant differences.

It used to be a sort of mini-trial, but it has now evolved into an opportunity for each side to familiarize itself with some of the evidence the other might present.

Unlike the American grand jury, a Canadian preliminary hearing is heard by a single person, either a judge or a magistrate. If there is to be a jury, it will not be selected until the next stage when the case goes to trial.

But whether the preliminary hearing is of today's variety or follows the standard that was practised in 1942, the primary purpose remains unchanged. It is intended to determine whether there is enough evidence to proceed with a trial, or whether the judge should save everyone's time, not to mention the taxpayers' money, by staying the charges.

The Crown presents evidence against the person known properly in Canada as the accused. In the United States, he would be the defendant.

The defence attorney tries to minimize the incriminating value of the Crown's evidence. In short, he attempts to convince the judge that the case is not sufficiently strong to proceed to trial. Should he feel the need to do so, he can call witnesses on his client's behalf. He contends that any reasonable jury would quickly render a verdict of not guilty.

The judge must decide if a properly instructed jury acting reasonably could return a guilty verdict on the evidence that has been presented.

It is true that the bar is not set high in a preliminary hearing. It is, after all, not a trial. It is just a scratching of the surface and even evidence that may be inadmissible in a formal trial can be heard. Once the trial itself is under way, admissibility can be challenged, but that course of action is rarely taken in a preliminary hearing.

Nevertheless, despite its relative informality, the preliminary hearing is a crucial step on the road to determining a defendant's guilt or innocence. Its evidence is given under oath and its transcript can be used in the trial, so a witness whose testimony during the trial differs even slightly from that given during the preliminary hearing can be exposed and discredited.

Even if all the evidence in a preliminary hearing is accepted by both sides as presented, a capable defence lawyer can sometimes convince a judge that while the Crown's evidence might be interesting, it in no way proves the guilt of his client. This is especially true in a case like Tom's, one that was based totally on circumstantial evidence. An imaginative defence lawyer can use the facts presented by the Crown and weave a story that is equally plausible. He may even be able to do it in two or three ways.

If that's the case, the judge may well decide that the charges should be dismissed because there is too much 'reasonable doubt'.

In American baseball, there is a saying regarding whether a batter running to a base is safe or out. 'Tie goes to the runner', the Americans say. Canadian criminal lawyers have modified that saying. Their rule of thumb is: 'In a preliminary, tie goes to the Crown. In circumstantial evidence, tie goes to the defendant.'

Since almost all of the evidence against Tom was circumstantial, his lawyer should have hammered that latter point again and again in the preliminary. For every piece of Crown 'evidence', he should have been saying, 'It's circumstantial. Tie goes to the defendant, which means that the so-called evidence has no weight.'

Then, when the time arrived for the judge to decide whether the case should proceed to trial, he could say that the Crown had produced no substantive evidence and as a result, the charges must be dropped. After all, the defendant is innocent until proven guilty and the Crown had produced no evidence of guilt, just a few guesses.

But Tom's defence lawyer at the preliminary hearing said no such thing for one simple reason. There was no defence lawyer.

It is nothing short of astonishing, and for that matter, disgraceful, that a preliminary hearing on capital charges of rape and murder was held without the accused having any sort of legal representation.

And yet that was the case. The RAF, still concerned about its status as a guest in a foreign country, decided not to intercede. An observer, Flight Lieutenant W. T. Elverston, was sent to keep his superiors informed of the events as they unfolded, but he did not get directly involved.

The Canadian judicial system, specifically the New Brunswick attorney general, hadn't got around to selecting a lawyer to defend Tom Hutchings. As a result, the Supreme Court of New Brunswick began its deliberations to determine whether a man should live or die without providing him with any sort of legal representation.

So Tom Roland Hutchings stood quietly in the box, watching the preliminary hearing unfold, listening to the testimony of thirty-six witnesses and saying nothing except 'No your honour', when asked, after each of the thirty-six, if he wished to cross-examine.

Chapter Nine

Tom's preliminary hearing took place in front of Ellis A. Nason, a Black's Harbour magistrate.

A magistrate is a step down the judicial ladder from a judge, qualified only to handle lesser matters before the court. In New Brunswick in 1942, a magistrate was not required to have had any formal legal training.

This was just one of the many instances of Tom getting the dirty end of the judicial stick. In theory, using magistrates to handle minor matters, thereby reducing the workload that would otherwise fall to judges, makes sense. Since there was no chance of Tom being sentenced to a jail term as a direct result of findings in the preliminary hearing, it was regarded as a minor matter.

But in a case like Tom's, it would have been far more equitable to have the preliminary hearing treated like the serious matter that it was. There was nothing to prevent the appointment of a judge to handle the proceedings. After all, the judicial system was not dealing with two counts of shoplifting here. The accused was charged with two capital crimes and this hearing theoretically could have resulted in those charges being dropped.

It was shameful enough that a man who was new to Canada had been provided with no legal assistance, would be unrepresented at the preliminary hearing and had been given no opportunity to evaluate the Crown's evidence. Surely he deserved to have someone of higher status than the village magistrate sitting in authority.

Naturally enough, with there being no opposition, the Crown was allowed to dictate the manner in which the hearing unfolded. Tom stood quietly in the box while the parade of witnesses took the stand. Not a single one of them was challenged about the evidence he or she provided. Not a single one of the many inconsistencies was questioned. Not a single one of the oversights was pointed out. Not a single one of the many instances of police work being shoddy, inefficient, inept or biased was brought to the fore.

Most of the inconsistencies and inequities were to arise again at the trial, but just to provide a single example of the way the preliminary hearing progressed, we can focus on the testimony regarding the blood stains that had been introduced as evidence.

The Crown's expert in the matter was Dr John M. Roussell of Montreal. He had been provided with the clothes that had been found near Bernice Connors' body as well as the uniform that Tom had surrendered to Staff Sergeant Davis on 8 June. He agreed with Davis's earlier testimony that the clothes he was shown were those in question, and was asked about the stains on the RAF uniform.

He said he had determined that they were human blood, but was not asked what tests he had done to arrive at his conclusions. Obviously, therefore, there was no follow-up question asking what percentage of accuracy might normally be expected from such tests. As might be surmised, the Crown did not feel the need to press Dr Roussell for any further elucidation.

Instead, Dr Roussell simply moved on from his imprecise observation concerning the bloodstains to give a recitation of the location of these stains on the uniform.

But even the Crown could not avoid the issue of blood type. It was a question that simply had to be asked in order to show the link between Tom and the crime.

Once again, Dr Roussell's testimony was inadequate at best. He admitted that he had been unable to ascertain blood type anywhere – not on Tom's tunic or trousers, not on Tom's leather belt, not even on Bernice's skirt or blouse. This he attributed to the fact that in some cases, the fabric had been subjected to heat. In other cases, he said, the blood had been on the cloth for some time and as a result, typing was impossible.

This testimony was given on 3 July. The items to which he was referring were in the hands of the police on 8 June. If too much time had elapsed to facilitate proper testing, whose fault was that?

Once again, this potentially probing line of questioning was ignored. The answer, though, is that it was clearly the fault of the RCMP. Staff Sergeant Davis testified that in addition to all the other items mentioned, he had found a blood-stained handkerchief near the kitchen door of Forrister Hall on 10 June. Even though the handkerchief could have been left by anyone, he gave it and all the other items to be tested to Dr Roussell on 25 June.

A good defence attorney would have approached Davis and said, 'So if I've got this right sir, you gathered some of this evidence on 7 June, some more on 8 June and the final item on 10 June, but you didn't submit it for forensic examination until 25 June? That was your testimony, wasn't it?'

Davis would have no option but to admit that this was the case, thereby opening the door for the defence attorney to challenge his competence. Was he not aware that blood deteriorates fairly rapidly, and that the more it deteriorates, the less likely it is that it will reveal useful evidence? Was it his custom to allow crucial time-sensitive evidence to be rendered useless? Was he aware that Bernice's blood had been classified as Group 4 and Tom's was Group 2, so identification of the blood group found at the crime scene might have virtually proved Tom's innocence?

At that point, the attorney, showing suitable indignation, would have approached the judge and said, 'Your Worship, this is indefensible! It is our contention that proper typing of this blood would have shown that none of it matched the blood of Bernice Connors. The RCMP officers, by mishandling the evidence, have removed the evidence that would have shown my client to be innocent. I must therefore demand that the charges be stayed.'

But of course, there was no defence attorney to say this. The judicial system in New Brunswick had not provided one. And even if there had been, there was no judge to hear it, just a village magistrate accustomed to handling remands and minor cases.

So Tom was bound over for a trial that could potentially bring about his execution.

Chapter Ten

For Tom Hutchings Sr, 29 June 1942 started out like any other day in the life of an older Englishman trying to make his contribution to the war effort.

He was one of 15,000 people working for the British Ministry of Food, trying to maintain a system that enabled the country's population to buy healthy food at reasonable prices and thereby remain well fed despite the war.

The substantial amount of food coming across the Atlantic as a result of the Lend-Lease Act meant that there was no shortage of staples. Even so, rationing was necessary to make sure that supplies were distributed fairly and used wisely, and that a black market either did not develop or was minimized.

But any sense of serenity that Tom Sr might have felt that day was shattered when he received two visitors from Scotland Yard. He was told that his younger son, the RAF sergeant, had been charged with murder in Canada.

The Scotland Yard officials made it clear that they were just passing along a message. There was nothing they could do to help. Frantic, Tom Sr immediately contacted the Air Ministry, but they too said the matter was out of their hands.

The next day, at the offices of the High Commissioner for Canada in Great Britain, he pleaded desperately for further information.

Since the original notification had emanated from RCMP national headquarters in Ottawa, that's where Tom Sr assumed his son had been arrested. Because of the nature of wartime security, he would have had no idea where his son was stationed.

Also, for reasons of security, his message would have been sent in code, and when the plain-language version landed on a desk in the Department of External Affairs in Ottawa, it referred to an RAF sergeant being detained in Ottawa. Although, in yet another concession to security, the

High Commissioner for Canada was not named in the message, the man who held the post at the time was Right Honourable Vincent Massey who went on to become Canada's governor general after the war. He seemed to sympathise with Tom Sr.

'Naturally, he is very upset,' his message read. 'Can you give me any particulars about the case which I could pass on to him? He also wishes to know what steps are being taken for his son's defence and what he can do to help his son.'

That message arrived in Canada on Tuesday, 30 June, and it was decided in the external-affairs department that it warranted a request for information from the RCMP. Following a one-day break for Dominion Day, a national holiday, that request was sent on 2 July.

On 3 July in London, Tom Hutchings Sr, was still frantically trying to find out information about his son's charge and the status of his defence.

On 3 July in Ottawa, the Secretary of State for External Affairs, having received a reply from the RCMP, was in the process of sending a coded message back to Vincent Massey.

On 3 July in Black's Harbour, Tom Roland Hutchings was committed to trial by a preliminary hearing in which he was unrepresented by counsel.

That trial could not begin for more than two months, even if it started on time – which, as it happened, it didn't.

Therefore, using the kind of logic that could make sense only to a bureaucrat, it was decided that Tom should be moved to Saint John because the security in the St Andrews Gaol in Charlotte County was somehow lacking.

On 9 July, an order-in-council of the New Brunswick government decreed that because of 'the unfitness of the said common gaol for the safe custody of prisoners', the move was necessary. A letter notifying Charlotte County Sheriff Charles W. Mallory of that fact was sent by J. Bacon Dickson, the clerk of the executive council.

Tom was being held in solitary confinement in St Andrews and had two options if he wanted to break out of the jail. He could find a way to unlock four iron doors that had maintained their security for more than a century, or he could somehow use his fingernails to chisel his way through the 30 inches of solid granite that composed the outer wall. Furthermore, the jailer lived on the premises and kept a close eye on his charges.

Nevertheless, because New Brunswick had reacted to concerns expressed by Canada's attorney general, who worked in Ottawa, Constable

Duncan Dunn of the RCMP's St George detachment drove to St Andrews in a police car on 24 July. Then he and Sheriff Mallory took Tom to Saint John in Mallory's car.

In his report on the matter, Constable Dunn duly noted that 'time spent on this duty was from 10 a.m. to 5 p.m.' and added that 'no expenses had been incurred on this duty'.

For two reasons, neither of which had anything to do with security, the transfer made Tom's existence more bearable. First, he was more comfortable in his new location. After all, the accommodation could hardly be more rudimentary than that which he had been enduring in St Andrews. But much more important was the medical attention he received.

Finally, Tom appeared to be getting a guiding hand. His plight came to the attention of Dr Ernest C. Menzies.

Dr Menzies was arguably the most highly regarded medical practitioner in New Brunswick at the time, and justifiably so. He had devoted his life to the study and care of the mentally ill and combined this dedication with selflessness and boundless empathy.

In 1945, three years after Tom's trial, public criticism of The Provincial Hospital, a psychiatric hospital operated by the government of New Brunswick, reached such an intolerable level that a Royal Commission was established to look into the matter.

Dr Menzies had been the head of that hospital since 1934 and usually, in inquiries of this nature, it is the man at the top who receives the lion's share of the blame. In fact, a resignation or a firing is the normal conclusion of the process.

But after sixty-three hearings to gather submissions from the public, and numerous unannounced visits, both day and night, to the hospital itself, the commissioners concluded that Dr Menzies deserved nothing but praise for the job he had done with limited staff, limited facilities, limited funding and a decaying building.

In its submission to the premier of New Brunswick at the conclusion of their investigation, the Royal Commission pointed out that among many other commendable actions taken during his tenure, Dr Menzies:

- Opened the doors at night so that patients would have access to bathrooms;
- Established an open-door ward for a group of about 100 male patients nearing return to society to allow them full access to the grounds in the daytime;

- Obtained the services of local practitioners who were specialists in surgery, gynaecology, genito-urinary disorders, eye, ear, nose and throat problems, metabolism, internal medicine and radiology;
- Set up an X-ray department, a laboratory, a dental room and an operating room with a sterilizing room;
- Set up a minor medical and surgical room, with the work of management and construction being done entirely by his staff;
- Arranged for every patient and all of the staff to be X-rayed – and found more than 350 open tuberculosis infectors;
- Established the first Sakel treatment in Canada – the hypo-glycaemia treatment, or insulin reaction. To this, he added electric shock therapy as well as malaria treatment;
- Organized repairs and alteration of the buildings while they were occupied by patients, thereby giving beneficial occupation to both chronic and recoverable patients under staff supervision;
- Created two cafeterias, and provided a modern admitting and treatment ward for women.

These were just a few of Dr Menzies' achievements cited by the Royal Commission. It is therefore clear that this man was much more than a general practitioner and that his evaluation of Tom ought not to be casually disregarded by anyone who wanted to see justice done.

Prior to being moved to Saint John, Tom had been subjected to only the most cursory of medical evaluations. But Dr Menzies, an expert on the subject of psychiatric afflictions, needed only a few minutes to realize that Tom suffered a significant mental deficiency.

Dr Menzies' achievements during his supervision of The Provincial Hospital illustrated his compassion for his patients. In Tom, he saw a man who had been deserted by the RAF and the New Brunswick justice system, and who was now left alone to fight a battle for his life. He also saw a patient in need of both support and empathy.

But unlike most cases at the hospital, this time Dr Menzies was dealing with a patient who needed more than direct medical intervention. He continued to interview Tom on a regular basis, visiting him six times in the Saint John Jail, fully aware that if he were to appear in court, his assessment had to be beyond reproach. But his experience told him that the kind of affliction he had seen exhibited in Saint John had to have been in existence for some time, so he began to delve into Tom's background.

He later explained that although he recognized the nature of Tom's affliction right away, he withheld making a submission to the court until he received what he referred to as 'confirmatory statements'.

He sent telegrams to Captain Tom Hutchings Sr in England to get as much information as he could about Tom's medical history. He contacted the RAF to see if Tom's friends could offer any insights. He consulted his medical textbooks.

Dr Menzies could have stopped there. After all, he was such a highly regarded authority on psychological matters that his assessment alone would have to be given significant weight by the court. Also, he was a very busy man. But such was his nature that he went on to enlist the opinion of world-renowned psychologists.

He spoke to RAF Wing Commander Christopher Mann, who had been a lecturer in psychology at the University of Manchester in England. Before the war, Dr Mann and Dr R. D. Gillespie had been co-workers.

Dr Gillespie was the chief psychiatrist for the RAF and the author of the highly regarded *Textbook of Psychiatry*. He had been a lecturer in psychopathology at the University of Aberdeen and in addition to his RAF duties was a lecturer in psychiatric medicine at Guy's Hospital and Medical School in London.

Now, finally, Tom was no longer alone. In his corner he had renowned medical specialists who believed that given the nature of his affliction, he had probably murdered no one, but even if he had done so, he was not culpable.

During Tom's time in jail in Saint John, the New Brunswick Law Society found a lawyer who would act as his defence counsel – Benjamin R. Guss of Saint John.

As far as Dr Menzies was concerned, this was a man who was to be seen as an ally, and he was therefore the man to whom he offered his services. He was convinced that his medical evaluation would go a long way to convincing a jury that Tom was not guilty of murder and he made it clear to Guss that he was willing to testify to that point in court.

Chapter Eleven

Tom's trial was a potential minefield for the New Brunswick Department of Justice. First of all, it was a capital trial and therefore, by definition, closely scrutinized, not only by the judiciary and the public but also by highly volatile special-interest groups.

Furthermore, it was as politically charged as a 1942 trial in Canada could be. It was quite possible that Canada, specifically the province of New Brunswick, might decide to execute an Englishman. And not just an Englishman, but an English serviceman who had come to Canada in order to improve the ongoing war effort of both countries by training armourers. The execution of an ally is not a task any country takes lightly.

It was no surprise then, that when it came time to select a judge for Tom's trial, the man chosen was The Honourable Mr Justice Charles Dow Richards, indisputably the star of the New Brunswick judiciary, at least as far as profile was concerned.

He was much more than a judge. In fact, at that time, his name would have been recognized by almost every resident of the province. Sitting on the bench was merely the latest calling in a long career in the public service.

Born in 1879 in the village of Southampton N.B., he had first turned to teaching, but that was simply a means to an end. He attended law school in his spare time, and by the time he was 33, he had graduated from the University of New Brunswick and been called to the bar. But he wasn't satisfied with being merely a lawyer. He immersed himself in politics and, when he was 41, was elected as the Conservative Member of the Legislative Assembly for the New Brunswick riding of York.

That was in 1920. He rose steadily through the ranks of provincial government and by 1931, he was at the top. He was the premier of New Brunswick.

But in the 1930s, the world was in the throes of the Great Depression and rare was the politician who escaped public censure. Richards headed the provincial government for two years and during that time, tried to shake the economy out of its lethargy by selling off government-owned assets – primarily fishing rights and land. In 1933, worn down by the demands of political life, he left politics and accepted a position as a judge for the Supreme Court of New Brunswick.

By 1942, he had established a reputation for taking a scholarly approach to the law and was regarded within the profession as a dignified and capable judge.

So this was the man who was to handle Tom's trial, not merely a widely recognizable, experienced judge but a former premier of the province.

The government had been every bit as painstaking in its selection of a Crown to prosecute the case. It had spared no expense in acquiring the services of Peter J. Hughes of Fredericton, a King's Counsel and one of the more highly regarded lawyers in eastern Canada. He had already featured in major New Brunswick cases, and had represented clients before the Supreme Court of Canada. The year after the Hutchings trial, he was named president of the Uniform Law Conference of Canada, an institution charged with standardizing laws across the nation.

Hughes also was also provided with an assistant, Harry Groom of nearby St Stephen, the man who had acted for the Crown during the preliminary hearing that had culminated with Tom being charged.

The expense of providing Tom with a defence was considerably less. The New Brunswick Bar Association simply told Benjamin R. Guss, a 37-year-old lawyer from Saint John, that the job was his. As Guss later admitted in a letter to the court, 'I did not seek this case, on the contrary, I tried to get out of it.'

The NB Bar Association refused to pay Guss for his services and would not even reimburse him for his expenses, but the power of the bar association was such that he had no choice other than to accept its edict.

Once again, Tom had been abandoned by those who should have been making sure that he was properly represented.

It was not a matter of Guss being a poor lawyer, or even an uncommitted lawyer, but he lagged far behind the team of Hughes and Groom in legal expertise and experience.

While the Crown's resources appeared to be unlimited, Guss was paying out of his own pocket for court documents, filing fees, travel to and from St Andrews, lodgings and so on. Furthermore, his own practice, and therefore his income, ceased to exist while he worked on Tom's case.

The preliminary hearing had been held in the community hall in Black's Harbour. But the majesty of the New Brunswick judiciary was to be put on display for a capital trial so, although there were a number of suitable courthouses fairly close to Black's Harbour, the magnificent edifice in St Andrews was selected for the occasion.

Built in 1840, it is an impressive white building in the classical style fronted by four grand columns. The cornice above the columns features a superb rendition of the British coat of arms with its lion and unicorn in vivid colours and the *Dieu et mon droit* written on an unfolding scroll. Still in use, it is the oldest operating courthouse in Canada, and its interior is every bit as elegant as its exterior. Its well-preserved Victorian glory is in marked contrast to the stark, gloomy jail only a few steps away where Tom was once again being held in solitary confinement after his return from Saint John on 24 September. There had still been no serious aid to Tom's cause provided by anyone in England, even though Vincent Massey, the High Commissioner for Canada, had received a reply to his 30 June request for information.

Canada's under-secretary of state, Norman A. Robertson, had sent a coded message on 3 July that the RCMP had confirmed to him that Tom Roland Hutchings had been charged with 'the murder of a young girl under particularly unpleasant circumstances', and had suggested that Tom Sr contact New Brunswick's attorney general if he wanted any legal advice. Robertson added that the RCMP had informed him 'that it is their understanding that RAF Headquarters in Canada will take steps to see that this man's defence is properly looked after.'

The RAF did no such thing. It limited its involvement to sending Flight Lieutenant W. T. Elverston to act as an observer. Before the trial began, Judge Richards clarified Elverston's status and asked if he was right in believing that Elverston was 'not appearing for any party at all other than as an observer for and on behalf of the Royal Air Force'.

'Yes, my lord,' answered Elverston. 'I am here in accordance with the instructions of my commanding officer and the custom and rules of the service which say that when any member of the force is charged with an offence in the civil courts, an officer shall attend and give the court such assistance as he may be able, and if required give evidence as to the accused's service and character.'

He might as well have said, 'The RAF couldn't care less what happens to our man, but the rules say someone has to be here, and I got stuck with the job.'

Having dispensed with the niceties, the judge saw no need to respond. He simply looked down to the Crown's table. 'Do you move for trial Mr Hughes?' he asked.

The trial of Tom Roland Hutchings for murder and rape was under way.

Chapter Twelve

Hughes confirmed that he was ready for trial. Then, in his turn, so did Guss. However, a problem arose immediately.

The law required that a list of forty-two petit jurors be submitted. Of these, twelve would be selected to sit on the trial jury. All were men because women were not allowed to serve on juries. Unfortunately, while he was attempting to compile the list, the sheriff had encountered six men who were not available.

One was ill; one had been excused by the judge for a confidential reason; one was over-age; one was dead; one was the janitor at the post office and thereby excused by virtue of being a member of the civil service; and one was in the army.

But instead of submitting the list of the forty-two who remained, the sheriff submitted the list of the forty-eight who had been considered.

The judge arrived at the logical conclusion that 'insofar as practical results are concerned, it doesn't seem to be of any importance.' Nevertheless, as a judge and a lawyer, he knew that logic is not always the ultimate arbiter in legal matters. 'The technical features may be of importance,' he added.

He therefore asked Hughes, but not Guss, for his 'considered view' and between the two of them – Hughes suggesting and the judge agreeing – they decided that court should be adjourned immediately so that the matter could be considered overnight.

Court had convened at 3.45 p.m. and was adjourned at 4.55 p.m.

When it reconvened at 10 a.m. the next day – 30 September – Hughes was well armed with legal arguments based upon the New Brunswick Jury Act. Unfortunately, none related directly to a problem of this nature.

Even so, Hughes and Judge Richards entered into a lengthy discussion, the only really salient point of which was the judge's observation that the first forty-two names on the list were the ones who were present and the last six on the list were absent. Therefore, he concluded, he would accept the first forty-two names and disregard the last six.

By this point, it must have become clear to Guss – even if it had not been earlier – that no matter what the judge's reputation for fairness might be within the legal community, Hughes was going to be well served by rulings from the bench.

The Crown and the judge travelled in the elite circles of the New Brunswick judiciary and were almost certainly social acquaintances. One was a King's Counsel, a significant step above an ordinary lawyer, and the other's standing in the province was such that he had been given a place on the Supreme Court bench simply because he asked for it.

Guss, on the other hand, was 37, a much younger man and an outsider. Although the circumstances need not be dwelled upon, they must be mentioned because of the realities of life in 1942. Guss was a Jew born in Europe, and New Brunswick was very much a Christian province populated by Canadians of long standing. In 1942, New Brunswick had never had a Jewish judge.

The first witness called was Dennison Guptill, the Black's Harbour police chief, and early in his testimony Hughes asked him why he was on Deadman's Harbour Road on the evening the body was found.

'I had been informed that a shoe had been found at that particular spot,' Guptill said.

Judge Richards intervened. '"As a result of information which you had received," would be a better way to put it,' he said.

Hughes wasted no time establishing his elevated status within the court. 'Nothing turns on it,' he said dismissively, before resuming his questioning.

Less than a minute later, he asked a leading question when he said to Guptill, 'Did you see any signs or marks on the road?'

At this point, Guss decided that it was time to make a stand. 'I'm sure my learned friend knows that he's not giving evidence,' he said. 'Let the witness tell what he saw. Don't suggest. What the witness saw is for the witness to say.'

The judge agreed that Guss was right and the questioning moved on. A little later in Guptill's testimony, a photograph was introduced and Hughes said, 'I see what looks like a stake there.'

Guss objected. 'My learned friend is suggesting again,' he said. 'My learned friend knows as well as I do, if not better, that he should not suggest anything to the witness.'

The judge wasn't so sure.

'If it was vital, that would be quite right,' he said.

'We don't know, my lord, what is vital and what is not,' said Guss.

In his defence, Hughes pointed out that he could easily arrive at the same conclusion by asking more questions. Guss replied that if that were indeed the case, then that was the way to do it.

The judge sided with Hughes. 'I think we do not need to be as particular as that about everything, Mr Guss,' he said.

For the most part, this is the way the trial was to unfold. Hughes repeatedly pushed the limits of permissibility – and often went past them. Frequently, perhaps because he realized that the judge had decided that he did 'not need to be as particular as that', Guss let Hughes continue unchallenged. Sometimes the judge accepted Guss's objections; more often he didn't. But at no time did Guss try to match Hughes' tactics.

Guss was always deferential, invariably referring to the judge as 'my lord', and Hughes as his 'learned friend'. Hughes often chose not to bother with such niceties, even though they were traditional in a New Brunswick supreme court.

When it came to dealing with witnesses, Guss tended to stay within the bounds of legal decorum and, on occasion, brought law textbooks to court to point out Hughes' transgressions. Even that tactic was not always successful. Judge Richards simply decreed that times had changed since the textbook was written and allowed Hughes to carry on.

Guptill was the first to testify because he set the stage for the Crown. In a lengthy, step-by-step examination by Hughes, he told of the phone call from Royden Connors that prompted the search for Bernice, the finding of some of her effects and the discovery of her body. He described the surrounding area, the injuries to Bernice's face, and his subsequent actions.

In his cross-examination, Guss tried to establish that the body was a good distance from the hall, but focused primarily on the area in which the first shoe was found and what Guptill had said were nearby signs of a struggle.

Guss pointed out that the road was a busy one and that the scuffle allegedly took place on Friday night. He wanted Guptill to admit that by Sunday evening, after two days of people passing and re-passing on their way to and from town, children playing and cars driving, 'there wouldn't be much to see.'

'I wouldn't admit that,' said Guptill.

He mentioned Guptill's testimony that an indentation in the dirt at the side of the road seemed to match the shoe found by Thomas Gaudet. 'You did not set that shoe into that mark to compare them?' he asked.

Guptill conceded that he did not.

Guptill stuck to his story that he saw Bernice's exposed foot, even though that testimony was not to be corroborated later by Constable Dunn who was at Guptill's side and admitted, 'I did not see that.'

It was also Guptill's contention that he first spotted the body and shouted, 'There she is!' That too was disputed by others at the scene.

There were other aspects of Guptill's testimony that were equally open to debate, but they weren't of such importance that they would determine the guilt or innocence of Tom Hutchings.

Those points would come. Guptill's was only the first name on the list of the Crown's forty-three scheduled witnesses, a list to which three names would be added.

Chapter Thirteen

While Hughes intended to lay out his case in a roughly chronological manner, he also wanted to make sure that he maintained the interest of the jurors. He therefore began by establishing the fact that a girl had gone to a dance but afterwards was not seen for two days. At that point, her body had been found, and to all appearances, a murder had been committed.

In essence, that was the testimony of Chief Guptill.

Having set the stage for the jurors, Hughes then went back to the beginning of the story to establish how this came about.

His first witness in that regard was Leading Aircraftman Albert Dungey, who worked in the motor transport section at the Pennfield base. In a way, he had been Bernice's date for the dance.

Black's Harbour wasn't much of a town, but to the RAF men stationed at Pennfield Ridge, an ocean away from home, it provided some entertainment other than the limited variations found on the base. Dungey had been in Black's Harbour on the Wednesday before the dance and had met Bernice Connors for the first time. He saw her again on Thursday, and it had been arranged that she and her girlfriend Cavell Bradford would go to the dance the next night with Dungey and another airman, Leading Aircraftman Fred Frewin. Dungey didn't even know Bernice's surname. To him, she was just 'Niecie'.

It was far from a formal date. In cross-examination, Guss asked if it were true that the girls had said that they 'didn't like to be tied to anybody'. Dungey answered, 'Yes. And we said we were the same at a dance.'

The four were to meet at 7.30 p.m., but the two airmen were delayed at Pennfield and left two hours late. Nevertheless, the girls were still waiting. After all, it had been understood that the airmen would pay the admission fee for the dance.

It became clear as the trial proceeded that a good deal of drinking took place that night. Bernice and Cavell were 19 and 18 respectively and the legal drinking age in New Brunswick at that time was 21, but before they went into the dance, a bottle of rum was passed around. All four took regular turns.

For the first half of the dance – until the intermission – the four were together. Dungey took every dance with one of the two girls, but was vague – probably intentionally – about how often he took a break to go outside for another drink. And although neither Hughes nor Guss pressed him on the point, it seemed likely that the girls went out and had drinks as well.

To the two lawyers, though, the important matter was not the amount of alcohol consumed but the timing of Bernice's departure. Dungey testified that although he saw her constantly until the beginning of the intermission, he did not see her afterwards. Therefore, the exact time that the intermission began was to become a factor in the trial. Dungey estimated that it started between 11.30 and 11.45 p.m.

The logical person to call to substantiate Dungey's testimony was his colleague, Leading Aircraftman Frewin. But Frewin was not in attendance, so the trial moved on, and the only other living member of the foursome, Cavell Bradford, one of four members of the Bradford family on the Crown's witness list, took the stand.

Hughes decided that it was now time to establish for the jury the link between Bernice and the items she was wearing that night. He therefore first asked Cavell to specify what clothes Bernice had worn and was told that they were a white blouse; a flowered skirt; brown shoes; and a brown coat. Bernice's accessories that night, Cavell said, were a necklace, an identification bracelet, and a ring.

In order to establish that the necklace was the same one found in the middle of Deadman's Harbour Road by Oscar Craig, Hughes asked for a more detailed description. Cavell said that it was 'green celluloid and gold'.

'Green celluloid what?' asked Hughes.

'Rings,' Cavell responded.

Cavell described the shoes Bernice had been wearing as brown with 'medium low heels'. When shown the shoes, coat and skirt that had been found in the vicinity of the body and had been introduced as exhibits, Cavell had no difficulty confirming that they belonged to Bernice.

But when shown another piece of cloth, she could not identify it. Hughes, as he so often did, tried to lead his witness. 'It seems to have the remnants of a sleeve or armhole,' he pointed out.

After Hughes had tried four variations of the same question without success, the judge made him move on to other items, and Cavell readily identified Bernice's purse, bracelet and ring, as well as one of the rings from the necklace.

To this point, no link had been established between Bernice and Tom Hutchings. Hughes decided to see if he could find one, and again, overstepped the limits of courtroom protocol.

'Did you see the accused ... that is, the prisoner in the dock?' he asked Cavell. She said she didn't, so Guss let it pass.

But Hughes decided to press the matter and said, 'You can't recall him at all that night?' That was too much for Guss. He had had enough. He didn't need to state the specifics of his objection because it was glaringly obvious to seasoned veterans of the court like Hughes and Judge Richards. The Crown is not supposed to point out the accused. He can ask a witness if he or she recognizes the accused, but he can't point out who it is.

Hughes somewhat disingenuously suggested that he thought Cavell didn't understand what he meant by 'the accused' so out of the goodness of his heart, he was just helping her with her testimony.

Guss was equally willing to supply some guidance. 'I have Phipson here,' he said. (*Phipson on Evidence* is generally considered to be the leading textual authority on courtroom decorum and it explains the proper procedures for lawyers to follow during a trial.)

'Yes, I'm sure Mr Hughes is familiar with that,' said Judge Richards, even though there hadn't been a lot of evidence to support that view. He then told the court that there is a proper way to identify the accused, and added, for the benefit of Hughes, 'You know what it is as well as I.'

Hughes did not respond. He simply resumed his questioning and established that around 11.20 p.m., Cavell and Bernice, as well as two local friends, Harry Watson and Athenia Hanley, had stepped outside the hall. They had stayed outside briefly, then three of them went back in.

Bernice stayed outside, Cavell said, and she never saw her again.

Hughes' next line of questioning had to do with the Sunday afternoon hunt for Bernice's body. There was nothing new in it. Because she was one of the group of girls who formed part of the search party, Cavell was able to more or less confirm Guptill's testimony. But that's all Hughes wanted from her.

In his cross-examination, Guss tried to suggest that perhaps Bernice had returned to the dance unnoticed, but there was no evidence to support that view. He also tried to get Cavell to admit that when Dungey took a break for a drink, she had done the same. She denied it.

After she stepped down, Hughes, as might be expected, tried to add to the chain of evidence he had started to create. If Hanley and Watson were the last two people Cavell Bradford had seen with Bernice, then they were the two who should be called next.

Hanley did advance Hughes' case a little, but not much. In fact, an impartial observer listening to her testimony would have to conclude that it was of no value to the Crown whatsoever.

She did confirm that the exhibits she was shown were Bernice's effects. But then she said that when Harry Watson and Cavell Bradford had gone back into the dance, she had stayed outside and talked to other girls. Cavell Bradford had specifically stated that all three went in together.

Then Hanley insisted she had seen Bernice walking down Deadman's Harbour Road in the company of an RAF sergeant. She had seen his three stripes, she said, but she could not see his face. Even so, she was sure that she had 'never seen him before', and that she knew it wasn't Leading Aircraftman Dungey by his physique.

This man was 'quite a bit taller', and Bernice 'came up to his neck or ears'. That kind of precision should have been able to help Hughes establish his case since Tom was 5ft 11in and Bernice was 5ft 6in.

But Guss pointed out in cross-examination that when she testified in the preliminary hearing, Hanley had been asked about the height of the unidentified sergeant and had said, 'Well, I don't know.'

When the matter was raised again a little later, she had said, 'Well, I guess, I think he was taller.'

There had been no mention of either his neck or his ears.

Her testimony regarding the time frame wasn't any help to Hughes either. She had said at the trial that she hadn't seen Bernice after 11.20 p.m. But in the preliminary hearing, she had said it was 11.30 p.m.

'I didn't know exactly the time,' she conceded to Guss.

Even her assertion to Hughes that Bernice was in the company of an RAF sergeant couldn't be substantiated. Her preliminary testimony was that the man was 'in the RAF, I guess.'

Guss asked her if the man she saw could in fact have been in the RCAF since there were some Canadian sergeants at the dance that night.

'Yes,' she said.

To the average onlooker today, there might not be an appreciable difference between the 1942 uniforms of the RAF and the RCAF. But to those who lived in that era and saw uniforms every day, the variations were noticeable. One was that British sergeant stripes were much larger than their Canadian counterparts. And Hanley was basing her identification, such as it was, almost totally on the man's stripes.

Sixteen-year-old Harry Watson provided yet another variation on the order in which he and his friends went back into the building. He said that Cavell Bradford was already inside when he got there. Asked specifically about that point, he said, 'I never went in with Cavell.' Cavell had said that he did.

He also was clear on the time he last saw Bernice Connors, saying that it was 11.45 p.m. Dungey had been able to say only that it was between 11.30 and 11.45 p.m., so Watson provided a firm time which was later than any previous witness had testified, and in this case, the time factor was to be crucial.

In cross-examination, Guss once again returned to the issue of the height of the man who had been seen accompanying Bernice. Hughes had induced Watson to agree with his leading question concerning what he had seen when the two walked away. 'Her head would have come halfway up his head?'

Watson agreed that it would.

But Guss went back to Watson's testimony in the preliminary hearing when he had said, 'Oh, his head was above Bernice's. I don't know how far.'

The issue of doubt had been raised and Guss was fully aware that the more doubt he could instill in the jury's mind, the better. This was a trial based only on circumstantial evidence, and more than ever, reasonable doubt was a primary consideration.

But it was at this point that Guss slipped up a little bit. He missed an opportunity to make a rape-case jury aware of a fact that might have added one more item to the growing evidence of reasonable doubt.

In his testimony at the preliminary hearing, Watson had said that Bernice and her male companion were walking away from the dance with their heads leaning together. He added that their arms were around each other's waists.

Guss's mistake was to not get him to confirm this observation. But had it been placed before the jury, Guss would have put himself in a position to contend that Bernice was able to make friends with a man very quickly. After all, it had already been established by her girlfriends under oath that Bernice had never met Tom before the group of four stepped outside.

So it would have done Guss's case no harm to point out to the jury that she walked off towards the dark end of the road, leaning her head against the head of a man she had met only moments ago and that the two had their arms around each other's waists.

Perhaps, as the trial unfolded, there might never have arisen an occasion to remind the jurors of this point. But then again, perhaps it might have been important. It would have done Guss no harm to bring it up at this stage without comment.

Chapter Fourteen

By the time Harry Watson stepped down, Hughes had established to his satisfaction the fact that Tom Hutchings and Bernice Connors were on Deadman's Harbour Road together. Now he needed corroboration, and he looked to Sergeant Tom Edwards and Mildred Justason to provide it.

Theirs was important testimony because if it was accurate, it advanced the Crown's case and placed Tom and Bernice closer to the area in which Bernice's body was discovered.

Certainly, some of it was accurate. But Guss was faced with the difficult task of separating the wheat from the chaff, something he might have been better able to do had he been given the time and the money to authorize a private investigation prior to the trial.

Like a number of the others at the dance, Edwards was an RAF sergeant. But whereas the others were ground crew or support staff, Edwards was a pilot. As a result, even though he lived in the same building as the other sergeants, he would have travelled in a different circle and wouldn't have been in their company on a regular basis.

He knew who Tom was because their rooms were on opposite sides of a corridor but he didn't even know him well enough to call him Roy as did all the other RAF personnel. During the preliminary hearing, he admitted, 'I knew him just by Hutchings.'

The rooming arrangement had been in existence for only two weeks or so and, as Edwards admitted in his testimony, 'I don't know him very well. I knew him just to speak to.' In other words, they were merely nodding acquaintances.

Edwards also differed from the other sergeants in that he was carrying on a relationship with one of the Black's Harbour girls.

He had left Pennfield in the early evening on the Friday of the dance and by seven o'clock was at the home of 21-year-old Mildred Justason – four houses down Deadman's Harbour Road past the hall. The two stayed there for three hours, but neither Hughes nor Guss felt the need to establish what transpired during that time.

There is little doubt that by 10 p.m., Edwards and Justason were at the dance hall and according to Edwards, who testified first, it was about 10.55 when Tom Hutchings approached him. 'He asked me if I would like a drink,' he said.

'I said, not at the moment. I would let him know later.'

Only about five minutes had passed when he told Hutchings he was ready. The two went outside and walked past the line of parked cars – about 40 yards – to put some distance between themselves and the hall. Since Tom had suggested the drink, it was his bottle of rum that was produced first and each took a turn. Then Edwards reciprocated, getting out his bottle of Scotch and they both drank from that too.

This testimony fits perfectly with the account of the evening that Tom gave to Staff Sergeant Davis in his initial interview. He said that while he knew the names of his ground-crew friends, he had only a casual acquaintance with aircrew. Edwards was aircrew. Tom also said that while he drank rum for most of the night, he had taken one drink of whisky. This was it.

While the two men were having their drinks, Edwards noticed a woman approaching the hall and carrying a pail. In England, he would probably have been asked about a bucket, but in Canada, it was a pail and Edwards agreed with Hughes that he had seen it. He didn't say whether it was full or empty and wasn't asked. He went back inside, found Mildred again and they danced until 11.30 p.m. With the dance hall getting stuffy, they decided to take a walk down Deadman's Harbour Road. This time, he saw two women carrying one pail between them. (The women were not directly involved with the crime, but Hughes introduced their appearances so that he would later be able to establish a time frame. Running water was not common in New Brunswick towns in that era, and the women were taking well-water to the hall so that coffee and tea could be served at the intermission.)

Just beyond the beginning of the unmade portion of the road, which coincided with the last streetlight and was a little more than 200 yards from the hall, Edwards saw two other people heading towards the dance hall, not away from it.

He told Hughes he recognized Tom, but not the girl with him. Justason knew it was her friend Bernice, but Edwards had never met her before. Tom produced his bottle and offered it around, Edwards said, but he declined and

Mildred told him to put it away because they were near her house and under the streetlight. Bernice was not of legal drinking age.

The pairs then went their separate ways. Tom and Bernice continued towards the dance hall, while Edwards and Justason sauntered on for another 50 yards or so along the unlit portion of the road, then turned around and came back.

Before they returned to the illuminated area, they met two people but it was too dark to see them clearly. Mildred said in the preliminary hearing that she recognized Bernice's voice. Edwards said that it was 'very dark' but he recognized the man's voice, and it was Tom's.

According to Edwards, nobody said anything of substance. There was just a passing remark.

Mildred continued on to her house with Edwards and the two went inside for half an hour. Neither saw Bernice Connors again.

In cross-examination, Guss managed to get Edwards to admit that when he and Mildred had gone on their walk into the unlit area of Deadman's Harbour Road, he had finished off his Scotch and thrown away the bottle.

Guss also asked if, during that same sortie, Edwards remembered passing a group of four boys drinking beer. Said Edwards, 'I noticed some fellows there but – Oh yes, I believe there were two bicycles among them, but I didn't notice them drinking beer.'

He said that he couldn't remember how many boys were in the group, but he was of the opinion that one was a sailor. In the local parlance of the day, anyone in the navy was referred to as a being a sailor, just as anyone in the army was referred to as being 'in the soldiers'.

Once Edwards had been cross-examined and Hughes had finished his redirect, court was adjourned. It was 5.35 p.m. on the last day of September.

When court reconvened at 10 o'clock the next morning, Mildred Justason took the stand. Hughes took her through the events of the evening of 5 June as they related to her, and they tended to correspond to the account given by Edwards. This was not surprising since she had sat in court the day before and listened to his testimony.

Still, there were some inconsistencies. For example, Justason was quite certain that she was not the one who told Tom to put his bottle away. She said Bernice had done it and remembered her using the justification that Boots lived nearby. Bernice always called her Boots, she said.

There were also some matters that Hughes had not mentioned and Guss raised them. He got Justason to confirm, for instance, that about twenty minutes before Edwards left the dance hall to go for a drink with Tom, he and Mildred had taken a walk in the other direction. There, near a garage that was under construction, Edwards had been drinking from his bottle of Scotch.

Guss had no problem accepting the fact that Tom and Bernice had been seen walking towards the dance hall. But he zeroed in on the crucial matter of identification of the pair that Edwards and Justason said they had later seen walking away from the dance hall. Was it indeed Bernice and Tom?

He cast doubt on Justason's ability to give an accurate recollection by asking her about the group of boys. In her trial testimony, she had said that the boys were standing beside the road. But in her preliminary-hearing testimony, she had said that they passed her and Edwards. 'They were coming towards the dance hall, and we were going the other way.'

The testimony about bicycles was another concern. She told Hughes that she 'noticed there was a bicycle there, or maybe two bicycles.' The judge said he hadn't heard her so she repeated it.

That testimony dovetailed perfectly with what she had heard Edwards say the day before. Although no one was aware of it at the time, the testimony of the next witness, Alonzo Hall, would therefore come as something of a surprise. Hall, one of the boys in question, said that there had been no bicycles at all.

Justason had also said that she didn't recognize any of the boys. Guss read a list of four names. In three cases, Justason admitted knowing the person in question.

The four names he had read were those of the four boys. 'You didn't recognize them?' he asked. Justason said she didn't.

'Although you know them?' he persisted.

'I didn't recognize them.'

The implication was clear. If she didn't recognize three people that she said she knew, how could she recognize Bernice Connors whom she also knew?

But by far the most important portion of the testimonies of Justason and Edwards had to do with the identification of the two people they saw walking away from the dance hall.

Edwards said, 'I didn't identify either until the accused spoke to me.' No conversation was held. He said that Tom made a passing remark that he couldn't remember because it was of no consequence, but he recognized his voice.

'Did anyone speak besides you and the accused?' asked Hughes.

'Not that I remember sir, no, 'said Edwards.

It was not surprising that he couldn't remember. Except for the drink he gave Hutchings – which was countered by a drink of Hutchings' rum – he had consumed a bottle of Scotch whisky by that point. It is not inconceivable that during his three hours in Mildred's house he was accorded further potable hospitality, but there was no testimony in that regard.

In redirect, Hughes, perhaps not recognizing the implication, got Edwards to confirm the lack of conversation with Bernice at the second meeting. He asked what Bernice had said at that time and Edwards replied, 'I couldn't say. I didn't hear her say anything.'

Mildred, however, had quite a different recollection. She first of all confirmed that she and Bernice had spoken. Hughes asked her what had been said.

Justason's answer was: 'Bernice said, 'We don't know those people. We wouldn't even bother speaking to them.'

'What?' said the judge.

Justason gave her answer again. 'She said, "We don't even know these people. We won't bother speaking to them." In a joking sort of way.'

So although it seemed reasonable to accept Justason's testimony that the woman on the road was indeed Bernice, the identification of Tom was far from reliable.

Edwards, almost certainly drunk, said he could identify Tom by his voice even though he had admitted both in the preliminary hearing and earlier in the trial that he hardly knew him. Justason couldn't identify him at all. She remembered a man with a light moustache whereas Tom's was dark and heavy. She had seen him at the first meeting under the streetlight but when Hughes had asked, 'You had never seen him before in your life?' she had answered 'No.'

In summation, Hughes had not accomplished a lot. He had placed Bernice on Deadman's Harbour Road heading towards the area where her body was later found. But on the matter of Tom being her companion, he had received no confirmation whatsoever from Mildred Justason.

And from Sergeant Edwards, who had been drinking heavily at the time of the encounter, he had received nothing more than a qualified belief that it was Tom's voice.

Guss first got Edwards to admit that he had been known to make mistakes when identifying voices on the phone. Then he asked him about a more direct evaluation. 'You certainly wouldn't like to take a chance – put a number of airmen up, and blindfold you and attempt to recognize their voices? You wouldn't like to submit to such a test?'

Edwards answered, 'Not exactly, no. Unless I knew them and heard their voices quite a lot of times before.'

But by his own admissions under oath, he did not know Tom Hutchings and he had not heard his voice 'quite a lot of times before'.

Chapter Fifteen

Any experienced trial lawyer knows that it is never a good idea to assume that the jurors are paying close attention to every detail. Therefore, once evidence has been introduced, it should be substantiated as much as possible.

To that end, Hughes took the opportunity to introduce a string of witnesses who – he hoped – would corroborate earlier testimony from other witnesses.

Since both Sergeant Edwards and Mildred Justason had mentioned meeting a group of boys near the last streetlight on Deadman's Harbour Road, Hughes called two members of that group.

There had been four on 5 June, but two had since left the area. Foster Eldridge was in Ontario serving in the army and Gilbert Eldridge was doing convoy duty with the Royal Canadian Navy on a corvette in the North Atlantic.

That left two 17-year-olds, Alonzo Hall and Donald Adams, available for Hughes. Hall was the first to take the stand.

Hughes set the stage by establishing that the four boys had been at the dance hall shortly after 11 p.m. but had left and gone down Deadman's Harbour Road.

It is a basic rule of courtroom strategy that a lawyer should never ask his own witness a question to which he does not know the answer. But it appeared that on this occasion, Hughes strayed from that mandate.

Referring to the boys' departure from the area of the dance hall, and probably trying to confirm the presence of bicycles, he asked, 'Did you have anything with you?'

'Yes. We had a couple of bottles of beer,' said Hall.

'You had what?' responded the apparently shocked Hughes.

'A couple of bottles of beer,' repeated Hall.

'Anything else?' asked Hughes.

Hall said that was the extent of it. They had nothing else.

Readers of the trial transcript can almost see Hughes' brain working. He was probably thinking 'I've got a 17-year-old on the stand that I'm trying to present as a credible witness and he's telling me he's got beer when he's still four years away from the legal drinking age. All I want him to do is tell me about his bicycle.'

He decided to put it bluntly. 'Were you walking or riding or what were you doing?' he asked.

'We were walking.'

Again, Hughes' frustration is almost palpable. Having already had so much success getting Judge Richards to allow him to use leading questions, he posed another one. 'There has been some reference to a bicycle. Was there a bicycle in your party?'

The answer could not have been further from what Hughes wanted to hear.

'No.'

Hughes was no doubt fully aware that he had just provided Guss with a superb opportunity to discredit the two previous witnesses. Edwards had been drinking heavily and had insisted there were bicycles. And it now appeared that Justason, who had sat in court during Edwards' time on the stand, had merely parroted her boyfriend's testimony. What other figments of Edwards' imagination had been confirmed by Justason?

The best tactic available to Hughes was a quick move in another direction, and that's exactly what he did.

He announced that while the boys were near the last streetlight, Bernice Connors had come along. He asked Hall if she had talked to the group.

Hall said that Bernice had said, 'Hello boys. I want you to meet Whitey.'

Guss immediately objected. According to the rules of court procedure, if the accused was not present, a conversation cannot be recounted.

Hughes contended that the accused was indeed present, but Guss was adamant that there had been no proof of that. Hall had said that Bernice was in the company of an airman, but that airman had not been identified.

Even though Hughes insisted that as a result of earlier testimony from his witnesses, the man had to be Tom Hutchings, the judge wasn't so sure. 'There is a possibility it may have been Bernice and someone else,' he said.

Hall was not allowed to give the particulars of the conversation, but he was allowed to say that he noticed the man had an English accent and that he offered them a drink of his rum.

The boys didn't accept his offer, Hall said, but when beer was offered, both Bernice and the airman drank some.

In his cross-examination, Guss reminded Hall that during the preliminary hearing, he had been asked about the height of the airman in comparison to Bernice. Hall agreed that he had said, 'I would say he was a little taller.'

The testimony of Donald Adams didn't differ much from that of Hall, and Hughes walked him through it, but this time he stayed away from any mention of bicycles.

In cross-examination, Guss again pursued the possibility that Bernice's companion was someone other than Tom Hutchings and, as he had done with Hall, referred to answers given at the preliminary hearing.

He pointed out that Adams had said the airman 'was a little taller than she', and that when asked about the airman's voice, he had said, 'I can't say much to the voice.' Adams did not deny having given that testimony.

Guss could have added more weight to his point by referring to a related question, to which Adams had responded, 'I couldn't tell you very much,' and added. 'I didn't hear him talk very much.'

Furthermore, the magistrate in the preliminary hearing was not as meticulous as Judge Richards. On that occasion, Foster Eldridge had been in town and the magistrate let him testify that when Bernice had met the boys, she had said, 'Meet Mr White.'

Whether it was Whitey or Mr White, it was not a name anyone had ever been known to use to refer to Tom Hutchings who was universally known as Roy.

The two women who had been seen carrying pails of water, Alice Mitchell and Grace Glennie, were also called. Hughes was constantly trying to pin down the time frame, which was central to his case, and because the women were involved only with the intermission and not with the dance, their testimony was likely to be more specific.

They knew what time they needed to show up with the water for hot drinks and judged themselves accordingly. They were able to say with certainty that they had seen Mildred Justason 'with an Air Force fellow', between 11.30 and 11.35 p.m.

Guss conducted only a cursory cross-examination of Glennie and had no questions at all for Mitchell. The fact that the two women had seen Edwards and Justason didn't really affect what he considered to be the key point in his case. To him, the crucial factor was that they had not seen Tom Hutchings.

To this point, the Crown had called eleven witnesses, yet there was still no one who had visually identified Bernice and Tom going back down Deadman's Harbour Road after they had been seen walking back towards the dance hall.

Chapter Sixteen

At this stage of the proceedings, it was possible that Hughes believed he had convinced the jury that Tom Hutchings was the man accompanying Bernice Connors when she met the group of four boys.

After all, he had tried to persuade Judge Richards to allow Alonzo Hall to describe the conversation on the premise that Tom was present. It may have been nothing more than a lawyer's little trick – and Hughes was never in short supply of those – to make a statement he knew would be disallowed because he also knew it would nevertheless stick in the minds of the jurors.

But more likely, he believed that Tom was guilty and that the evidence had piled up to the point that the jury had already adopted the same view.

Even so, Hughes had to realize that there was a very weak link in the chain of evidence – and it had been there from the beginning.

As far back as 12 June, five days after discovery of the body, when Staff Sergeant Davis had submitted his report to the RCMP's J Division (serious crimes) headquarters in Fredericton, Davis had also been aware of the flaw. His report to his superiors detailed how he had gathered witnesses, taken statements, collected exhibits, and drawn his conclusion that Tom Hutchings was 'a sexual pervert of the most violent type'.

But he knew there was more to be done. As he explained:

> Whilst discussing this case with Inspector Bullard, O.C. (officer commanding) Fredericton Sub-Division; on the 10 instant; it was agreed that further attention should be given to search the locality at the scene of the crime with the hope that some article may yet be found which would place the accused actually on the spot.

That was a major void in the body of evidence. There was not a scrap of physical evidence to put Tom at the scene. No popped buttons. No skin under Bernice's fingernails. No blood matching Tom's type. No missing hat. No pubic hair. No footprints. Nothing.

It was at this stage of the trial that Hughes tried to develop some sort of proof that Tom had indeed, at some point, been near the site of the moss-covered body.

He couldn't do it with physical evidence. As Davis had promised, he had sent his men back to the scene. However, they had found nothing more than a dirty, old, well-worn table knife that did not match any cutlery in use at the Pennfield base.

So Hughes tried to counter the evidentiary gap with the testimony of three related witnesses he called in sequence. The first was Gerald Humphries, a fitter in the RAF. Given that the British wartime slang for German military was Jerry, it is not surprising that Gerald Humphries went by the nickname of Jeff, not Jerry.

After arriving at the Friday-night dance, Humphries had spent most of his time with the second witness, Sylvia Gaudet, a Black's Harbour teenager who had agreed to meet him there. Following the accepted pattern at these dances, she was not his date in the true sense of the word, but it was understood that they were more or less together for the evening. And Humphries admitted that at the time he learned that Bernice's body had been found – on Sunday evening – he was with Sylvia again, this time visiting her at her house.

The third in this series of witnesses was Leading Aircraftman Robert Moore, a man from Northern Ireland who was a carpenter in the RAF and a close friend of Humphries. They had gone to Black's Harbour together, gone to the movies together and then gone to the dance, arriving at approximately 10.30 p.m.

Much of the testimony given by those three overlaps, but the essence is this: Shortly after midnight, Humphries and Gaudet decided to take a stroll down Deadman's Harbour Road. They were more than 400 yards from the hall when they heard what they thought was the sound of someone vomiting. Even though the sky was overcast and the nearest streetlight was at least 200 yards away, Humphries thought he saw a couple having sex.

It was so dark that, as Humphries admitted during the preliminary hearing, 'If it hadn't been for those sounds, I should have passed right by and not known them.' This was an important point but Guss did not raise it at the trial.

Humphries shepherded his 15-year-old companion away from the scene and accompanied her back to dance hall. There, he sought out Moore and enlisted his aid. The two went back to the place where Humphries had seen the couple and discovered that they were still there. The RAF men suggested to the couple that they should curtail their activities, then went back to the dance hall, arriving there around 12.40 or 12.45 a.m.

When Hughes tried to pinpoint the location of the incident, Humphries said that he and Gaudet had been 'two or three telephone poles' past a culvert on the unmade portion of the road and had been walking away from the hall.

As for what he saw there, Humphries said, 'I could see the naked leg of one person and the other appeared to be on top and when I realized what was taking place, I promptly got hold of the girl's arm and took her straight back to the dance hall.'

The person on top, Humphries said, was wearing an air force uniform.

Because of the level of decorum that existed in 1942, there followed a further twenty questions from Hughes regarding the placement of feet, the direction in which the bodies were facing and so on. Judge Richards chimed in with three questions of his own and added three comments regarding the nature of the questioning. At no point did anyone state directly that the two appeared to be engaged in sexual intercourse, but eventually, the conclusion was inescapable.

Guss's cross-examination was not at all aggressive. He asked some questions regarding elapsed times and got Humphries to admit he could identify neither of the two people on the ground.

Then Guss ended with this question: 'You cannot swear that Bernice Connors had any improper relations on the night of 5 June?'

Humphries said he could not.

Sylvia Gaudet's testimony regarding the event differed significantly. Whereas Humphries said they were 'on the way out', she said they had been on the left side of the road when they headed out and that when they saw something moving just off the right side, it had caught their attention. They 'walked past fast', then came back on the side closer to the site of the movement.

Whereas Humphries saw a couple on the ground, Gaudet 'saw a person crawling or moving'. When she was urged to be more specific, she said she saw 'something white that appeared to be a person unclothed'.

She said she heard a man speak with what appeared to be an English accent. Humphries had said, 'I can't remember the words,' but confirmed that he had heard 'a few softly spoken'. They were so quiet, in fact, that he had to admit that he couldn't identify the gender of the person who spoke. 'I would not be sure,' he answered when asked if it were a man or a woman.

Humphries and Gaudet were standing so close together that he was able to grab the girl's arm, yet whereas he saw two people, one of whom was in uniform, Gaudet saw only 'a person unclothed'.

When Hughes put the question, 'Did you notice any clothed person at that time?' her answer was simple and unequivocal.

'No.'

So one of them saw a naked leg and two people on the ground; the other saw a nude person crawling. One heard a man speaking with an English accent, but the other, an Englishman well-attuned to the dialects of his country, heard no accent and couldn't determine whether the speaker was male or female.

Apparently, Gaudet was unable to visually establish the gender of the crawling person, but must have assumed it was a male since she saw only one person and heard only a male voice.

For some reason, Guss did not pursue these inconsistencies in his cross-examination. He merely asked Gaudet about the number of English servicemen at the dance and her knowledge of English dialects – which she confirmed was non-existent. Then he put one final question: 'Would you swear that you saw Roy Hutchings, Sergeant Roy Hutchings, the accused, kill Bernice Connors on the night of 5 June?'

Of course, she would swear no such thing.

Leading Aircraftman Robert Moore said he remembered his friend Jeff Humphries coming back to the dance hall and asking him to accompany him down Deadman's Harbour Road. He also remembered going past the culvert covered with boards. 'I tripped over it,' he said.

He thought the distance from the culvert to the couple was '40 or 50 yards'.

His testimony was very close to that of Humphries. In fact, on some occasions, it was delivered using almost the same phraseology. He had seen a bare leg, 'from the hip downwards', which he assumed to be a woman's leg.

Like Humphries, he said the man was wearing an air force uniform but neither man could say whether it was RAF or RCAF. Neither of them could see any signs of rank. And for that matter, the area was so dark, as both of them admitted under oath, that it had been impossible to see the face of either person.

But Moore did say that he had spoken to the couple, and a man's voice had answered him. During the preliminary hearing, Moore recalled saying, 'Better break it up chum in case the police get here.'

He said the response had been, 'Okay chum.' The judge did not allow the testimony of that brief conversation to be heard in the trial.

Moore also said that neither of the people on the ground moved while he was there.

Again, Guss's cross-examination took a strange tack. He did not ask Moore to explain how, since it was too dark to see the faces of the couple, he could be sure that there was no movement. He merely confirmed the time of the incident and the fact that it was too dark to tell which type of uniform the man had been wearing.

Fourteen witnesses into his list, Hughes still had been unable to establish the identity of the person accompanying Bernice after she had been seen walking back towards the dance hall with Tom. He had no evidence whatsoever of rape because if the person who may or may not have been crawling around past the culvert had been under some duress, surely she could have said so. And for that matter, he didn't even have any evidence of murder.

Chapter Seventeen

The trial was now well into the afternoon of its second day – third day if the wrangling over the selection of jurors was included.

Yet so far, Hughes had done very little to prove that Tom Roland Hutchings had murdered and raped Bernice Connors.

While it certainly seemed highly likely that Bernice had been murdered, there was no incontrovertible evidence. The wounds on her face could have been self-inflicted by someone who was intoxicated enough to fall repeatedly. Her body could subsequently have been found by someone who, through some misguided sense of decorum, had decided to cover it with moss and place her arms and legs in what Staff Sergeant Davis called a 'normal position'. While such a turn of events did not have a high degree of probability, a court of law considering a charge of murder requires proof that a murder had indeed been committed and so far, Hughes had produced none.

The only evidence to support the rape charge was the scratch on Bernice's inner thigh, a minor wound that was nowhere close to meeting the standards required to prove rape. And even if it were shown that a rape had been committed, there was nothing to indicate that Tom had been the rapist. As Davis was only too aware, nothing at the scene indicated that Tom had ever been there.

As for the murder, any evidence proving Tom to be the culprit was scanty at best. A number of people had seen him at the dance. That was not in doubt. But the last time he and Bernice had definitely been seen together, they were walking towards the dance hall, not away from it. After that, there had been no reliable identification of Tom at all, just speculation, guesswork and assumption.

Sergeant Edwards, who by his own admission, had nothing more than a passing acquaintance with Tom and had drunk a bottle of Scotch, said he recognized him by his voice. His girlfriend, standing beside him, did not recognize Tom at all. Both of them saw boys with bicycles when there were no bicycles.

Sergeant Humphries, Leading Aircraftman Moore and Sylvia Gaudet said they saw variations of a couple (although Gaudet admitted to seeing only one person) involved in an amorous encounter, but it was far too dark for them to see either face.

Since these collective reminiscences were the essence of Hughes' case to that stage of the trial, he had a lot left to prove. Granted, there would be much more evidence to come, and those who considered Tom to be guilty had to assume that it would be a lot more damning than what had been produced so far. But on the other hand, if the Crown had a good deal of incontrovertible evidence, why bother with the witnesses who had taken the stand so far and presented testimony which was, at best, circumstantial, and at worst, vague and contradictory?

The answer was to be found in the report of an incident that was never mentioned at the trial but which appeared to have convinced Davis that Tom Hutchings was not only guilty of the attack on Bernice but had been guilty of an attack on another woman. This report, attained from RCMP files, was based upon an account that lacked solid evidence, to say the least. Nevertheless, it seems to have had a profound effect on Davis's approach to the Bernice Connors murder.

The alleged incident had occurred while Tom was stationed in Nova Scotia prior to being transferred to Pennfield. Mabel Richmond, a 23-year-old woman who had been separated from her husband for two years, knew Tom by his nickname of Roy. She had agreed to a date with him on the evening of 30 April; they went together to her friend's house shortly after 8.30 p.m. but found no one home. What follows is her statement to the RCMP with minor editing changes for the sake of clarity:

> We decided to go down to the river and have a drink. We sat on Roy's tunic and drank a bottle of whisky between us. The next thing I recall was Roy wanting to go a little further than I did, and when I refused, he hit me on the right side of the face with his fist. The next thing I can recall was when a car, driven by a man and with a woman in the front seat, let me off at my mother's home in Salem N.S.
>
> I don't remember taking my clothes off and wanting to go in for a swim, although I may have, and although I know that

Roy hit me, I am not certain as to whether I had my clothes on at the time or not.

All I had on when I got home was shoes, stockings and Roy's tunic. I do not remember putting his tunic on. On Saturday, Mrs Trefry (her landlady) gave me my clothes, and said that Roy had left them with her the night previous. There was a jacket, dress, slip, girdle, brassiere, pants and purse. None of my clothes were torn and they were all in good condition. It was about 11.30 p.m. when I got home on Thursday night. My right eye was black and the right side of my face was swollen. I also had a small cut under my chin.

I next saw Roy on Sat. night, May 2 1932 [sic]. He came up to Mrs Frery's [sic]. He asked me what was the matter with my face and I told him that he had hit me. He said he didn't. He told me that I had taken my clothes off and wanted to go in for a swim. He also told me that I had taken his tunic and gone up the road. I had quite a few drinks and was feeling pretty good.

On Friday morning May 1, I told my mother that a man had attacked me with a knife as I did not want her to know what happened. She did not know that I had come home without my clothes. As far as I know, Roy did not assault me or touch me in any other way than hit me in the face, and then I passed out.

I have seen Roy on two occasions since but I have not been out with him. I told him the story that I had told my mother. I do not know who the people were that drove me home.

There are a number of reasons why Hughes did not call Mabel Richmond as a witness, one of which may have been that he did not know of her. For some reason, Davis appears to have kept this information to himself and did not submit it to his RCMP superiors until a week after Tom's trial had concluded.

But if we accept that Hughes had seen her report, he would certainly be aware that any capable defence attorney would have shredded her testimony on the stand. By her own admission, she was drunk. She concedes that she may have got undressed without any help from Tom. She's an admitted liar, having made up the story of being attacked by a man with a knife and telling it to more than one person. She can't confirm any sexual transgressions, and even though it is possible that a woman could be raped and not be aware of it the next morning, it is highly unlikely. And if there are no signs of rape, it is difficult for someone who was too drunk to remember the occasion, to confirm an attempted rape.

So even though there is virtually no chance that Mabel Richmond's testimony could have swayed the jury, it certainly seems to have swayed Staff Sergeant Davis.

He believed he was seeking 'a sexual pervert of the most violent type', and because Tom could offer no supportable alibi, Davis had quickly targeted him as the murderer. By October, he had no problem equating the dubious Nova Scotia incident to the murder and rape of Bernice Connors.

In his tardy report to his superiors, he wrote, 'prisoner was investigated by our Force in Nova Scotia for alleged Rape ...' This is untrue. The original RCMP file says that Tom was investigated for 'alleged *attempted* rape'.

Davis went on to say, 'the Modus Operandi in the alleged Rape Case was identical with the murder of Bernice Connors.' It is hard to see how he saw a murder case as identical to an alleged attempted rape case lacking a murder, but apparently, he did.

But he went even further than that. He said that he 'was given a chance to peruse the Prisoner's personal fyle [*sic*]. There is an adverse comment on his fyle concerning his behaviour towards certain females whilst enroute to Canada from England on the boat.'

The nature of this adverse comment is unknown. The females are never identified. The specific nature of the transgression is unknown. Considering the level of decorum that existed in 1942, it could easily have been nothing more than using coarse language in mixed company.

Yet Davis appears to have put these two unsupported allegations together and decided that they proved that Tom was guilty of rape and murder.

He quoted Mabel Richmond's letter in his report and added that 'Complainant did not desire any further action and the matter was dropped.' As a seasoned policeman, he would have known that on evidence as flimsy as that provided on this occasion, the matter would have been dropped whether Richmond desired it or not.

Davis also wrote, 'I refer you to the footnote on the report by Insp. J. M. McIntosh, in which he states that disciplinary action has been taken against Sergeant Hutchings, resulting in several charges being placed against him.'

In fact, if there ever was a footnote to this report, from Insp. McIntosh or anyone else, Davis failed to file it.

And unless RAF Flight Lieutenant Elverston lied in his testimony to the court, there were never any charges against Hutchings at any time. Elverston told the court that Tom's conduct during his three years in the RAF was 'very good'.

But Davis was the man in charge of the RCMP investigation and as such, he would have been the driving force behind the Crown's decision to prosecute Tom Hutchings. After all, as far as Davis was concerned, he had positively identified the guilty party long ago. He had no intention of being embarrassed in court by a not-guilty verdict, even if it sent an innocent man to his death.

Chapter Eighteen

In every trial, there are witnesses who can swing the verdict. If their testimony is used properly by the Crown, it will convince the jury that the accused is guilty. If used properly by the defence, it will bring about an acquittal.

Hughes was now ready to call two men who fitted that categorization, and both of them had cleaned blood off Tom's face.

The first was another RAF witness, William Protheroe, who described his job title as 'ACHGD – aircraft hand, general duties'.

Hughes tried to pin him down on the crucial issue of timing but had no success, despite repeated efforts. Protheroe said he been in the dance hall throughout the entire evening, so it all ran together.

He was much more specific about his involvement with Tom. He testified that he had been standing at the door – 'right on the doorstep' – when he had seen Tom approaching with blood on his face.

His first reaction was to ask him if he had been in a fight. Tom did not respond in any fashion.

The blood, Protheroe testified, was on the left side of Tom's face, from his temple to his chin and in some parts, it was thick. He asked Tom for his handkerchief and tried to wipe the blood off, but much of it was dried. He spit on the handkerchief to provide some moisture, removed what he could, and handed the handkerchief back. It was at that point that he noticed blood on Tom's left hand, especially around the knuckles, but not as thick as the blood on his face.

When asked by Hughes if he noticed anything special about Tom, Protheroe answered, 'Yes. He looked in a dazed condition.'

Hughes asked if Tom showed 'any signs of liquor'.

'No,' answered Protheroe. 'He seemed to walk straight toward me when I saw him.'

Hughes' next witness was David Christie, an RAF cook who had wiped the rest of the blood off Tom's face.

As was his custom, Hughes quickly tried to establish the time frame and unlike Protheroe, Christie was able to be precise.

He knew it was 'between quarter past twelve and half past'. He explained that he had arrived in Black's Harbour and gone bowling before noting the time and going to the dance shortly after 11 p.m. He had been there only about an hour-and-a-quarter, and the intermission had taken up part of the time, so within a range of a few minutes, he was certain about the time he had seen Tom.

He testified that he was standing at the door of the dance hall when he saw Hutchings beckon. Christie approached and Tom asked if he had blood on his face. When Christie confirmed that he did, Tom handed him a handkerchief and asked him to remove it.

Christie said he asked Tom if he had been in a fight, but 'he just shrugged his shoulders and didn't say anything.'

Christie dipped the handkerchief in the ditch to get it wet, then removed almost all the remaining blood although, thanks to Protheroe's efforts, there wasn't much left. Again, he asked Tom if he had been fighting. This time, the answer was 'Yes.'

As he continued his ministrations, Christie pointed out that the blood must have come from someone else because there were no cuts on Tom's face.

Finally, Christie testified, Tom responded. 'He said that the blood had come off the other fellow.'

In his redirect, Guss wondered whether either witness had done a test to see if the substance removed from Tom's face was indeed blood. They hadn't.

He got Protheroe's agreement that Tom had appeared not to know that there was any blood on his face; and got Christie to confirm that the time was 'around a quarter after twelve'.

Then he went through the back door to get yet another confirmation of the time. He pointed out that during the preliminary hearing, Christie had been asked how much time had elapsed between wiping off the blood and the end of the dance. On that occasion, Christie had said it was, 'Anything from half an hour to three-quarters of an hour.'

'That is right,' confirmed Christie. There was no doubt that the dance had ended at 1 a.m.

The matter of the blood and the circumstances surrounding its removal were to become integral parts of the testimony presented during the trial.

CHAPTER EIGHTEEN

It therefore became crucial for each lawyer to try to use the testimony to establish his case.

From Hughes' point of view, he had managed to get two witnesses to break significant new ground. He now had placed Tom at the dance hall with enough blood on his face to require two people to remove it all. He got assertions from both men that there were no cuts on either Tom's face or his head, and a further statement from Protheroe that Tom had not appeared to have suffered a nosebleed.

When that information was linked with the fact that Bernice's face had been badly battered and that she had been bleeding profusely, it seemed to form an extremely strong case against Tom, even though it was circumstantial.

Clearly, from Hughes' point of view, the combined testimony of these two witnesses had sufficient potential to convince the jury of Tom's guilt.

But its circumstantial nature, although not of concern to Hughes, left Guss with an opportunity to capitalize on the testimony and more than negate the advantage that Hughes felt he had gained.

First of all, within very small parameters, Christie was absolutely certain of the time. Protheroe, on the other hand, was not able to say when he had wiped Tom's face but it was clear that he had done so a few minutes before Christie took over.

However, in previous testimony, two other airmen, Humphries and Moore, had been equally certain about the time of their activities. Humphries insisted that he had left the hall shortly after midnight and had returned to it with Sylvia Gaudet after spotting a couple at the side of the road. He immediately found Moore and at 12.20 a.m., they had gone back to the site to find the couple still there.

Yet if Christie's testimony were accepted, he and Protheroe were attending to Tom 500 yards from the site of the amorous couple at exactly the same time that the pair was seen twice by earlier witnesses.

Furthermore, Protheroe had been specific about Tom's demeanour. He said he had appeared to be 'in a dazed condition' but not drunk. This kind of behaviour conforms exactly to what had been seen occasionally by some of Tom's other colleagues, including Sergeant D.C. Huggett, Sergeant Edward Hutchings and Leading Aircraftman Sam Blakely. He sometimes lapsed into what might be best described as a trancelike state and had no memory of what happened during that time. Guss might have been able to capitalize on the fact that Tom, apparently not aware that

Protheroe had just wiped blood off his face, asked Christie if he had blood on his face.

Perhaps the combined testimony of Protheroe and Christie, instead of establishing Tom's guilt, represented an opportunity for Guss to utilize a defence of diminished responsibility – or even no responsibility at all.

Clearly, the evidence presented by Protheroe and Christie would have a profound effect upon the jury's thinking. But which lawyer would be able to make the most of it?

Chapter Nineteen

Whenever Staff Sergeant Davis referred to Vincent Bradford, an element of praise was involved.

In his initial report to his superiors a week after the murder, Davis's first description of Vincent called him 'a very intelligent young lad', an odd evaluation of a 13-year-old who was still in Grade 5. By the time the trial began, Vincent was 14.

In a later report, Davis praised the youngster for refusing to vary from his initial statement – which turned out to be accurate – even though it had seemed to contradict some other reports.

Davis and Hughes probably saw Vincent Bradford as a likeable boy who, by virtue of his age and his distinct Maritimes accent, would leave a favourable impression on the jury. They did everything they could to make sure that was the case, even though they weren't always successful.

On the stand, Bradford confirmed that he had seen Tom return to the dance hall 'a short while' after the intermission, and be attended to by Christie and Protheroe. He also confirmed that had seen the two men wipe off some blood, but he 'didn't take notice where it was around his face.'

Bradford did introduce some new evidence by saying that Tom's trouser legs were wet. In a confidential RCMP report, Davis had told his superiors that Bradford 'will testify that both trouser legs of the accused were soaking wet'.

On the stand, Bradford would not go that far. When Hughes asked him about the wetness, he said, 'Oh. Not as far up as the knees.'

When Hughes asked if 'the bottom of the trousers' was wet, Bradford answered, 'Yes.'

Pressed for more exact information, he said they were wet 'about half way up to his knees'.

Bradford was asked to confirm that the man whose face he saw being wiped had a moustache but was unable to do so.

Nevertheless, he did tell Hughes that he would be able to identify Tom. Had Guss been given access to the confidential report Davis had sent to his superiors a week after the murder, this certainty would have come as a surprise. In it, Davis specifically mentioned that Bradford 'does not say that he can identify the accused'.

Hughes asked Bradford to identify Tom, and the young man pointed in Tom's general direction. 'The prisoner in the dock?' asked Hughes.

This prompted an immediate objection from Guss who once again brandished his *Phipson on Evidence* and cited three precedents from the book which affirmed that the Crown Prosecutor can ask a witness to identify the accused but cannot do the identifying himself.

The judge, to no one's surprise, sided with Hughes, saying that the quoted precedents had to do with pictures of the accused, not the man himself, and allowed Hughes to continue.

When Guss persisted with his complaints, the judge chastised him saying, 'You could have made your objection a little earlier.'

Guss had, of course, done just that when Hughes identified Tom for the benefit of Vincent's sister, Cavell Bradford. On that occasion, the judge had disallowed Guss's objection, saying that court rules evolve. This time, Guss had made a point of saying that his *Phipson on Evidence* was the latest edition. It didn't matter. The judge would not be deterred from his support of the prosecution.

In his cross-examination, Guss was nowhere near as diligent. He asked only one question of Vincent and that was whether he could tell if the man he had seen was wearing an RAF uniform or an RCAF uniform. Vincent said he could not, even though Davis's report had stated that he could. With that, Vincent stepped down and with him went a golden opportunity for a mistrial or even an acquittal.

Had Guss been properly compensated for his work – or even allowed to claim his expenses – he might perhaps have hired an outside investigator to look into Vincent Bradford's testimony. After all, in the preliminary hearing, Bradford testified that he was with three friends – Franklin Lovett, Clarence Gaudet and Barton Justason – but none of them appeared in court. Had any one of them done so, would his testimony have contradicted that of Bradford?

If Tom Hutchings Sr had been allowed to send money from England to pay for a detective, as he wanted to do, perhaps that detective might have learned that Bradford's testimony was not all it appeared to be.

A small book about the Hutchings case published in 2002, *Occupation Murderer* by David A. Walsh, quotes Vincent Bradford as saying that he was frequently taken for car rides by policemen and lawyers, including Hughes. 'At the end of these meetings with detectives and lawyers, one of them would reach over and stuff dollar bills in my pockets.'

In 2001, Richard Blatchford, another researcher operating independently, spoke to Vincent Bradford who then lived in St George about 10 miles from Black's Harbour.

Bradford said he still remembered the events of 1942 clearly. He had gone to the movies on 5 June and saw Police Chief Dennison Guptill there but made nothing of it, even though Guptill had said in his sworn testimony that he had been on duty all evening.

'There was a hot-dog stand outside the dance hall, and that's where I stood until it closed,' Bradford recalled.

He recounted his testimony about seeing Tom having blood wiped off his face by two men. 'Actually, several airmen came out of the dance hall,' Bradford said. 'They set him down on the bumper of a car and cleaned him up.'

Then, unprompted, Bradford delivered information to Blatchford that would have dramatically changed the course of events had it been revealed at the time.

'They took me out to Pennfield and lined up hundreds of airmen,' he said. 'They wanted me to identify the man I had seen, but I couldn't.'

At no point did Davis include that fact in his reports to his superiors. However, he must have maintained his faith in Bradford as the type of witness who would gain the confidence of the jury, and passed that opinion along to Hughes. They obviously realized that they had found a witness who was young, malleable and, to put it as kindly as possible, susceptible to financial persuasion.

'Mr Hughes was really good to me,' Bradford told Blatchford. 'He gave me a lot of money. I don't remember how much, but it was a lot to me and he told me I could use it to buy candy and pop and stuff. For about ten days, the Mounties treated me like I was one of them. They let me ride around in their car through town so the other kids could see me. Then one day, they took me to the hotel and we were on the verandah and they said, 'All you've got to do is say you remember the guy in the box. He's the one who did it.'

'That's what I did.'

And to help make sure he got the right man, Hughes pointed him out.

Chapter Twenty

There had been a good deal of speculation concerning the time of the dance's intermission, so to get the matter settled to everyone's satisfaction, Hughes called the man who would know: James Watt, the band leader.

Watt was a company man – the manager of 'ladies and gents' furnishings' at the Connors Brothers Department Store in Black's Harbour. His band played at the dances regularly, and on 5 June the intermission began at the usual time – 'about a quarter of twelve'. In his preliminary-hearing testimony, he said he knew the time because he had looked at his watch.

It was twenty-five-minute intermission. 'That would take it to about 12.10,' Watt said when asked by Hughes. Because so many of the witnesses used the intermission to determine the time of their involvement, this was important testimony.

Watt answered a number of other questions while he was on the stand because he had also been the photographer at the crime scene, taking pictures before and after the moss was removed from Bernice's body. But there was nothing new in that testimony, just further confirmation of what the jury had already heard from other witnesses.

Guss had no questions for Watt.

It was now time for Hughes to call one of his star witnesses – RCMP Staff Sergeant Frank Davis, the man who had been in charge of the on-site investigation.

Davis spent two-and-half hours on the stand that afternoon, and it must have seemed like an eternity to the jurors.

Granted, Davis was responding to questions posed by Hughes, but it was an item-by-item recitation of exhibits taken from the crime scene and from Tom Hutchings. It was far from riveting.

Such was the inattentiveness of all concerned that no one queried it when Davis contradicted himself, saying, 'I took possession of the blouse and slip and handed them to Corporal Prime and left the skirt and the blouse to cover the body.' Then came an argument as to whether Davis had cautioned Hutchings by saying, 'Anything you say may be used against you at your trial.' Because a statement of that nature could be seen to presuppose guilt, the lawyers and judge spent some time arguing about it.

When the argument did not seem to be nearing a conclusion, Judge Richards sent the jury out for an hour while the lawyers argued some more and the three RAF officers who had been in the room during the interview were called to share their memories of the proceedings.

Eventually, after the judge had ruled in Hughes' favour, as was customary, Davis continued his testimony, listing more seized evidence and saying that on 10 June, five days after the murder, he had found a stained handkerchief near the dance hall.

This prompted further wrangling between lawyers with Guss contending that the handkerchief could have been left by anyone during the five days that had elapsed and could not be linked to Tom.

It was decided that, for the time being at least, the handkerchief would not be entered as an exhibit.

Davis also explained that although some of the evidence had been given to other Mounties for safe-keeping, he eventually had gathered it all and taken it to Montreal for testing.

He also said that he had conducted an experiment to see how long it took to cover a body with moss. Again, Guss objected, saying that he had been neither called nor notified about this experiment and that this evidence had been unreasonably sprung upon him.

The judge said it was Guss's responsibility to be ready for the Crown Prosecutor's attempts to test the limits of courtroom procedure. 'We can't always anticipate what may be done in this respect,' he said. 'You would have to be prepared for things of this nature.'

In his cross-examination, which took place the following morning, Guss focused on the handling, collection and transportation of evidence – making sure that the exhibits had not been tampered with on their way to the Montreal laboratory. He also argued about the manner in which Davis had acquired Tom's ring on the Saturday after the murder, but that was more a matter of legal procedure than anything of substance.

Once again, as was so often the case, Guss failed to zero in on the aspects of a witness's testimony that were open to attack.

During his recitation of evidence, Davis said he had found a rock on the road near the body and that it appeared to be blood-stained. Guss did not ask if he had had the rock tested for fingerprints.

Davis had insisted that all the sergeants except Tom could be accounted for. But Guss did not press him on the possibility of there being sergeants in town who had not attended the dance. Black's Harbour was serviced by buses and taxis, and private cars were available. It was a fishing village, not a gated community. What was to stop another sergeant showing up later in the evening?

Guss did not ask Davis what physical evidence he had found to indicate that Tom had been at the scene of the crime. Davis knew this was a weak spot in the Crown's case and Guss could have made him squirm by asking, item by item, if one object or another had been found. Davis would have had to repeatedly answer, 'No.'

But most important of all, with proper questioning, Guss could have highlighted Davis's inept handling of blood-stained items. It was indefensible that items collected on 7 June, 8 June and 10 June were not submitted for testing until 25 June, by which time it was impossible to determine the type of the blood being tested.

If none of the blood on Tom's clothing matched Bernice's blood type, then surely he could not be found guilty. But that path to freedom had been barricaded, not by anything Tom had done, but by the RCMP which had virtually destroyed the most important evidence in the entire case.

And Guss never mentioned it.

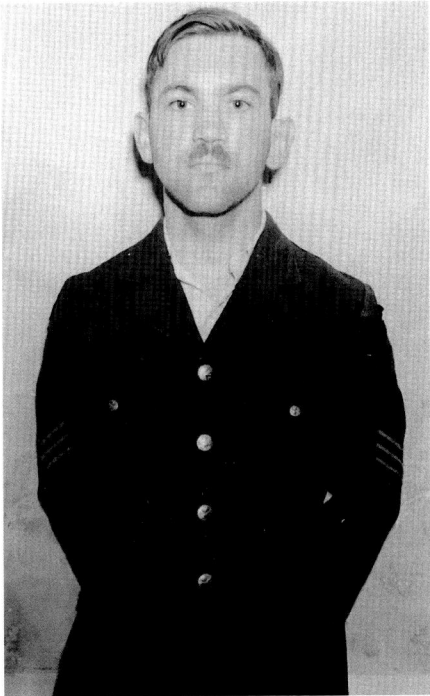

Above left: *RCMP file photo of Sergeant Tom Hutchings.* (RCMP files)

Above right: *Bernice Connors on 11 February 1942.* (Richard Blatchford)

Right: *Bernice Connors in 1941 with Mildred Justason.* (Beaver Harbour Archives)

Left: *Bernice Connors two days before her death with LAC Dungey.* (Beaver Harbour Archives)

Below: *Map of south-west New Brunswick.* (Public domain)

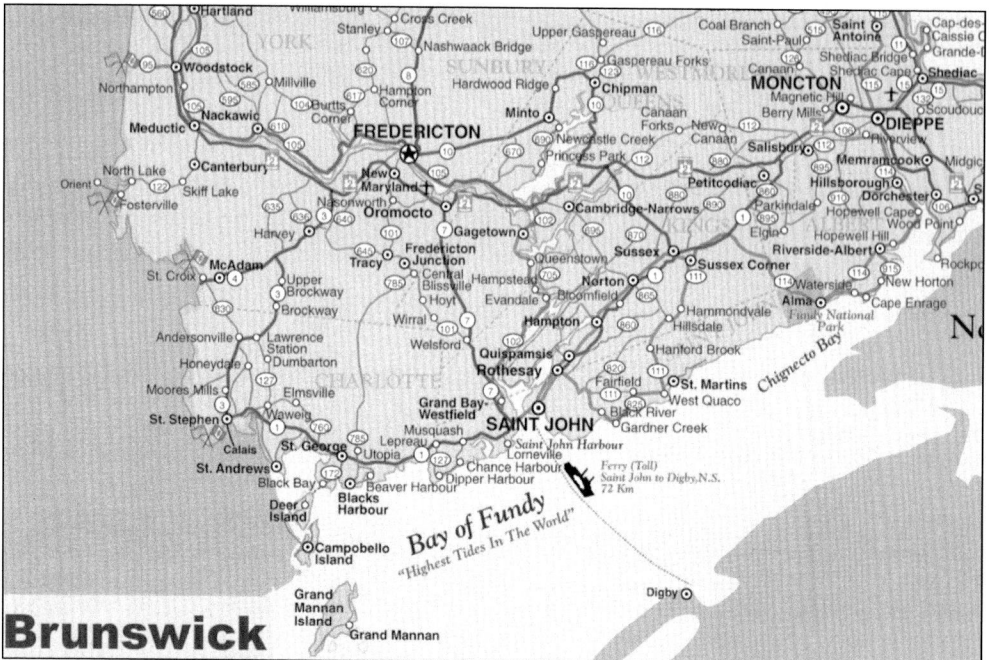

Black's Harbour map. (Library and Archives Canada)

Charlotte County Court House. (Alan Strachan)

Above: *Charlotte County Court room with lawyers' table at centre.* (Alan Strachan)

Left: *Trial judge Rt. Hon. Charles Dow Richards.* (Richard Blatchford)

Above: *Charlotte County Court House and St Andrews Gaol.* (Alan Strachan)

Right: *Hutchings' cell door in St Andrews Gaol.* (Sheryl Crighton)

Above: *Cell corridor in St Andrews Gaol.* (Charlotte County Archives)

Left: *Secondary door at the end of the four-cell corridor.* (Alexandra Crighton)

Above left: *Hutchings' cell from doorway in 2022 as a museum exhibit.* (Alexandra Crighton)

Above right: *Main door at the end of the four-cell corridor.* (Sheryl Crighton)

Right: *Tom Hutchings and lawyer Bernard Guss leaving St Andrews Gaol.* (Charlotte County Archives)

RCMP examining the area where Bernice Connors' body was found. (Charlotte County Archives)

Crime scene showing transmission line installed for lighting. (Charlotte County Archives)

Above: *Crime scene cordoned off by police.*
(Charlotte County Archives)

Right: *Black's Harbour Police Chief Dennison P. Guptill.*
(Beaver Harbour Archives)

Below: *RAF 34 Operational Training Unit.*
(Heritage Charlotte)

Pennfield Ridge

Lockheed Venturas from 34 OTU on patrol. (Heritage Charlotte)

Above left: *Contemporary RCAF recruiting poster.* (Heritage Charlotte)

Above right: *Royal Canadian Air Force 1942 recruiting poster.* (Library and Archives Canada)

Above: *Tom Hutchings' fingerprints.*
(RCMP Files)

Right: *List of trial exhibits.*
(Library and Archives Canada)

CAPITAL CASE

No. 67933
S. OF S.

YEAR
1942

C.C. 551
JUSTICE

Department of the Secretary of State
CANADA

Capital Case of   TOM ROLAND HUTCHINGS

Trial Held at   Saint Andrews, N. B.

Before   The Honourable Mr. Justice Richards,

Address   Fredericton, N. B.

Date Fixed for Execution   the 16th day of December, 1942.

Reprieved by   Until

EXECUTED	COMMUTED
Date	Date
At	Nature

Ottawa,   October 22,   19 42.

Referred to the Honourable the Minister of Justice for his consideration.

BY COMMAND,

[signature]

UNDER-SECRETARY OF STATE

OTTAWA, January 9, 1943.

REFERRED to the Honourable the Minister of Justice for his information in connection with papers hereto attached relative to the execution of TOM ROLAND HUTCHINGS.

BY COMMAND,

[signature]

UNDER-SECRETARY OF STATE

Proceedings duly noted: papers may be filed.

[signature]
for D. M. G.

000361

Cover of trial transcript. (Library and Archives Canada)

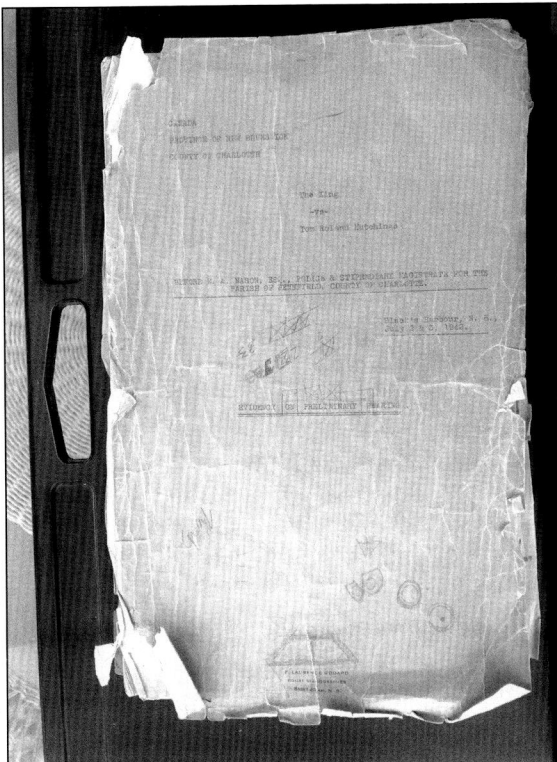

Cover of the original transcript of the preliminary hearing.
(Al Strachan)

onset, and lived very happily
with his wife & child until
drafted to Canada.

I may add that my son
has always been a very affectionate
obedient and loveable boy, causing
no anxiety apart from illness.

I must thank you very much
indeed for your very kind interest
you are taking in my son, and
may God bless & help him in his
great trouble and give him
strength to bear the great strain
and agony that he must be
suffering.

your sincerely,
J. Hutchings

P.S. The answer to the cable sent
by Dr Menzies regarding Dr. report
on my sons illness was given
to the Air Ministry to forward last
Monday August 24th to prevent
delay.

J.H.

Secretary of State memorandum confirming death sentence.
(Library and Archives Canada)

The gallows. (Charlotte County Archives)

Tom Hutchings' birth certificate. (Richard Blatchford)

Tom Hutchings' death certificate. (Charlotte County Archives)

Above left: *Early marker on Hutchings' grave.* (Charlotte County Archives)

Above right: *Hutchings' grave in 2019.* (Alan Strachan)

Above: *Bernice's headstone in Black's Harbour.*
(Alan Strachan)

Left: *Hutchings' headstone provided by an anonymous donor in 2021.*
(Sheryl Crighton)

Chapter Twenty-one

The trial was now entering its crucial phase. The RCMP's version of the series of events had been presented and the chain of evidence had been established. If there were ever a time to 'prove beyond reasonable doubt' that Bernice Connors was murdered and that Tom Roland Hutchings was the perpetrator, this was it. But within the ranks of the RCMP, there was still some concern.

The attempt to find some hard evidence placing Tom at the site where the body had been found had proved fruitless. Nothing there, or on Bernice's body, tied Tom to the murder. The handkerchief that Davis had found near the dance hall and that he hoped would add to the pile of evidence, proved to be worthless. It was marked with what appeared to be a regimental number but that number did not match anyone stationed at Pennfield. It also had a laundry mark, but checks with every laundry in Yarmouth, Saint John and St George had failed to uncover any indication that the handkerchief had ever been in Tom's possession.

The table knife that had been found near the scene by a soldier one week after the murder had been shown to residents of nearby houses in Black's Harbour and compared to cutlery used at the Pennfield base but no match was found. It turned out to be nothing more than a cheap, widely distributed knife sold by T. Eaton Company.

Even the Fredericton RCMP detachment's dog, Cliffe, had been dragooned into duty but he too had been unable to find any evidence of Tom's presence anywhere near the scene.

Nevertheless, for various reasons, the Mounties remained determined that they had fingered the right man. In the case of Davis's superior, Inspector S. Bullard, that determination was tied to his reasoning that Tom was guilty because he hadn't said anything to the contrary.

On 29 July, he had sent a memo to Davis saying:

> In thinking about this case, it has occurred to me that at no
> time has Hutchings ever pronounced his innocence and at
> no time has he stated to the investigators 'You have got the
> wrong man,' or 'You are wasting your time.' This seems
> an extraordinary thing to me as I am sure that almost every
> average man if innocent and charged with a serious crime
> would have energetically proclaimed his innocence before
> now. … While this is not exactly evidence, yet in my opinion
> it is very strong proof that the accused is guilty, I mean looking
> at this fact alone without all the other evidence.

It apparently had not dawned on Bullard that Tom, whom he had never
met, might not be an 'average man' because of a mental affliction that
prevented him from knowing whether he was guilty or not, and that he was
too honourable to lie.

Further up the RCMP ladder, Superintendent R. E. Mercer, the head
of J Division, the serious-crimes specialists, had sent a letter to New
Brunswick's attorney general saying:

> I would request that the background of the accused in England
> be enquired into. In view of the complaint made against him
> in Yarmouth N.S. it is quite possible that he has been involved
> in serious occurrences in the Old Country. Could you arrange
> for the necessary enquiries to be made through Scotland Yard
> please and advise me on this point.

The 'enquiries' were made and proved negative. Tom had no criminal record
in England. This was another setback for the Mounties, but not impactful
enough to encourage them to look elsewhere for their culprit.

Mercer was also concerned about the implications being made regarding
the signs of struggle at the side of the road – the ones that had been originally
noticed by Thomas Gaudet and Oscar Craig during their Sunday afternoon
stroll.

Mercer went right to the top. He sent a letter addressed simply to
'R.C.M. Police Commissioner, Ottawa'. (The man in question was Stuart
T. Wood, a great-great grandson of United States president Zachary Taylor.)
Mercer mentioned that it was a distance of 200 yards from the indications

of a struggle to the mound that covered Bernice's body. 'The reason that this is pointed out,' he wrote, 'is that although the accused is quite a strong man, it would seem a long distance to have carried the girl in an insensible condition. It would appear more likely that he dragged her along in a daze.'

Really? If that were the case, where were the signs of anyone being dragged? It was, after all, an unmade road and since one of Bernice's shoes was found near the scene, it would surely have left a mark on the road had she been dragged 200 yards wearing a shoe. And furthermore, why drag her such a long distance? The last street light had already been passed and there were no more houses between that spot and the eventual location of the body on either side of the road.

Mercer was also facing a dilemma with regard to the proper forensic examination of Tom's clothing.

'In this very important case,' he wrote, 'it is felt that the clothing of the accused should be thoroughly examined, not only for the blood, but also to see if human hair can be found on same and traces of moss which are not visible to the naked eye'.

He, an RCMP lawyer and the New Brunswick deputy attorney general had decided that only one expert should examine it for those elements.

As the New Brunswick pathologist, Dr Arnold Branch should be doing the testing for blood, a procedure that would require the clothing to be cut up.

But if Branch had first crack, Mercer reasoned, 'to then take the tunic on to some other expert for examination for hair specimens and then on to someone else for examination for moss specimens seems unwise.'

Branch could test for blood but not for moss and hair, wrote Mercer, because 'he has no equipment such as a special vacuum cleaner for this purpose.'

Even providing him with a vacuum cleaner wouldn't work, Mercer continued, because Branch was 'purely a hospital pathologist and has very little experience in criminal matters'.

To make the point clear, he added: 'He, himself, has in other cases expressed the opinion that he is not in a position to examine hair specimens.'

In the end, the tunic 'in this very important case' was subjected only to Branch's blood testing, and, except for examination with the naked eye, never tested for hair or moss.

Once most of the ground-level investigation had been completed, the RCMP internally distributed a document entitled *Official Summary of Evidence*, which detailed the exhibits and gave a brief version of the testimony that could be expected from each witness. It contained a number of errors, but the most glaring one was the assertion that Tom had been seen at the dance but had left around 11.30 p.m. and 'no one noticed him in the hall or around the hall until approximately 12.45 a.m.'

Simply put, this was a lie.

Davis certainly knew it was a lie because he had gathered the evidence, and his superiors should have known it was a lie because he submitted regular reports to them.

But they all continued to perpetuate the lie.

Three witnesses who testified at the trial – Protheroe, Christie and Vincent Bradford, all gave evidence that indicated Tom was at the dance hall around 12.20 a.m., if not earlier.

Two other RAF men interviewed by the Mounties, Corporal Harold Walker and Corporal Cyril Griffiths reported seeing Tom at the hall around 12.15 a.m. Their testimony was included in internal reports, but they were not called to testify.

In fact, after a step-by-step examination of his movements prompted by Guss, Eddie Hutchings places Tom at the dance hall at 11.59 p.m.

But it was the RCMP's version of the time frame that was to endure, despite the obvious fact that either it was wrong, or six people at the scene were wrong.

It may be best to designate it as the RCMP Big Lie. It is repeated again and again throughout the course of the proceedings. One official after another accepts the RCMP Big Lie as representing the truth, which it clearly wasn't, and it plays a major role in the outcome.

Indulging in a brief foray into self-praise, the report stated: 'All of this would seem to be as good a line of evidence as you could expect to get, unless you saw the act actually committed.'

Therein lay the problem. Nobody did see it committed – probably because it wasn't.

Chapter Twenty-two

In any trial devoid of eyewitnesses and therefore based totally on circumstantial evidence, the most important person to take the stand is usually the pathologist. He is the one who can confirm the death, state its cause, and precisely detail any injuries sustained by the victim. Armed with that information, the Crown hopes to forge links to the accused and convince the jury that no one else could have been the culprit.

In the Hutchings case, the pathologist was Dr Arnold Branch who, for the previous fifteen months, had been the designated pathologist for the province of New Brunswick.

Branch was British and had served in the Royal Navy in the First World War, but he was registered as a doctor under the New Brunswick Medical Act and the Canadian Medical Act. Since 1920, his practice had been limited to pathology and research.

Both Hughes and Guss were aware of how important his observations were likely to be, and there is little doubt that Branch's arrival on the stand prompted each man to produce his best performance of the trial.

Being the Crown, Hughes went first.

He painstakingly confirmed the basic particulars of the autopsy – the time, the place, and the peripheral evidence. Then he got Branch to enumerate the injuries Bernice had suffered.

There were many.

Although Branch occasionally used medical terms, whenever he did so, Hughes asked him to explain in layman's language.

In those terms, Branch said that Bernice's lips were swollen; her eyelids were black and blue; she had a ¾-inch cut on the left side of her head just above the hairline and a 2-inch cut under her chin; her tongue was swollen and the tip was purplish; there were two cuts on the inside of her cheek; the right side of her face was black and blue; her face had an over-all bluish appearance. He also said there were two recent abrasions 'at the lower side' of the hymen., 'a membrane which covers the lower entrance to the vagina.'.

In addition to listing the specific injuries, Branch, responding to Hughes' urging, made a number of other observations.

For instance, he said that he attributed the purplish tone at the end of Bernice's tongue to her teeth closing on it when she was hit. He thought the cuts on her cheek were also caused by blows from her assailant.

As for the bluish tinge to her face, he suggested that 'the most probable cause was from blows, black and blue.'

But he suggested a further option: 'The other possibility would be of sealing up of the circulation by the veins of the neck being obstructed.'

Not surprisingly, Hughes did not understand that answer. Branch tried to clarify his response, although it is not certain that he succeeded: 'If you tied a ligature around your arm and obstructed the vein and not the artery, you will notice that your hand will get a deep colour due to the dark colour of the venomous [sic] blood.'

Therefore, Branch went on to explain, the bluish tinge on Bernice's face could have been caused 'by pressure on the neck'.

Hughes moved on to Branch's description of the rest of Bernice's body as being pale. That was due, the doctor said, 'to a large quantity of blood lost'.

With regard to the sexual aspect of the crime, Branch said that he had found a sticky matter inside the vagina which subsequent testing showed to be spermatozoa and therefore indicated that sexual intercourse had taken place.

Judge Richards interrupted to ask if this information could be used to determine the time of the intercourse. Branch's response was that he had heard of spermatozoa living for seven days.

As for the internal examination of Bernice's body, Branch said he noticed that when he put his hand into the peritoneal cavity, the organs felt cold. This too, he attributed to loss of blood.

He went on to say that by this time 'an experienced person' such as himself, would have noticed an aroma that signified the presence of alcohol. He therefore extracted the contents of the stomach and sent them for further analysis.

Branch had now listed all the injuries to Bernice, and given all his conclusions regarding the cause of those injuries. Hughes therefore switched his focus to the cause of death. What was it?

Branch was not quick to answer.

There was no oedema (watery swelling) in the brain, he said.

He had already ruled out asphyxiation during his testimony.

The bleeding of the nose and ears had 'no significance'.

He had said there was no internal hemorrhage.

There was no skull fracture.

The blood-alcohol level, even though being .204 per cent (.08 in a driver of today is enough to be considered impairment. In some jurisdictions, it's 0.5 per cent) was 'a level insufficient to cause death'.

Keeping all these non-causes in mind, said Branch, he felt constrained to find an answer to Hughes' question. 'I gave the cause of death as shock.'

As for the time when this shock took effect, Branch provided the somewhat confusing answer of: 'I would be willing to say she had died within three days and at least thirty-six hours previously.'

He went on to explain that the autopsy had started at 5 p.m. Monday, so he was sure Bernice had died between 5 p.m. Friday and 5 a.m. Sunday.

At that point, Hughes felt he had done his job. At his urging, an experienced pathologist had confirmed that a murder had taken place, enumerated the damage to the victim's body, established the possibility of a sex crime and provided a time of death that would allow Tom Hutchings to be seen as the murderer and rapist.

Now it was up to Guss to go to work. This time, he couldn't settle for a cross-examination that was either irrelevant or inconsequential as had so often been the case. He had to go after Branch and discredit either his qualifications or his conclusions – or better still, both.

There had been other witnesses on the stand and there would be more to come. But if Guss could take the entire sting out of Branch's testimony, he would be well on his way to getting Tom acquitted.

He began with an attack on Branch's determination of the cause of death. This made sense. After all, once all the medical terminology had been shunted aside, what Branch had essentially said was 'I couldn't find a cause of death, so I guess I'll call it shock.'

In fact, that was more or less his statement on the stand when he said at one point, 'I didn't find any other natural cause I could lay my hands on.'

As Guss said to him, 'There is really no constant finding in shock, is there?'

Branch had to agree that there was 'no constant pathological finding'.

The judge wasn't sure what he meant, so Branch produced an answer that was more of a desperate attempt at justification than a source of enlightenment.

'Shock is a clinical term that is followed by lower blood pressure and so on but we use that pathologically. Particularly the word traumatic shock, when we find on our estimation sufficient damage to an organ that we think would result in shock, particularly if that organ is richly supplied with nerves.'

Guss's questioning in this area was persistent and Branch's answers continued to dance around the issue. But on more than one occasion, Guss got a direct answer to a telling question. Here are some verbatim excerpts, with Guss being the questioner in each case:

Q: Shock is a changing picture?
A: Yes.

Q: (Shock) is actually a vague term.
A: Yes.

Q: Can you say there is a definite anatomical reason for death in this case?
A: No.

Q: You were really puzzled by the reason for death, weren't you?
A: One is always puzzled.

At that point, Guss went in another direction, although it might have been better to ask Branch what he was doing on the stand if he was always puzzled.

Instead, he started listing potential causes of death that did not exist in Bernice's case, and getting Branch to agree that each had been ruled out. It was a clever way of emphasizing Branch's inability to identify the cause of death without giving the Crown the chance to object that he had asked the same question twice.

He got Branch to admit that while he had conceded spermatozoa can live for seven days, there had been recorded cases of them living seventeen days.

He suggested, and Branch agreed, that a blood-alcohol level of .204 would bring about intoxication, especially in a non-alcoholic young person whose stomach was devoid of food, as was the case with Bernice.

He even got Branch to admit that the bleeding from Bernice's nose and ears was of 'no significance' as a cause of murder, and that it was quite conceivable that the injuries were caused by her falling repeatedly because she was drunk.

And for that matter, Guss said, the blows to Bernice's face may well have been inflicted by more than one person. Branch could not disagree.

That brought Guss to an aspect of the autopsy that was of major significance: The alcohol.

First, he asked Branch if the tests that determined Bernice's blood-alcohol level had tested the alcohol itself. Had Branch requested a test for methyl alcohol, as opposed to ethyl alcohol which is found in legal, store-bought potables such as rum and whisky?

He hadn't.

Had he requested a test for fusel oil (a mixture of several alcohols, especially amyl alcohol)? He hadn't.

This was probably the best opportunity for acquittal that Guss was to get in the entire trial. The path was open. If he could pin Branch down, he could establish the cause of death not as shock, but as methyl-alcohol poisoning. Since it would be all but impossible for Hughes to show that Tom had force-fed the alcohol to Bernice, her cause of death would have to be seen as self-inflicted. And self-inflicted death is not murder.

Guss started well. He got Branch to admit that it was widely accepted in the medical community that people under the influence of alcohol were more susceptible to injuries than those who were sober.

Guss referred to a respected medical text which said that 'intoxicated people will often die from injuries that would not affect people who aren't intoxicated.' Branch said he hadn't read the book in question, but would not refute the assertion.

Guss referred then to Branch's testimony in the preliminary hearing in which he had said that Bernice had some 'congestion in the brain'.

Branch remembered that he had done so.

'And in poisoning from alcohol,' Guss continued, 'isn't it an accepted fact that death may generally be traced to congestion of the brain?'

Branch conceded this was true but said the brain tends to gain some weight in the process. Guss pointed out that since he had no idea of the weight of Bernice's brain when she was alive, that observation was irrelevant in this case.

Guss then moved into another area, one offered to him by Dr E.C. Menzies, the man who had interviewed Tom at least six times in Saint John. He raised Dr Menzies' diagnosis of pathological intoxication.

Guss almost certainly expected a battle from Branch on this front. He must have been both shocked and delighted when Branch admitted that he not only knew of the condition but had treated it.

Guss started off with an exploratory question about 'people have done things and been places when intoxicated and then have no recollection whatever of it the next day.'

Branch said he concurred, and Guss gingerly dissected the question, putting it to Branch bit by bit. Branch kept agreeing, and finally volunteered, 'I have known two cases of it myself.'

Guss appeared to be shocked. 'So you can really say (it exists)?' he asked.

'I believe it's called pathological intoxication,' announced Branch.

'You say accepted in the medical world?' asked Guss.

'Yes,' said Branch.

Psychiatry was not as widely established in 1942 as it is today. Pathological intoxication was well known to the world's top psychiatrists, but would have been quite unfamiliar – and perhaps seen as ridiculous – to a jury composed of men from small New Brunswick towns.

Guss had every opportunity at this point to get Branch to speak more about pathological intoxication, to discuss its frequency and to make it a credible explanation for Tom's actions on the night of 5 June.

He could not have related it directly to Tom's situation because Branch was dealing only with the pathology of the case, not with the investigation of the crime. But he could nevertheless have instilled in the minds of the jurors that this was not some lunatic concept dreamed up by bearded tweed-jacketed Europeans, but a very real, very credible affliction that was fully recognized and accepted in the medical world.

But he didn't.

Instead, Guss moved to a discussion of cuts – those on Bernice's face and those on Tom's hands.

After that, Guss went to work on the matter of the rape, which prompted all four men – the two lawyers, the judge and the witness – to get involved in a lengthy exchange concerning the legalities and definition of rape.

But on two separate occasions, Guss got an important concession from Branch.

First, he wondered if Branch would agree that the presumed assault 'If it were a crime, were not necessarily a sex crime.' Branch's response was an unequivocal, 'Yes.'

Then, after Guss had established the legal definition of rape, Branch admitted, 'I understand that rape implied consent, and I am not prepared to state that there was rape.' He presumably meant that a determination of rape required a determination of whether there had been consent, but either way, he would not say Bernice was raped.

Other than getting Branch to establish that he had not tested the water in Bernice's hair to see if it was salt or fresh, Guss had no further questions.

It was clearly his best cross-examination of the trial and he had wheedled a number of important concessions out of a major Crown witness. But he had nevertheless, as usual, fallen tantalizingly short.

Three glorious opportunities to devastate the Crown's case had opened up, and while Guss had danced around all three, he had not taken advantage of a single one.

First was the matter of alcohol poisoning. Tom had been drinking bootleg liquor and there is little doubt that Bernice had consumed some on her way to a .204 blood-alcohol level. Bootleg liquor is quite likely to contain methyl alcohol and sometimes fusel oil.

A sign of methyl-alcohol poisoning is a bluish tinge to the face – which Branch noticed in Bernice. Another sign is 'congestion in the brain', which Branch admitted existed in this case. A third sign is a purplish tongue – which Branch noticed in Bernice. Guss should have asked if there were teeth marks or abrasions on the allegedly bitten tongue. Almost certainly, there weren't, or Branch would have mentioned them in his list of injuries.

In the preliminary hearing, Branch had not speculated that Bernice had bitten her tongue to cause the discolouration. He had simply referred to 'purplish marks as if blood had oozed out into the tissue of the tongue'.

In the trial, Branch contended that the bluish tinge to her face could have been caused by the sealing of veins, the result of 'pressure on the neck'. If so, where were the marks that would show this pressure had been applied?

Although Branch was arguing against the idea of Bernice dying as a result of methyl-alcohol poisoning, it was less than three years later, in 1945, that a detailed medical study of acute methyl-alcohol poisoning was produced by the Bureau of Laboratories, Province of New Brunswick and the Saint John General Hospital. At the time, methyl alcohol was so prevalent in New Brunswick that in a three-day span, thirteen people in Saint John, then a city of approximately 50,000, died from drinking it. One of the common symptoms, the report said, was a flushed face. And it pointed out that a large intake was not required. One of the thirteen people who died in the three-day 'epidemic' had taken only one drink of methanol.

The co-author of the report was Arnold Branch MD.

Guss should have pressed Branch on the impact of alcohol poisoning and got him to admit that, given the symptoms, it was much more likely to have caused Bernice's death than shock. After all, Branch had insisted he identified shock as the cause of death because shock is a result of significant blood loss. The reason Bernice's body was pale, he said, was because of 'a large quantity of blood lost'. During the preliminary hearing, he twice referred to 'considerable' bleeding. But Guss failed to ask him where he thought that blood had come from. The ¾-inch cut on her scalp? The 2-inch cut under her chin? A couple of small cuts on the inside of her cheek? There aren't a lot of arteries in those areas. Branch had said there was no internal bleeding. How did a 'large quantity of blood' manage to escape?

The simple truth of the matter was that the symptoms did not come close to supporting a diagnosis of shock due to blood loss. But they strongly supported a diagnosis of methyl-alcohol poisoning.

The second opportunity that opened up to Guss was the concept of pathological intoxication. Dr Menzies could have given him all the background he needed to make sure that it was developed as a serious alternative. Guss would have to wait until it was time to present his defence to call Menzies, but he could have established a lot more groundwork than he did while Branch was on the stand.

And as for the rape, Guss left a couple of key points unchallenged. First, Branch said he had done a vaginal examination of the body. Had he found any pubic hairs belonging to anyone other than Bernice? After all, Tom had willingly given the Mounties samples of his. Obviously, Branch would have answered in the negative because if the situation were otherwise, the rogue hair would have already been presented as evidence by Staff Sergeant Davis.

Branch had mentioned two abrasions close to her genitalia and conceded, in passing, that they could be chronic. Guss should have got him to stress that they quite possibly had nothing to do with any recent sexual activity and were simply minor abrasions possibly caused by the friction of clothing, and were common in women.

But more than anything, he should have pointed out that the Crown's star witness, the pathologist, twice testified under oath that he couldn't say there was a rape. Then why was the accused on trial for rape? If the pathologist can't say there was a rape, who was the person who had made that determination? A policeman? A lawyer? How would they be more qualified in this area than a pathologist?

Guss should have put it to Branch point blank. 'You have no evidence of rape, do you?' Branch would have had to admit that he didn't.

Then Guss could have continued, 'You were the pathologist. Other than the participants, is there anyone in the world better able to make that determination than you?'

Instead, Guss had established some options and tossed them out for consideration. But instead of fortifying them, he left them vulnerable to an assault from Hughes. And that's what came next.

It was like the ancient Chinese torture of death by a thousand cuts. Hughes went after the concessions made during Guss's cross-examinations and picked away at them bit by bit. At times, his questioning was so innocuous that he even seemed to be confirming the points that Guss had elicited, and at times, he got some help from the judge. Gradually, the relentless assault took its toll.

Hughes started by confirming that a doctor can't confirm rape but 'In some cases, I suppose, it might pretty well be told from the condition of the body, might it not?'

Branch confirmed that he supposed it as well.

Hughes got Branch to enumerate the injuries to the face again and although Guss should have objected, he didn't.

Hughes returned to the definition of shock, and Branch produced yet another variation on his definition. 'It indicates a certain lack of blood in circulation if that means anything to you – that the blood from your blood veins go [*sic*] out into your own tissues instead of staying in the vessels.'

This, he confirmed when Hughes asked, was the condition he noted in Bernice's body.

Hughes wondered why Branch might say that he was always puzzled in determining a cause of death.

'I mean if you approach a dead body, Mr Hughes, even knowing something about the death, it is always more or less puzzling to say exactly what caused death. If you find certain things, they are accepted as a cause of death,' Branch said.

'A man with a gun wound in his head,' offered the always helpful judge.

Hughes then went a step further. 'And these cuts that you found would indicate sufficient [*sic*] to cause death?'

'In my estimation, yes,' said Branch, without appearing to wonder which particular commodity was sufficient.

Guss had referred to the diagnosis of congestion in the brain as a symptom of alcohol poisoning. Hughes suggested it might have been the result 'of a body lying on its back for a length of time'.

'Yes, I would think so,' answered Branch.

The shelf life of sperm was considered and Branch thought that a seventeen-day term was probably just the result of someone's test, not something likely to happen on a regular basis.

Hughes scoffed at the idea of pathological intoxication and Branch, despite having treated it twice, did nothing to dissuade him. Under pressure from Hughes, he was forced to concede that he did not know with certainty that the examples he had seen in the Royal Navy were indeed pathological intoxication. Hughes suggested that the sufferers could have been lying and each diagnosis could have been wrong. 'I wouldn't absolutely know it was correct, no.' admitted Branch.

Hughes tried to get Branch to change his testimony and say there had definitely been a rape. Even though he wasn't successful, he still managed to sow some doubt, as he had done so often during his re-examination.

Branch stated that he was sure that Bernice had been involved in a sexual encounter, but added that it might have occurred two days before she died. Even so, Hughes had opened the door for the possibility of it happening on the night of 5 June.

Hughes tried to get Branch to admit that he had found no indication of methyl alcohol in Bernice's stomach. That avenue closed quickly when Branch said he hadn't tested for it.

The fact that alcohol poisoning causes the face to be bloated was mentioned and discussed. Bernice's face was definitely swollen, Branch said, but he had never seen that much swelling from alcohol alone.

A defence attorney might have asked, 'What about a combination of alcohol poisoning and blows? Would that do it?' But Hughes was not the defence attorney, so he didn't ask it.

Branch also said after prompting from Hughes that alcohol causes a red face. That might be so for ethyl alcohol – legally sold liquor. But methyl alcohol, which was probably present in the illicit rum Tom had bought in Black's Harbour, induces a blue face. Hughes did not point out the shortcoming in Branch's answer.

The result of the head-to-head matchup of Guss and Hughes was inescapable. Guss had made some valid points, scattered some seeds of doubt and presented alternative theories for the events that had led to Bernice's death. But he had failed to take full advantage of his openings.

He had been given an opportunity to show that the rape wasn't a rape and the murder wasn't a murder. But both scenarios were left waiting at the altar. He had missed an excellent chance to validate the pathological-intoxication theory, but had left it unfulfilled as well, and would now have to rely on Dr Menzies to do the job when the defence presented its case.

He had failed to challenge Branch's qualifications even though there were whispers in medical quarters that his expertise was both dated and limited. It had been twenty-two years since he had treated a living patient.

Guss hadn't even asked whether Branch had been told Bernice's likely time of death before making his determination. In that part of New Brunswick, news travels quickly and the autopsy didn't commence until late Monday afternoon.

Hughes, on the other hand, had got away with presenting Branch as a credible, knowledgeable medical witness. He had made sure that Guss's primary avenues to an acquittal had been clogged, if not barricaded altogether.

There was still no real evidence against Tom. There were still no witnesses and still no tangible evidence of his presence at the scene. Even his personality spoke against his guilt in that he had always been forthcoming and, according to Guss, had asked for a blood test to show that he was innocent.

But there was an inescapable and ominous aura to the trial now, a feeling that the chances of pinning the murder of Bernice Connors on someone other than Tom Roland Hutchings were evaporating more and more with every witness who took the stand.

Chapter Twenty-three

Eddie and Roy were fast friends. They hadn't known each other before the RAF lumped them together in 1941, but ever since then, they had got along famously and were all but inseparable.

Eddie was Sergeant Edward John William Hutchings. Roy was Tom Roland Reginald Hutchings, known to all his RAF acquaintances as Roy, the nickname his father had given him as a child.

Eddie and Roy travelled together. They roomed together. They worked together. They spent much of their spare time together.

And there is one other unassailable fact that must never be forgotten. They drank together. A lot.

Even though they were in Canada temporarily and enjoying a much easier life than their colleagues back in Europe, there was no escaping the fact that they were in the middle of a war – a war that, at the time, wasn't going particularly well for the Allies.

Eddie and Roy were armourers. They spent their working hours repairing, installing and maintaining machine guns, and trained others to do the same.

Together, the Hutchings duo had crossed the treacherous, submarine-infested North Atlantic. On at least two occasions, before meeting Eddie, Tom/Roy had encountered a Luftwaffe blitz, when German bombs rained down every night. Theirs was a stress-filled life and like most of their colleagues, when they were given a chance to relax with alcohol, they took it.

It has already been seen that their acquaintance, Sergeant Thomas Edwards, a pilot, singlehandedly consumed a bottle of whisky on the night of 5 June and later testified to seeing bicycles that didn't exist.

When Tom's group – Eddie, Leading Aircraftman Morgan, Leading Aircraftman Blakely and himself – arrived in Black's Harbour that night, they quickly went through the whisky they had brought and immediately set about trying to get more.

It should therefore come as no surprise that when Eddie Hutchings gave his testimony at the murder trial of his friend, there was not always a high degree of precision in his recollections and sometimes his memory needed to be jogged.

He would not intentionally have been misleading, but his statements wouldn't have shown the same degree of clarity as those of someone sober. And Eddie Hutchings was far from sober that night.

As a result, a capable, experienced Crown like Hughes was able to get Eddie to testify to a chain of events that was particularly damning to Tom.

To make sure there was little doubt who Eddie was talking about, on four separate occasions during his questioning, Hughes asked him to confirm that when he said 'Roy', he was talking about Tom Hutchings.

Hughes started with the drinking – the quick consumption of the group's first bottle and the subsequent quest for more. While Tom went in pursuit of the bootleg liquor, Eddie went to the bowling alley and waited for a lane to become available. Upon Tom's return, they bowled, so Eddie was quite aware of the time the pair got to the dance. 'Around eleven o'clock.'

Now that they had restocked their liquor supply – a small bottle for Blakely; a large bottle for Tom – they made the most of it. After a quick survey of the dance hall, the four airmen who had travelled to Black's Harbour together went outside for drinks – at least two. They went back in for a while, then the two Hutchings and two other sergeants went out for nips of rum. After going back inside again, they went out once more. This time, the two Hutchings went with Sergeant Edwards.

Hughes asked the time of the third drink. 'Oh, it would be around 11.30,' Eddie estimated.

At that point, Eddie said, he lost contact with Tom and didn't see him again until after the dance.

But when they did meet up, they agreed to head back to Pennfield as soon as Tom had made a quick dash into the dance hall to look for his missing cap. Once the men were under way towards the taxi rank, they noticed a pair of girls walking in front of them. Eddie followed one and Tom the other, but both girls soon went into houses, so the two men retraced their steps and resumed their wait for a taxi.

In response to questions from Hughes, Eddie testified that because Tom had said he was feeling sick, he put his arm around his neck. At that point, he had noticed that the arm of Tom's tunic was damp.

Hughes then turned his attention to Saturday afternoon when the two men were in their quarters and Tom was cleaning his uniform in preparation for his Monday duties as orderly sergeant. He had laundered his shirts and handkerchiefs and was sponging and pressing his battle dress – the tunic and trousers.

Hughes focused particularly on one incident. When Tom was pressing the arm of his tunic using a damp cloth to prevent a sheen developing, the cloth took on the outline of his stripes in a brownish stain. He showed it to Eddie then washed it out.

Hughes moved on to the activities of the pair on Sunday. In the evening, they had gone back to Black's Harbour and walked down Deadman's Harbour Road until they came to a spot where a number of local residents were milling about. It was adjacent to the mound where Bernice's body had been found.

As he had done on Friday night, Eddie asked Tom where he had been when he was absent from the dance. On both occasions, Tom merely answered that he had been drinking.

As a result of a strained conversation with Mildred Justason, the woman they knew through Sergeant Edwards, they learned that the murder victim was Bernice Connors. At first, they thought Mildred was joking when she said that the victim had been seen with an airman who had a moustache. 'Roy said jokingly that he had better shave his off,' said Eddie.

But when it became clear that Mildred was serious, Eddie made a remark suggesting that perhaps Bernice shouldn't have spent so much time with men. Tom told him not to be so callous.

Black's Harbour, like most company towns, has an inherent suspicion of outsiders and Eddie sensed that the two RAF men were being accorded some unfriendly glances. He felt it was time to return to Pennfield, so they left.

The news of the murder had reached Pennfield and all returning airmen were required to report to the guardroom to record their movements on Friday evening. Tom said that he had been with Eddie all night. 'Not all night,' corrected Eddie.

There was much for Guss to counter here. As a result of Eddie's testimony, it appeared that Tom had been absent for at least ninety minutes on Friday night, and had subsequently considered changing his appearance to avoid suspicion. Furthermore, the condition of his uniform indicated that he had not been sitting quietly indoors after he separated from Eddie.

Guss began with an assault on the time frame. He took Eddie through it step by step, getting an assessment of the time required for each aspect – each trip down the road and back – each drinking session, each stay in the dance hall. Then he totalled it up and announced his conclusion.

CHAPTER TWENTY-THREE

'I make it 11.59 when you went back to the dance hall the last time.'

Eddie conceded that this may have been the case.

Guss stressed the point. With regards to Eddie's statement that the two men split up at 11.30 p.m., he asked, 'You could not have been altogether correct?'

'No sir. That was only approximate,' agreed Eddie.

Guss asked if the estimate of 11.59 was more likely than 11.30.

'Figuring it out that way, it could not have been anything else,' Eddie conceded.

Guss also reminded Eddie that during the preliminary hearing, he had said that Tom walked ahead of him when they went back to the dance hall for the last time. Even though he didn't see Tom afterwards, that placed him at the hall around midnight.

The judge seemed confused so Guss explained. 'He says it was 11.59,' he said.

'According to your figures,' snapped the judge.

Not really. No matter who calculated the figures, Eddie had agreed with them.

This was obviously important testimony, so Hughes tried to join the judge in discrediting it. Guss got Eddie to confirm that he had said Tom had walked in front of him.

'He didn't say that,' Hughes interrupted.

Guss picked up the preliminary-hearing transcript and read Eddie's testimony from it. 'Did Sergeant R. Hutchings come back with you? Yes, he was in front of me.'

'Does that say the accused came back?' asked Hughes. Clearly, it did.

Guss also managed to take some of the impact out of Tom's remark regarding shaving off his moustache.

It was not an admission of guilt. It was just a quip typical of English humour. Guss again read Eddie's testimony from the preliminary hearing:

'There were several rumours going about that she was with RAF boys and someone said it was a corporal and somebody else said it was a sergeant-pilot and somebody else said it was a sergeant with a moustache.'

Guss now turned his attention to Eddie. 'Didn't you say something?' he asked.

'Somebody said she was last seen with a tall sergeant,' said Eddie. 'I told him to call me 'Shorty'. He then testified that he was 'About 5ft 11in'.

With regard to the brown stain on the cloth Tom used while ironing his uniform, Guss got Eddie to admit that it was Tom who drew his attention to it, not something he would be likely to do if the stain were blood, as the Crown had hinted.

And for that matter, Eddie himself had a nosebleed that Saturday afternoon while Tom was working on his uniform. Guss brought up that fact and Eddie agreed. It was a stretch, but following a favorite tactic of Hughes, Guss was muddying the waters a bit by laying out the possibility that Eddie's nosebleed was the source of the blood on Tom's tunic.

As for the wet uniform, Eddie admitted under questioning that it had rained in the early evening on 5 June.

On redirect, Hughes tried, to no avail, to get Eddie to admit that he was wrong when he said that Tom preceded him when they walked back to the dance hall. Eddie willingly agreed that he didn't see Tom after that, but wouldn't change his testimony that after the third drinking session, they returned together.

So there it was. One more witness had narrowed the time span that Tom was absent from the dance hall, even though all the official RCMP files and internal correspondence continued to insist he was absent from 11.30 p.m. until 1 a.m.

Chapter Twenty-four

A capital trial can never be considered enjoyable. However, it can proceed in an efficient manner and be made tolerable, should the three most-active participants – the judge, the Crown and the defence – endeavour to control the rancour and disdain that tends to arise as a case drags on.

But once the proceedings opened on Saturday, 3 October, it quickly became apparent that the attempts to make the process bearable in this case were a thing of the past. Each of the main participants was at odds with the other two; civility was at a minimum; both sides were reduced to pettiness; and the judge's most frequent response to the defence's repeated procedural complaints was open hostility.

In retrospect, it would appear that the judge was jealous and therefore became petulant. It was clear from the many objections that Guss put forward that he was the better versed of the two in the areas of courtroom precedent and evidence admissibility. This would stand to reason. Guss had been in law school more recently and had immediately made the law his vocation, whereas the judge was granted a sinecure on the bench after the collapse of his political career. But it was the judge who wielded the ultimate authority and he used it.

At one point, Guss asked a witness about a building attached to the dance hall and said, 'I wonder if the witness knows, of his own knowledge, what it is used for.'

'That can not affect anything,' interrupted the judge. Since Guss was asking about an abutment to the only building of any real importance in the trial, surely that was for him to decide.

Another incident that was typical of the day's proceedings came when Leading Aircraftman Jack Morgan said he had seen Eddie Hutchings looking around the dance hall for Tom Hutchings.

Guss was of the opinion that Morgan could not know who Eddie was looking for unless he had been told. But if the accused is not present when a conversation takes place, it is considered hearsay and its contents are not admissible. Therefore, he interrupted the questioning to say, 'I don't think this witness can say that at all.'

'He is saying it,' snapped Hughes.

'He may as well tell the conversation if he can give it that way,' responded Guss.

'It is a fact,' said Hughes disdainfully. 'Facts are always provable.'

For once, the judge sided with Guss, saying that Morgan couldn't know who Eddie was looking for unless he had been told.

Hughes' somewhat incomprehensible response was, 'That is true, but that is a fact which must be able to be proved. If it weren't, you couldn't prove it at all.'

'You can prove it by the man who did it,' said Guss.

'You may not have the man who did it,' said Hughes, thereby more or less making the same point as Guss.

This is the way it went all day. No more 'My learned friend'. No mention of 'If it please the court'. Just arguments, interruptions, objections and a general tone of nastiness and discord.

It started with the introduction of Percy Rigby, a civil engineer by trade, who held the post of district highway engineer for Charlotte County. He had created a diagram showing all the pertinent points relating to the case – the dance hall, the roads, the street lights, the places at which exhibits were discovered, and so on. Guss, of course, had not been given a copy. It was agreed that he would get one. Eventually.

Fifteen seconds later, Guss objected to the contents of the plan. He was ignored.

There followed a series of tedious arguments relating to the source of the evidence and its admissibility. As Rigby patiently tried to explain the notations on his diagram, more and more arguments arose. A half-hour passed and most of the time was spent with the lawyers making points and counter-points, while the judge interjected his own observations that may or may not have been relevant.

Eventually, Rigby was sent off to draw another plan, using only the notes he had made at the scene, as opposed to information the RCMP had given him.

Even though the court did not adjourn until after five o'clock, very little useful or new information emerged during the proceedings. In fact, it is impossible to consider the attitude of the jurors without being convinced that at least once during the day, every single one of them must have thought, 'What am I doing here spending my Saturday listening to all this?'

When the disagreeable tone of the proceedings abated a bit, it was replaced by boredom.

CHAPTER TWENTY-FOUR

Hughes produced witness after witness who did little more than confirm what had already been well established. The interview in Tom's room was again discussed at length, as were the actions of the four airmen at the centre of the story who travelled to Black's Harbour together. RCMP evidence was confirmed piece by piece and exhibit number by exhibit number. Again, the provenance of the items found along Deadman's Harbour Road was discussed.

It is understandable that Hughes was doing this. He had no hard evidence to link Tom to the crime, so he kept adding to the pile of soft evidence in the hope that it would eventually accumulate enough weight to convince the jurors of Tom's guilt.

Perhaps Guss was as bored as the jurors. Perhaps he was worn down from his intellectual battles with the judge and the Crown. But whatever the reason, he once again failed to capitalize on the one nugget that did emerge.

The occasion arose when Leading Aircraftman Samuel Blakely, the airman who had accompanied Tom on the quest for bootleg liquor, was on the stand. As he often did, Guss came tantalizingly close to striking a solid blow in Tom's defence but missed his chance.

Hughes had raised the question of the liquor the men drank and Blakely had said that he didn't know what it was.

Guss referred to that response in his cross-examination and queried, 'You had never tasted whisky before?' Blakely said he had indeed tasted whisky but he didn't recognize the drink he was given. 'It tasted like methylated spirits,' he said.

He went on to say that at the time, he told his colleagues that the drink 'burned my tongue'.

Guss could then have taken a step towards making the jury aware of the possibility of Bernice dying from methyl-alcohol poisoning. Since Blakely had raised the subject unprompted, Guss had every right to pursue the matter and ask, 'Are you aware that drinking methyl alcohol can be fatal and that those who die from it exhibit a bluish tinge to the face and a purplish tinge to the tongue?'

Instead, he merely moved on to the other events of the evening.

It is quite likely that Hughes fully realized the import of Blakely's observation even if Guss didn't. In his redirect, he got Blakely to admit that he wasn't accustomed to drinking methylated spirits and didn't really know what they tasted like.

Another opportunity had slipped through Guss's hands only to be negated by Hughes.

Chapter Twenty-five

The Crown's presentation of evidence was clearly nearing its conclusion when proceedings resumed on Monday morning, but any hope that the combination of a day of rest and the proximity of the finish line would improve the atmosphere was quickly shown to be unfounded.

Again, Hughes seemed determined to bludgeon the jurors into submission with repetition and tedium. Three more Mounties – Duncan Dunn, Frank Tudor and David Evans – were called to testify to a series of events that was already well established.

Guss even said to Constable Tudor, who had spent half an hour on the stand and offered no new evidence, 'Your story is the same as told by Staff Sergeant Davis.'

'I presume it is,' said the Mountie.

His two colleagues could have been presented with the same remark and could have given the same response.

When civil engineer Rigby was recalled to present the latest version of his diagram showing the dance hall and surrounding area, this too was less than enthralling. Location after location was designated, identified by its distance (to the nearest inch) from another location, and assigned a letter of the alphabet. Since the jurors could not see the diagram, they could do little more than sit and twiddle their thumbs and wish they were elsewhere.

Again, as had been the case on Saturday, the animosity among the judge, Crown and defence was obvious.

The examples were many, but here is one that was typical. On the stand was RCMP Constable Duncan Dunn who conceded that even though he had talked about the events of 5 June, he had not been at the dance.

Therefore, suggested Guss, it was 'hearsay from someone else'.

As Dunn began to answer, the judge interrupted. 'You are basing that on the information you got from the people you spoke to?'

Dunn said he was, and Guss said, 'That is hearsay, I would say.'

'That is another matter,' snapped the judge.

But really, it wasn't another matter. Dunn was testifying about events that he himself had not witnessed. His evidence was based on what people told him. That's hearsay. Guss had been right, but the judge would not accept that view and allowed the testimony.

Only a few moments later, with Dunn still on the stand, Guss referred to testimony made during the preliminary hearing. Hughes interrupted to ask, 'Aren't you going to read the next question?'

'I have read the whole thing to the question,' answered Guss.

'You read it in the wrong order,' said Hughes.

'I did not read it in the wrong order,' countered Guss. 'I read it just as it stands.'

Perhaps Hughes was feeling the strain of the long trial. Certainly, one series of questions would indicate that this was the case.

When Bernice's sister, Etta was on the stand, this exchange took place with Hughes doing the questioning:

'Was she married or single?'

'Single.'

'And of course she was not married to the accused.'

'Pardon?'

'Then of course she was not married to the accused. She was single you say.'

'She was single. No, she was not married to anyone.'

During testimony on Saturday, Bernadine Bradford had said that she had found a pair of panties near the road, and on Monday, Etta Connors confirmed that they were the type that her sister wore but could not positively identify them.

She was followed to the stand by the third Mountie of the day, Constable David Evans.

Even though the RCMP testimony produced no new evidence of any significance, it provided an opening for Guss to gain some ground. He had been given the opportunity to make the case that Bernice Connors drank herself to death. But again, he fumbled the ball.

Although Dunn was asked about nothing more than the swelling on Bernice's face, he had had spontaneously added that he noticed its bluish colour.

Similarly, Constable Evans had said, 'The face was a kind of blue colour.'

Perhaps Hughes did not like these repeated references to a blue face because their implication had not escaped him, or perhaps it simply slipped his mind. But whatever the reason, he did not ask Constable Tudor, the third Mountie of the day, about Bernice's colouring, even though Tudor had testified that he was at the scene where the body was found on Sunday night. Guss did not introduce the matter either.

Guss did engage Dunn in a lengthy cross-examination, but most of it had to do with the items that had been entered in evidence – the places they had been found and their subsequent treatment. He got Dunn to agree that he had seen Bernice's face, but quickly changed the tenor of his questioning, not asking him for any illumination of his observation to Hughes regarding the bluish tinge.

The cross-examination of Evans was little more than perfunctory. Guss simply determined that Evans was not in Black's Harbour between 11 p.m. 5 June and 1 a.m. 6 June. Nothing more.

It was an astonishingly lackadaisical performance, one that was not ameliorated by Guss's approach to the next – and final – witness for the Crown. That was Rigby, who had been recalled brandishing his new map. When Guss's turn came, he simply ascertained that Rigby had not been in Black's Harbour on the night Bernice disappeared.

Still, this kind of letdown by a defence attorney at this stage is not terribly uncommon. Guss was aware that Rigby's testimony represented the final piece of evidence from the Crown, and that it would now be his turn to instill reasonable doubt into the minds of the jurors.

Defence attorneys, with their minds on their plans to introduce a series of qualified experts in a specific area, as well as a string of rebuttal witnesses, often find their intensity flagging as the Crown's case winds down.

The Crown had done its best, but still had been unable to cite any real evidence to show that Tom Roland Hutchings had murdered Bernice Connors. In fact, it hadn't even been proved beyond reasonable doubt that a murder had been committed. And there was certainly no evidence of rape.

The last time Tom and Bernice had positively been seen together, they had been walking towards the dance hall, not away from it. The only person to identify Tom with Bernice walking away from the dance hall made that identification by voice only, even though he was nothing more than a nodding acquaintance, had just finished a bottle of whisky, and had seen two bicycles where there were none.

At least three witnesses placed Tom at the dance hall at the time three other witnesses in an area too dark to allow visual identification, saw what they thought was a sexual coupling between Bernice and Tom taking place 1,465 feet 7 inches away from that dance hall (using the Crown's measurements provided by Percy Rigby).

And, as has been well established, there was not even the most minute particle of evidence that would show that Tom had ever been at the place where the body had been found, let alone that he was there at the time of the incident.

That brings up another point. No evidence had been presented to show where Bernice's life had ended. The coroner's jury had made the assumption that she died where she was found, but no proof of that assumption had been forthcoming, either in the inquest, the preliminary hearing or the trial itself.

Now was the time for Guss to bring forth a fully qualified doctor who could testify about the impact of methyl alcohol on the body, and the symptoms that are evident when it has caused death. He danced around that point when Dr Branch was on the stand. Now was the time to hammer it home.

It was time to bring forth Earl Watson who knew the provenance of the bootleg liquor and how it was made.

It was the time to bring forth Dr E.C. Menzies who had examined Tom six times and knew him to be suffering from pathological intoxication and therefore not always able to give a complete account of his whereabouts.

It was the time to bring forth his own witnesses: the three boys who had been with Vincent Bradford on the night of 5 June but were never called; anyone who had seen Hughes and the Mounties paying Vincent to do their bidding; the RAF officers who would have had to be present when Vincent was unable to identify any of the hundreds of airmen who were paraded before him; Corporal Harold Walker and Corporal Cyril Griffiths who had been interviewed by the RCMP and said they saw Tom at the dance hall at 12.15 a.m. but were never called by Hughes; and Sergeant D.C. Huggett who had seen Tom in the throes of pathological intoxication during their time in Yarmouth.

It was even the time to put Tom himself on the stand. He had cooperated with the authorities at every turn and, if he were to testify after the medical experts had been heard, his explanation that he had no knowledge of the events of that night, would not be seen as far-fetched and would probably be accepted.

It was therefore an exciting moment in the court. Everyone turned expectantly to Guss as the judge asked what his next move was to be.

'The defence calls no witnesses,' he answered.

Chapter Twenty-six

In the summer of 1942, conversation in Charlotte County, New Brunswick tended to drift into one of two areas. You either talked about the war or you talked about the murder of Bernice Connors.

As far as the ongoing developments in the war were concerned, there wasn't much ambiguity. The German army was advancing relentlessly on the eastern front and there was a widespread fear that Stalingrad would soon capitulate and the Wehrmacht would continue its advance to Moscow. The outlook was not much better on the North Atlantic as the U-boat wolfpacks were sinking millions of tons of Allied shipping every year and the battleship Tirpitz was terrorizing convoys on the Murmansk run. Tobruk fell in late June and the armoured divisions of Rommel's Afrika Korps were heading across North Africa towards the Suez Canal, a vital waterway if the Allies were to maintain control of the Mediterranean. In the Pacific, the Americans were still reeling after the 7 December 1941 attack by the Japanese on Pearl Harbor. In Asia, the Japanese were advancing inexorably – into Hong Kong, the Philippines and even the Aleutian Islands.

But in Charlotte County, where both Black's Harbour and St Andrews are situated, the other topic, the one relating to the fact that the ancient jail now held a man widely seen as a vicious murderer, was every bit as prevalent. And everyone had an opinion.

Carman Eldridge remembers it well. He was in the Royal Canadian Navy at the time, serving on corvette shepherding convoys across the North Atlantic, but because he lived on the east coast, he was able to get home on leave, and he had family who kept him informed while he was away.

Two of Carman's cousins, Foster and Gilbert Eldridge, had been among the four boys Bernice Connors had spoken to on her last walk along Deadman's Harbour Road.

Carman and five others made up the graduation class of Black's Harbour High School in 1939. Until his death in 2019, he had a memento of that graduation framed on his living-room wall. It was a small photograph of the high school itself surrounded by seven cameo photographs – six students and the teacher.

Carman didn't live in Black's Harbour. He lived in Beaver Harbour, at the other end of Deadman's Harbour Road. 'It was 4 miles,' he said in a 2016 interview at his home in St Andrews. 'Each way. And there were no school buses.' But as far as the locals were concerned, Beaver Harbour and Black's Harbour were essentially the same community. They were both fishing villages on the same coast, and they both supplied the Connors plant.

Carman explained that news spread primarily by word of mouth in that part of the world in 1942. It had to. There were no televisions. Very few people in Charlotte County had radios. And for the many who were illiterate, newspapers were no help either.

'There wasn't much formal education,' Carman said, 'but that didn't mean people were stupid. There was a man named Ossie Waite who built up quite a haulage business that is still being run by his family today. He was a smart businessman. Every morning, he used to deliver newspapers from Pennfield Ridge to Black's Harbour – 7 miles. Then he'd stop at the café. He couldn't read, but he didn't want people to know that, so he'd spread out a newspaper while he had his breakfast and pretend to read it.

'One day, someone said, 'Ossie, you've got the paper upside down.'

He said, 'Well any fool can read it right side up.'

Because the trial of Tom Hutchings was such a momentous occasion, Eldridge has not forgotten the way it was perceived in Charlotte County.

'I don't think there were too many people who thought he didn't do it,' he said. 'Maybe a few, but not too many. But most of us thought that even though we were sure he did it, it was accidental.

'I knew Bernice and her sisters and she was used to going out with men. But she was a teenager. She shouldn't have been there at a dance like that. It's not like it is today with teenaged girls. Most people thought maybe it got carried a bit too far and he didn't mean to do it. But we all thought that because the police had charged him and he was on trial, he must be guilty. The police must be right. That was the way people thought.'

Carman remembered there being a fair degree of sympathy for Tom – a widespread feeling that although he must certainly be punished, he shouldn't be hanged. Even so, as is always the case when human beings are involved, there was no unanimity of opinion.

'There were some people who just didn't like the military,' said Carman. 'I don't know why, but they didn't. And there were others who didn't mind our military but didn't like the Englishmen. There was that sense of them coming over here and taking up with our women while our men were overseas.'

Neither sentiment is uncommon in wartime. In England after the United States entered the war, the common complaint about American soldiers was that they were 'Overpaid, over-sexed and over here'.

In St Andrews, where Tom was being held in solitary confinement, everyone knew that his cell was the one closest to the road. Children were told that they must not walk past the jail, even if it was on the shortest route to and from the nearby school. But there were some adults who made a point of going there to shout abuse towards Tom's window.

'Some did,' conceded Eldridge, 'but not the thinking ones.'

Still, there are always non-thinkers, and in a society where gossip is the universal currency, rumours and speculation are quickly transformed into widely accepted facts.

Consider a letter that was passed to the RCMP by one of the Canadian postal censors. Astonishingly, it was written only hours after Bernice's body had been found. The author was a woman named Dot Denyea who lived in St Stephen, about 40 miles by road from Black's Harbour and was writing to a friend in Portland, Maine.

> Something horrible happened down at Black's Harbour Friday night. Here's how I heard the story. A Conner's [*sic*] girl who lives down there was at a dance there dancing and she went out with an English Air Force, and that was the last seen of her until yesterday when the girl was found covered with moss behind the dance hall with a large gash in the back of her head and she was cut up quite badly and her clothes were all torn off her. This English 'Dog' had a couple of helpers (so I heard) and one was a Canadian Air Force and I guess the other one was an Englishman. The girl was buried before she was dead because when she was found, her knees were shoved up through the moss where, I imagine, she tried to get out but suffocated instead. The one who took her out down there is said to have been up here Saturday night with another girl. I imagine it will give the fellows down at the airport quite a name after this happening so soon after landing here. Pauline said the crowd of Air Force up at the dance were terribly rough and I don't doubt it if the rest of them boys down there are like those other three.

With the exception of the fact that a girl had been murdered, very few of the circumstances mentioned in the letter conformed to reality. But accounts of this nature were rampant and with only limited media coverage, the rumours perpetuated unchecked.

In St Andrews, the informal triumvirate comprised of jailer George Goodeill, county sheriff Charles Mallory and town marshal Norman Johnson stayed alert and focused on the mood of the town. All three were local men with deeply rooted ties to the community and as a result, little that transpired escaped them.

They heard of the occasional threats of vigilante groups planning to attack the jail and lynch the murderer. They knew that there was a strong current of discontent at the Pennfield base and that there were occasional rumblings of a different sort of vigilante action. In this case, the jail would be attacked and Tom Hutchings freed.

But, as was invariably the case, these rumblings amounted to nothing more than talk.

Even so, when the unfounded rumours reached the bureaucrats in the provincial capital of Fredericton, it was decreed that Tom should be moved to more secure surroundings in Saint John. Accordingly, on 24 July, Sheriff Mallory and Constable Duncan Dunn of the RCMP bundled Tom into Mallory's car and took him to the Saint John County Jail.

The federal taxpayers would no doubt have been pleased to know, as Dunn pointed out in his report to J Division, that because no RCMP car was used, 'no expenses were incurred in this connection'.

Tom stayed in Saint John until 24 September and during that time, Goodeill and Johnson transferred another prisoner from St Andrews to Saint John. Because both men had come to know and like Tom during his time in St Andrews, they stopped in to visit him. It was not until they were on their way home that Goodeill pointed out that without thinking, both men had been carrying loaded sidearms while they were talking with Tom, who was under no restraints.

So much for the increased security in Saint John.

But while it was a pleasant respite for Tom to chat with two men he saw as friends, his frequent conversations with Dr E.C. Menzies were more likely to have a beneficial result.

Because of the interest that the doctor took in Tom's case while he was in Saint John, a clear line of communication was established between Menzies and Tom Hutchings Sr in England.

The documentation of his son's illnesses, sent by Tom Sr, enabled Menzies to conclude that there was no doubt he was right about his initial speculation that Tom was prone to bouts of pathological intoxication.

But Menzies didn't keep his opinion to himself. He met with Guss and passed along his evaluation. He also offered to testify under oath that even if were proved that Tom had committed the crime, he could not be considered culpable.

But Guss didn't accept the offer. The court proceedings moved directly from the Crown's evidence to the Crown's summation.

And by that time, M. Camille Branchaud of Montreal, a professional hangman, had received a letter from Sheriff Mallory:

> Dear Sir:
>
> I have a prisoner who is to be tried for MURDER on the 26 of this month and if he is convicted, I shall be compelled to have him executed.
>
> If this man is found guilty the execution will probably take place late in December or early in January. You have been recommended to me by Sheriff M. Colby Smith of Saint John to be a very capable man and that I should get in touch with you early in order that I might have dates to present to the Judge.
>
> Should your services be available, at what date and what is your fee?
>
> Yours truly
> Charles W. Mallory

Chapter Twenty-seven

Court resumed at 10 a.m. on the 6 October. This was the day the case was to be sent to the jury. The Crown and the defence would make their summations, then the judge would give his charge, and the jurors would leave the courtroom to begin their deliberations.

But before that series of events began, Judge Richards sent out the jury and sought some advice from Guss. Was he intending to use drunkenness as a defence and thereby make a case for manslaughter?

'My lord, I have not directed my thoughts to that,' said Guss. 'It has always appeared to me it was murder or nothing.'

The judge made it clear that his only interest in the matter was whether he would need to instruct the jury on the value of a defence of reduced culpability due to drunkenness. As far as the judge was concerned, there was no legal precedent of eliminating guilt. 'It is not a defence,' he said. 'It is only an amelioration.'

Clearly, Guss was not quite sure what the judge was getting at. He had already said that he hadn't been thinking of a drunkenness defence, but he began to warm to the judge's point, 'If he were drunk, that he did not have the intent? Could not have the intent? Well, I think …'

The judge cut him off. 'It is only a question of whether or not you are going to ask me to give any special instructions on that point,' he said. 'That does raise the other question of manslaughter.'

Manslaughter had never been under consideration, not even by Guss, as he had just admitted. For the judge to mention the option of manslaughter to the defence attorney at this stage of a capital trial involving rape was unusual, to say the least.

Guss, suddenly sensing the opening of an opportunity where he had believed that none existed, said, 'I think there is sufficient to show that there was considerable drunkenness by the accused and by others and under those circumstances. I think that it might be well to instruct the jury in that way.'

The judge said that he would consider it, but for some reason, Guss backed off. 'I must confess,' he said, 'I was not proposing to touch on that point, your lordship, during my address to the jury.'

When Hughes was asked for his opinion on the matter, he suggested that the law was quite clear on the point and that the evidence was what mattered. He was not expecting drunkenness to be a consideration because as far as he was concerned, there was ample evidence that Tom was not drunk.

Guss was given a few minutes to leave and consider his position, and when he came back, he explained his views to the judge.

'My lord, the position of the defence is that the accused did not do it and that the Crown has not brought home the offence to him, but at the same time, in all fairness that the jury might be instructed to this effect, if they should come to the conclusion that he is in fact guilty that they should further consider that intoxication – that is drunkenness if they find it in him – would warrant their returning a verdict of manslaughter, if they should think that he is guilty.'

'So that raises the matter definitely then,' responded the judge. It did. That much was clear. Judge Richards had accepted that manslaughter was an option.

The legal sparring had taken fifteen minutes. The jury was recalled, and at 10.17 a.m., Hughes took centre stage for his summation.

'Culpable homicide is murder whether or not death was meant to ensue,' he began.

It was a point he was to make more than once. As far as he was concerned, Bernice Connors was dead and Tom was the culprit. Nothing else was really relevant.

Hughes was a skilled attorney. He had been through these courtroom battles before, even at the level of the Supreme Court of Canada, and he knew that truth was an option, but certainly not a necessity. As long as he stayed close to some facts, pushed the limits of others and ignored whatever might not help his cause, he could weave a narrative that exuded nothing but guilt for Tom Roland Hutchings.

Also, he was patient. He knew, as he had shown when he paraded witness after witness to the stand to give the same testimony, that no matter how ridiculous the principle might be in the real world, in the courtroom, a pound of feathers far outweighs a pound of lead.

He intended to recount the testimony of each witness, but first, he had to establish what he saw as the basic unvarnished truth.

'The accused was the person with Bernice Connors when she was last seen alive on Deadman's Harbour Road,' said Hughes. He presented it as a fact. It was an opinion. The identity of the person with whom she was last seen alive was very much in doubt.

Tom had been seen walking towards the dance hall with Bernice Connors. After that she was seen leaving with a man identified only by the testimony of a drunken acquaintance of Tom who barely knew him and couldn't see him but thought he recognized his voice.

Hughes was never averse to a bit of theatrics either. Brandishing Bernice's blood-stained blouse, he asked the jury, 'Would any logical person come to any conclusion other than that the girl had been taken and raped and murdered?'

In fact, a logical person might ask if every blood-stained blouse in the world came from a murdered rape victim.

But Hughes rolled on. He brought up the struggle that was indicated by the marks at the side of the road, a piece of evidence that even RCMP Superintendent Mercer had found spurious. Hughes spoke of the nearby shoe, even though it was found two days after the dance and could easily have been moved. He spoke of the 'mound of moss' under which lay Bernice's body.

She was killed, he said, because she had repelled Tom's attempt to have sex with her. He saw it as a universal truth that when a woman finds herself in such a situation, 'if consent is not given, a determined man will beat her.'

Then he returned to his initial theme. 'In the case of rape, culpable homicide is murder, whether death is meant to ensue or not.'

He produced the crime-scene photographs and again called upon the jurors to apply logic. 'Common sense means he is responsible for what he did,' he said. 'It is murder.'

Once again, the application of common sense would render those statements somewhat less iron-clad than Hughes' assertion, but he quickly returned to a recital of injuries to the body. It was evidence that had been presented before, but he wanted to hammer home his point.

Wary of what the judge had discussed with the two attorneys earlier in the morning, he then moved to a new area. 'The accused had a few drinks before he went to the dance,' he said, 'and had a few while he was there. No one said he was drunk. And if he was drunk, it would be the duty of his counsel to establish it. In fact, there is evidence that he wasn't drunk.'

That was certainly true. William Protheroe had said that Tom did not seem drunk but was in 'a dazed condition'. Since this could open the door to a defence of pathological intoxication, Hughes was not specific about the source of his information.

Instead, he moved to the testimony of Eddie Hutchings and said that he had looked for Tom and 'missed him for 90 minutes. And that is the hour and a half that is involved in this case.'

Again, those statements are true. But they have nothing to do with Tom's guilt or innocence. They could also have been said of most people in the world that night.

Hughes recalled the evidence that Bernice was seen 'going up Deadman's Harbour Road with a sergeant'.

He also pointed out that the couple encountered another couple – Sergeant Edwards and Mildred Justason.

'Edwards knew the accused,' said Hughes. 'Spoke to him. Miss Justason who was well acquainted with Bernice identified her.

Edwards knew the accused but would not swear who the girl was. She was identified as Bernice Connors by Edwards' companion, Mildred Justason. At about 11 o'clock they met the accused and Bernice Connors under the last street light on Deadman's Harbour Road. 'We don't know those people we won't even bother speaking to them,' were the joking words used by Bernice at that second encounter.

In this case, Hughes got away with a half-truth and an outright lie.

To say that Edwards 'knew the accused' was a stretch. He had admitted that he recognized him from Pennfield but didn't even know his first name. And that second encounter was in an unlit area of the road, well past the last street light.

Hughes told the jurors that the combined testimony of his witnesses clearly established the identity of Tom and Bernice.

He moved on to the testimony of Sergeant Humphries – that he had seen a man wearing an Air Force uniform involved in a sexual encounter. He recalled that Humphries had taken his 15-year-old date, Sylvia Gaudet, back to the dance hall, collected his friend Leading Aircraftman Moore, returned to the scene and found the couple still there.

Hughes made no mention of the fact that Sylvia Gaudet had testified that she had seen only one person 'crawling or moving', and that it was too dark to see the faces of people 5 feet away.

The issue of blood was crucial, and it was to that aspect that Hughes next turned his attention. He told the jury that Tom Hutchings had returned to dance hall with blood on his face, but no cut.

He spent a lot of time discussing Eddie's testimony and Tom's assertion that the two had been together all evening. He said that Tom was trying to establish an alibi when he had not been in attendance for the latter part of the dance.

Then he went back to the blood. 'Where did this blood come from?' he asked. 'From the body of the victim. And the blood on the face of the murdered girl? The fist of the accused when he struck her with his left hand and he is left-handed.'

No evidence whatsoever had been presented to support either of the last two statements.

'There were six Air Force sergeants at the dance that night,' said Hughes, 'five British and one Canadian. They are all accounted for with the exception of the accused. He's not accounted for because he wasn't there. He's not accounted for because he was up the road.'

Hughes was working up to his conclusion. 'The British Air Force men are the same as our own,' he said, 'and must be judged by the same standards as by which we judge our own.

'On this matter, there can be but one conclusion. That conclusion is that the accused has committed this murder. And that you find him guilty of the charge which has been laid against him.'

It was now 12.46 p.m., so the judge adjourned the court until 2 p.m. when it became Guss's turn.

He began with a full broadside on the evidence presented by Hughes. Every bit of it was circumstantial, he said, and therefore highly suspect.

Like Hughes, he had a theme. No one, he said repeatedly, had seen Tom Roland Hutchings either kill Bernice Connors or have sex with her. He also questioned the time element as it had been presented by the Crown and the importance of solid proof.

'The Magna Carta was produced by the people of the birthplace of this man,' he said, pointing to Tom Hutchings. 'The Crown must produce evidence beyond a reasonable doubt that he is guilty.'

Like Hughes, Guss dealt with each witness, and pointed out that not one of them had been able to testify that he or she had seen Roy Hutchings kill Bernice Connors.

'A chain is no stronger than its weakest link,' he said. 'The same applies to the chain of circumstantial evidence.'

So far, he was on solid ground. His broadside was effective. A man is on trial for his life here. Where is the solid evidence?

But then he began to lose his focus. His broadside became a scattergun approach. He made points that were of little consequence, and when he made valid points, he failed to fully develop them.

He questioned the reluctance of Eddie Hutchings to mention that he had a nosebleed the day Tom was ironing his uniform, as if the jury should now start to consider Eddie as the murderer.

He suggested that the discovery of an old, worn kitchen knife a week after the murder proved his client's innocence. Despite searches of the scene, nothing had been found that would implicate Tom.

When he got to the testimony of Dr Branch, the field was wide open. 'Reasonable doubt,' said Guss, reminding the jury of their charge. 'The doctor's evidence is full of it.'

And so it was. But Guss didn't take advantage of it.

He did quote Branch as saying 'I am not prepared to say that this was rape,' and concluded that 'The doctor's evidence has eliminated the possibility that this was a sex crime.'

He should have hammered that point. He should have forced the jury to put the murder out of their minds for the time being and consider the rape charge in depth. He should have shown them that there was no evidence of rape whatsoever. But he didn't.

He made a number of valid points – points that needed to be made. But he didn't drive them home as Hughes did. And unlike Hughes, he didn't mix half-truths in with the facts, thereby getting the jury to accept a set of circumstances that couldn't be supported by the evidence.

He made the case that his client had voluntarily acceded to every police request and had agreed to blood test.

Like Hughes, he mentioned the blood and said, 'That blood does not connect Roy Hutchings with the crime.' This too was true. But Guss made no mention of the fact that proper blood testing could have proved his client's innocence had the RCMP not waited so long to have it tested.

He hinted at pathological intoxication, when he asked, 'Wouldn't he know he had blood on his face?' But he went no further. A hint was not enough to counter the case Hughes had made.

As his summation moved on, Guss seemed increasingly lost – more and more like a drowning man clutching at any bit of flotsam in the hope it would keep him afloat.

He contended that there was no sign of decomposition and said that Branch's testimony showed that Bernice might have been alive on Sunday afternoon. 'Someone may have seen her alive and had good reason for not coming forward,' he suggested.

'I contend that witness after witness have come forward and given facts consistent with the innocence of this man.' That much was true but Guss didn't properly enumerate and present those facts.

126

He said that Bernice's body was put in the only open spot in the road. 'Would a man unfamiliar with the country choose that spot?' A juror would have a hard time seeing that development as something that vindicated Tom.

'I suggest there is more in this than meets the eye,' he continued. 'A knife planted. Seaweed. Wet hair.'

He told the jury that testimony showed Tom Hutchings to be in more than one place at the same time. That too was true, but like so many other points, it needed to be developed.

Guss had encountered two major problems when making his summation. The first was that he was no match for Hughes in a courtroom. He was too inexperienced in the bare-knuckle brawling at which Hughes excelled.

The second was that he had introduced no witnesses of his own. Instead, he had to dredge up wild theories about Bernice being alive on Sunday afternoon and Eddie's nosebleed pointing to his guilt.

As a result, he could not refer to an assertion made by Hughes and say something along the lines of, 'My learned friend would have you believe X but you heard my expert witness made it very clear that Y is the case.'

At 3.38 p.m., Guss finished. The judge recessed the court until 4 p.m.

Chapter Twenty-eight

In Canada, it is customary to seal the court once the judge begins his charge to the jury. Security officers move to the doors and no one is allowed to come in or go out until the judge either finishes his charge or calls a recess.

By nature, judges' charges are rarely stirring, and legal lore has it that this is the reason for the doors being barred. If they weren't, everyone would leave. But the judges are in a difficult position. It is their duty to explain the law to the jurors and to remind them, step by step, of the evidence that they have heard.

Unfortunately, in the case of Judge Richards, his explanations of the law were repetitive, unduly verbose and occasionally incomprehensible. His recollections of the evidence were often vague or incorrect.

Again and again, he would admit that he was recalling testimony that he thought was right, but he wasn't sure. And in some cases, the accuracy of this testimony could be crucial to the determination of innocence or guilt.

For instance, a vital aspect of the case was the time at which Leading Aircraftman David Christie wiped blood off Tom's face. Judge Richards reminded the jurors of the testimony in which 'Christie guesses the time'.

In fact, Christie's determination of the time was much more precise than most. He knew it was 'between quarter past twelve and half past', because he had gone bowling before looking at his watch and realizing that it was time to go to the dance.

Said Judge Richards to the jury: 'I have not got the exact time. I'm not sure. It was a little after 12 o'clock. I have not that exact time. You will probably recall these times. There are a great many of them and I know how difficult it is to keep them exactly.'

But Leading Aircraftman Robert Moore said he too was sure of the exact time that he saw two people he assumed to be Tom Hutchings and Bernice Connors 500 yards from the dance hall. It was 12.25 a.m.

Tom's life depended on the jurors' determination as to whether Bernice was raped on Friday night. The judge told them that Dr Branch had said the scratches in Bernice's vaginal area occurred up to two days before the autopsy which began at 5 p.m. on Monday. In fact, Branch said no such thing. The time reference he gave initially on the stand was 'days rather than weeks', before death. Hughes got him to narrow the gap down to two days and when Guss queried it, Hughes answered, 'He meant two days before death.'

Branch did not disagree.

In describing the injuries to Bernice, the judge mentioned the bluish tinge to her face and ascribed it to an obstruction applied to her neck. But he did not mention that there were no marks indicating any obstruction had been applied.

In another instance, the judge referred to Leading Aircraftman Humphries, Leading Aircraftman Moore and Sylvia Gaudet 'seeing some woman, some girl, near the side of the road with a man on top of her.' Sylvia Gaudet saw no such thing. She testified that she saw a person crawling.

The testimony of Alonzo Hall and Donald Adams, two of the four teenagers drinking beer on Deadman's Harbour Road, was also misrepresented by the judge who said they 'spoke of having been in a car.' They didn't. They spoke of having looked in a car that had a clock in it. If the judge was going to refer to their testimony at all, justice would have been better served if he had mentioned that they said they had no bicycles, even though Sergeant Edwards and his date, Mildred Justason, said they had seen them.

By 5.35 p.m., even the judge was wearing down and he sent the jurors to the jury room where dinner was waiting for them. But at 7 p.m., he began again and spoke until 9 p.m. Over the course of their day, the jurors had been compelled to sit and listen to approximately seven-and-a-half hours of speeches – and expected to absorb everything that was said.

The judge had begun his remarks with a lengthy consideration of points of law. He explained and evaluated: burden of proof; reasonable doubt; murder as opposed to manslaughter; culpability; treason; piracy; intent and circumstantial evidence.

Since that last point represented the very basis of the Crown's evidence, the judge spent a good deal of time on it, summing it up for the time being, as follows:

Now the established rule which I ask you to observe with respect to this class of evidence is that where proof of the guilt of an accused person depends upon circumstantial evidence, you as a jury must be satisfied not only that the circumstances are consistent with the guilt of the accused, but are inconsistent with any other reasonable conclusion. That is in practically in [sic] the terms as they were stated to you by counsel for the accused in repeating the words of a famous English judge in respect of that principle of our law – 'Where the proof of the guilt of an accused person depends upon circumstantial evidence, you must be satisfied not only that the circumstances are consistent with the guilt of the accused but are inconsistent with any other reasonable conclusion.'

It seems safe to assume that the fishermen, labourers and menial workers on the jury had not spent a lot of their leisure hours considering the opinions held by English judges on the requirements of valid circumstantial evidence.

Granted, Judge Richards had a difficult job. He wanted to be as precise as possible, and given that restriction, he did what a lawyer is likely to do. He resorted to legal terms. But instead of repeating his evaluations using legalistic phraseology – as he did at length with regard to the legal definitions of rape and circumstantial evidence – he might have, at some point, tried to use language more likely to be in common use in Charlotte County, where adult illiteracy was rampant in 1942 and remains so to this day.

All the evidence points to the fact that the jurors were more confused than enlightened by the judge's charge, partly because of his verbose meanderings, partly because he kept suggesting that a reduction of the charge was a reality. As had been the case when he spoke only to the lawyers with the jury out, he repeatedly raised the possibility of a verdict of manslaughter.

On one occasion, he said to the jury: 'If you think the evidence justifies a verdict of manslaughter, not murder, under the instructions I have given, you may so find.'

The phrase 'under the instructions I have given', was crucial. Did the jurors understand what he meant? After all, he had been giving instructions since four o'clock and it was now nearing 9 p.m.

It must be said, in all fairness, that the instructions to which he referred were quite explicit. But they were given much earlier in the charge, and even though Judge Richards repeated many points of law, he did not repeat the one that needed to be stressed the most. It was this:

Now in the present case, to reduce the offence from murder to manslaughter, you would of course have to find the accused was the person involved and that he inflicted the injuries upon Bernice Connors and those injuries caused her death. So far, the essential features are the same as for murder, At this point, a difference arises. The other features are not the same. You would have to come to the conclusion that there was no rape.

There it was, albeit somewhat vaguely. If Bernice had died during the commission of a rape, the charge could not be reduced from murder.

As the judge neared the conclusion of his charge, he tried to offer a summation and said:

If, after an honest and impartial consideration of all the evidence, you have a reasonable doubt in your minds of the guilt of the accused, you must find him not guilty. But if, on the other hand, you are satisfied beyond a reasonable doubt, then it is equally your duty to find him guilty of murder or manslaughter in accordance with the instructions I have given you.

Again, there was a reference to instructions. But which instructions?

Then, to finish his charge, Judge Richards delivered a lengthy *mea culpa* which was supposed to make up for his omission of a minor point.

To a legal mind, this speech did make clear the relationship of rape and murder. But this was a Charlotte County jury, made up of men who had very little formal education. And this is what they heard:

If you find the accused inflicted grievous bodily harm, for either of these things, to facilitate the commission of rape or facilitate the escape after the commission or attempted commission of that offence, and death resulted from those injuries, then the accused is guilty of murder. Practically using the words of the definition. Subsequently I did not refer, or perhaps I did but I had no intention of referring to the matter of the attempt, dealing only with the commission of the rape itself. I think there was one case I remember where I perhaps went a little farther than that; speaking of rape, and asking the question: 'Were the injuries inflicted by someone in furtherance of the commission of rape?' I did say something there. I do not recall at the moment what it was. Were they done for the purpose of rape? That includes, as I think I said, an attempt as well as the actual commission. I had in mind then of the definition. The definition refers to the attempts as well as the commission. But here it is only the commission of rape I was speaking of – if the act was done in furtherance of the commission of rape. You may forget as far as the attempt of rape is concerned, I did not intend to refer to that and that may be disregarded. The evidence was directed, of course, to the rape and when I spoke of the furtherance of rape, I meant the commission of rape itself, nothing to do with the attempt.

That ended the charge. The judge then asked the lawyers if there was anything they wanted to add. Hughes brought up the fact that Leading Aircraftman Humphries insisted he had returned to the dance hall at 12.20 a.m. after seeing an intertwined couple 500 yards away.

Guss wanted it noted that Leading Aircraftman Christie had testified that he saw Tom Hutchings outside the dance hall between 12.15 and 12.30 a.m.

There being nothing further, the judge now turned his attention to the jurors. 'Gentlemen of the jury, you will retire and consider your verdict and report to the constable when you are through.'

The jury left the courtroom to determine the fate of Sergeant Tom Roland Hutchings.

Chapter Twenty-nine

There is little doubt that the longer the trial went on, the less impressive Guss's performance became.

Even though the accused is presumed innocent until proven guilty, a capable defence attorney still must give the jurors a reasonable alternative to his client's guilt. The presumption of innocence may be the law of the courts, but the suspicion of guilt is the law of human nature. In 1942, when the police were held in higher esteem than is the case today, that suspicion of guilt was even more developed. The consensus was that if a man was on trial, he was guilty.

When Guss presented no defence, he threw away his chance to counter the testimony provided by the Crown, especially the crucial medical testimony.

His reasoning is unknown but it probably had a lot to do with his personal finances. He was receiving no income while he was in court in St Andrews. In fact, he would be losing money because his office in Saint John would be open and incurring the usual operating expenses while no business was being generated. He would not only be unavailable to new clients, some of his established clients would almost certainly have taken their business elsewhere to get help with matters that they considered pressing.

By virtue of the edict of the New Brunswick Bar Association, Guss was paying his own expenses for food and lodging, and had been told that he should not expect to be reimbursed. He had been required to pay for court documents – the transcript of the preliminary hearing, for example – and he knew that he wouldn't be reimbursed for those expenses either.

He didn't even have a client who might conceivably reward him by bringing him post-trial business. Hutchings lived in England as did all his friends.

So with all these factors in mind, Guss probably decided that the sooner the proceedings came to an end, the better. For most of the witnesses in the latter part of the trial, he either waived cross-examination or asked only cursory questions that seemed barely relevant.

If that were the extent of his failings, Guss could probably have been excused. But once the summations were over, it was clear that he had also made a grievous error in his tactics.

He had been given the opportunity. All the evidence was there for him. Or to be more precise, the lack of evidence was there for him.

But instead of floating out a series of conspiracy theories, he should have attacked the charges separately and made it clear to the jury that he was doing so.

He should have started with the rape. Two key factors determined that strategy. First, it was the charge most easily disputed. Second, it had the potential of maximizing the other charge. Without the rape, the killing could be reduced to manslaughter. With the rape, the killing was automatically considered to be capital murder.

Guss should have made it clear to the jurors that, until further notice, he wanted them to work with him while together, they considered only the evidence of rape. Absolutely nothing else. He might then have begun by asking the jury a question:

'And what evidence would that be?

'Where is the evidence that my client raped Bernice Connors? Or, let's put it more simply. Where is the evidence that she was raped at all?

'The pathologist said that she had sex and incurred some minor scratches up to two days before she died. Not two days before the Monday autopsy, but two days before the Friday-night dance. This point was clarified during cross-examination.

'The pathologist said in his estimation, there was no rape.

'The pathologist said in his estimation, this was not a sex crime.

'So why then, is my client still here, battling for his life fighting a charge of rape? If the pathologist, the Crown's own witness, doesn't think that a rape occurred, why are we in the midst of a rape trial? If the pathologist is not producing evidence of a rape because he doesn't believe there was a rape, then where is the evidence coming from?

'Rape has to do with forcing a woman to have sex. There is not the slightest piece of evidence to show my client was at the scene, forcing her to do anything. There are no boot marks, no fingerprints, no pubic hairs, no left items of clothing. Nothing.

'And even if he was there – which he wasn't – and even if he had sex with her – which he didn't – where is the evidence that it wasn't consensual sex? Where is the evidence that the facial injuries occurred before sex and not after? There is none.

'If I were to ask any one of you, where is the evidence of rape, what would you say? The fact that poor Bernice Connors had suffered bodily harm? That's not evidence; that's a circumstance. There's nothing there to link a crime to my client. The fact that she had had sex? Same thing. Nothing to link a crime to my client. The fact that he had blood on his face and hands?

'Now you might be getting close to a serious consideration. Under the right set of circumstances, that might be evidence. But let's not forget that my client asked for a blood test. He knew that the blood on his uniform didn't belong to Bernice and the only reason he wasn't able to prove it was that the RCMP kept the exhibits so long that they could no longer be tested for blood type.

'The RCMP destroyed this man's chance to prove he didn't commit a crime, then encouraged the Crown to prosecute him for rape using as its primary expert witness, a doctor who believes there was no rape.

'Any more so-called evidence? Nothing tangible was raised by any of the Crown witnesses, so you might grasp at straws and say that Tom had no alibi. If you do say that, you've forgotten the most vital, most basic premise of our system of jurisprudence, one that the judge reminded you about on a number of occasions. It is not the accused's job to prove his innocence. He is innocent until someone proves he isn't. And to do that you need evidence. I say again, there is none.

'You must not, under any circumstance, find Tom Roland Hutchings guilty of rape. There is no evidence. None at all.'

At that point, Guss should have paused and looked at each juror, making sure he made eye contact with every one. Then he should have moved on to the charge of murder.

In that regard, there was no shortage of inconsistencies and many of them have already been discussed. Guss should have enumerated them, reminding the jurors over and over, that there was reasonable doubt.

Once again, his own failing in not having provided rebuttal witnesses would be an issue, but there were still many reasons why there was too much doubt to convict a man of murder. He had to defuse a Crown case that relied on witnesses who saw bicycles that weren't there; who saw a greyish-blue air force uniform when it was too dark to see a face; who could ascribe no better cause of death than shock; who held on to evidence so long that its value was lost; who offered nothing more than a recitation of evidence that had already been submitted; and so on.

But the jury retired without any significant contribution from Guss in their minds. And by then, Sheriff Mallory had received a reply to his letter to Camille Branchaud:

Dear Sir:

During my absence from the city of Montreal, I received your letter of the 15 inst., requesting my services for a coming execution.

The regular fees for a hanging are:

$150.00 per head, plus all travelling expenses, such as transportation, taxis, etc. Also the rope and black cap which are supplied by myself.

$75.00 per head, if services are retained by authorized letter and said execution is changed to life sentence. If arrived at destination for said hanging and said execution is commuted to life sentence, the charge is also $75.00 per head. Plus travelling expenses.

At the moment, no dates have been reserved for late December or early January, but the Courts have just begun in Montreal. However, should the prisoner be sentenced to hang, kindly write air mail immediately and I will arrange for your chosen date not to interfere with the ones on my list for the Province of Québec.

Should my services be required, I will be in your city three or four days before execution in order to examine the dispositions of your jail for a hanging.

Hoping this will prove satisfactory, and awaiting an early reply, I remain,

Yours very truly
Camille Branchaud

Chapter Thirty

Less than two hours after being sent to deliberate – an hour and fifty minutes to be precise – the jury returned.

As might have been expected in a trial that stretched over a week with forty-three Crown witnesses, there had been disputes among the jurors regarding the specifics of some of the testimony.

To refresh – or perhaps alter – their memories, they wanted to hear again the evidence of Athenia Hanley, Sylvia Gaudet, Leading Aircraftman Gerald Humphries, Leading Aircraftman David Christie and Leading Aircraftman William Protheroe.

With the exception of Hanley, these witnesses had testified to key points.

Hanley said she saw Bernice walking away from the dance hall with a sergeant she had never seen before at about 11.20 p.m., but it might have been 11.30 and she wasn't really sure. At 12.20 a.m., Humphries and Gaudet had seen something in an area that was so dark that they would have blithely passed it by had it not been for the sound of someone vomiting. Humphries said he saw a couple intertwined on the ground; Gaudet, at Humphries' side and holding his hand, didn't. She saw one person crawling. Neither could see a face.

Christie and Protheroe had wiped blood off Tom's face. Protheroe was unsure of the time; Christie placed it close to 12.15 a.m.

It took the clerk almost an hour to read the five testimonies and at 11.48 p.m., the jury retired again.

Clearly, the re-reading had achieved the desired purpose and clarified any misconceptions. Only five minutes later, the jurors came back into the courtroom. They appeared to have arrived at a unanimous decision.

In response to a query from the judge, the foreman, W. W. Quartermain, confirmed at 11.55 that this was indeed the case. The verdict was then rendered: 'Guilty with a recommendation that mercy be shown to the accused.'

The silence of the courtroom quickly gave way to an outburst of gasps, shouts and even cheers, but order was just as quickly restored.

It is not known whether the judge was shocked by this verdict or merely wanted to make sure that there was no ambiguity. 'You say guilty of the offence as charged?' he asked.

'Yes, your lordship,' answered Quartermain.

'Murder?' asked the judge again.

'Yes, murder.'

Again, there was a clamour throughout the courtroom but again, it quickly died down as Hughes stood and made a motion for immediate sentencing. After all, to someone as well versed in the law as Hughes, a King's Counsel, there was no doubt now as to what the sentence would be. And since that was the case, why wait? It was midnight and time to bring the proceedings to a close.

Tom was ordered to stand and when he did so, the judge told him that he had been convicted of the murder of Bernice Connors. 'Have you anything to say why sentence should not be passed upon you according to law?'

Appearing totally composed, Tom stood to attention. Speaking to the court for the first time since he had said, 'Not guilty', six days earlier, he announced clearly and emphatically, 'My lord, I have been asked by my defence counsel not to make any remarks at all.'

This time, there was no doubt that the judge was shocked.

'Not to make any remarks at all?' he asked.

'Yes my lord,' Tom said.

Guss quickly jumped up and intervened. 'My lord, might I make a request?' he asked. 'Flight Lieutenant Elverston is here and he is familiar with the record in the service of Tom Roland Hutchings, and if your lordship would ask him, if you think it is in order, I'm sure he would be pleased to say something in that regard.'

The judge was not at all sure that he agreed that it was in order and promptly expressed his doubts.

'It might be a little irregular,' he said. 'Aren't you in a position to do it? It would be better if you would, perhaps.'

Guss battled on, undaunted. 'I understand the jury has brought in a recommendation of mercy,' he said. 'I would ask you to consider that. I am not familiar with the record myself, except from what I have been told, that he was in the Air Force for three years.'

The judge conceded. 'I will let Mr Elverston make a statement,' he said.

But really, Elverston had very little to contribute. He confirmed that Tom had joined the RAF in 1939 and added, 'His conduct has been very good according to his papers.'

Guss jumped in again. 'I would humbly ask that your lordship consider the youth of Tom Roland Hutchings who is only 21 years old,' he said. 'He has a young wife, a child who is just 12 months old. His father is a retired artillery captain, at present with the Ministry of Food Supply in England, being too old himself to serve, having served in the First Great War for four years. He has an older brother who is a wing commander and has already in this war earned his DFC for gallant service which he has rendered to his country. And to ask you again to consider the remarks by Flight Lieutenant Elverston who is in a position to know the record of Tom Roland Hutchings in the past has been clear. I ask you to give these matters your consideration and to exercise that mercy which the jury has recommended and which I know your lordship possesses in full measure.'

It was passionate speech, one that provided every incentive for the court to show mercy. But really, it was nothing more than window-dressing, perhaps delivered to ease Guss's conscience. Whether it achieved that aim or not, it indisputably illustrated his lack of understanding of the law. By making that plea, he proved what many had suspected. He had not provided Tom with a committed defence lawyer determined to prove his client's innocence. He had gone through the motions, limited his research to a reading of the transcript of the preliminary hearing, and wasn't even aware of Canadian law as it pertained to the charges his client was facing.

The judge waited patiently until Guss had finished but made no acknowledgement.

Instead, he directed his remarks to Tom, starting by saying what judges usually say at that point – that he had been well represented.

But he left no doubt that he felt the jury had made the right decision.

'It is difficult to understand what could have prompted you to commit this offence,' he said. 'You are wearing the king's uniform. You are sworn to preserve the king's subjects … It is clear that the jury have realized your position quite fully because they have added to the verdict a recommendation for mercy. Your counsel has spoken of your family position. Flight Lieutenant Elverston has told us of your military record. All of these things cause us a very great deal of concern and create an occasion that is extremely painful, as it must have been to the jury.'

He looked toward the jurors. 'In regard to recommendation of mercy that you gentlemen of the jury have made, I can only say this: so far as I am concerned, I am bound by the law to pass one sentence and one sentence only.'

This statement caused a stirring among the jurors. Clearly some of them wondered what this meant. Was the judge planning to impose capital punishment? That was not what they intended.

The judge carried on.

'I have no discretion,' he explained. He had said this during his charge, even though his explanation had clearly been lost on the jurors who didn't comprehend his legalistic meanderings. And apparently, Guss hadn't understood it either. But the judge now made it perfectly clear, something he should have done during his charge.

The jurors were stunned. They had reached a unanimous agreement to find Tom guilty but not have him executed. It was now evident that something had gone terribly wrong.

'There is only one sentence which can be passed upon the accused who is found guilty of the crime of murder,' the judge said. 'You know, of course, what it is.'

Perhaps, by now, they did. But they hadn't known when they emerged from their deliberations. They had expected that their recommendation of mercy would lessen the severity of sentence. The judge could see the shock in their faces and tried to let them down gently.

'But I shall communicate the recommendation which you have made to the governor-in-council at Ottawa,' he said. 'It will come before the minister of justice. They have the prerogative – the governor general of Canada has the prerogative – of mercy. The matter of your recommendation will be presented in the usual way before the governor general-in-council. What action they may take, I can, of course, say nothing about. It is a matter which is in the jurisdiction of the governor-in-council.'

The fact that the jurors were uniformly stunned by this development makes it clear that not a single one of the twelve had understood the message that the judge had tried to deliver in his summation. Had just one of them realized that a guilty verdict mandated the death sentence, surely that juror would have said as much to his colleagues during deliberations and there would therefore have been no surprise in the jury box when the judge rendered his sentence.

For that matter, had any of them realized the incontestable result of their verdict, they would not have added a recommendation of mercy.

The judge probably realized this, but could offer no real solace.

He told them, 'There is nothing further, I think, that I can say to you at this time. Nothing further that I can do.

'All that remains for me to do, painful as it is,' he said, turning his attention to the prisoner's dock, 'is to pass sentence upon you according to law.

'The sentence of this court is that you, Tom Roland Hutchings, be taken from this courthouse to the common jail of the County of Charlotte, the place from whence you came, there to be kept in some safe place within the said jail, and from all other prisoners until Wednesday the sixteenth of December next and on that day between the hours of one o'clock in the morning and twelve o'clock noon you be taken to the place of execution within the walls of said jail, and there be hanged by the neck until you are dead.

'And may God have mercy on your soul.'

Tom was led out. The jury was discharged.

Chapter Thirty-one

The jurors weren't the only ones who were shocked by the sentence imposed on Tom Hutchings. Dr E. C. Menzies was shocked as well. Furthermore, he was outraged.

As a result of his visits to Tom during the latter's stay in Saint John County Jail, he had no doubt whatsoever that Tom was incapable of knowingly murdering Bernice Connors. He recognized the possibility that Tom might have murdered Bernice unknowingly, but if that were the case, capital punishment should have been out of the question.

The hanging was scheduled to take place in approximately ten weeks, so Dr Menzies knew there was no time to waste. He had already compiled a large portfolio supporting his stance that Tom was not culpable and had passed it along to Guss. He had intended to supplement that information in the expectation that he would be called as a defence witness. But Guss had never made that call.

Because Dr Menzies had a heavy workload at the psychiatric hospital and was already taking time to stay abreast of trial developments, he had not completed his submission when the trial began.

But on 7 October, the day after the verdict was rendered, Menzies immediately started to fill in the gaps. His eventual intention was to get the guilty verdict overturned, but before that, there was a much more urgent priority – commutation of the death sentence.

In the next few days, he acquired statements from Sergeant D. G. Huggett, Sergeant Eddie Hutchings and Leading Aircraftman Samuel Blakely, (all of which were included in the earlier chapter detailing Tom's medical history) confirming that it was not unusual for Tom to leave a group of friends for a while, then come back and not know where he had been.

As an eminent psychiatrist, Menzies was able to elicit the supporting opinions of other notable practitioners in the field – men known worldwide in the psychiatric community – and add their views to his portfolio.

CHAPTER THIRTY-ONE

In less than two weeks, he was able to garner so much substantiation for his case that he felt ready to take the matter to the next level. Accordingly, he battled through the red tape and spoke on the telephone to M. F. Gallagher in Ottawa, a task much more difficult than it might seem. Not only were phones scarce in New Brunswick, but in 1942 communication with any government official in Canada was invariably done through mail or telegrams. It was only Dr Menzies' status as one of the country's pre-eminent medical authorities that earned him the opportunity to communicate with Gallagher directly.

Gallagher worked in the federal Ministry of Justice. His immediate superior was the deputy minister, but he himself held the title of Chief of Remission Services. After finally making direct contact with him, Dr Menzies pleaded his case, strongly urging Gallagher to look into the court proceedings more closely. Gallagher eventually relented and promised that he would give serious consideration to a written submission.

Menzies immediately sent Gallagher a memorandum 'Re Tom Roland Hutchings' that was as direct as it could be:

> After examining this prisoner on at least six different occasions before his trial, I informed Defence Counsel of my conclusions and placed myself at his disposal. Why I was not called at the trial, I do not know. Had I, at the time, had a more complete knowledge of the facts now available, I would have stated my honest belief that when he committed the act with which he is charged, the accused, because of a degree of mental impairment due to pathological intoxication, most likely did not know the nature and quality of his deed, and very probably, did not realize that he was doing wrong. I do not speak with certainty in the matter; I doubt whether anyone could, but I do believe that the mental infirmity with which this man was afflicted was such a controlling factor in his periods of stress that his responsibility would at least be materially decreased, if not likely obliterated.

The concept of pathological intoxication, sometimes referred to as pathological drunkenness, was not widely known outside the psychiatric community. In a footnote, Dr Menzies defined it as:

> a constitutional (congenital) diseased condition of the nervous system. The patient subject to it reacts to alcohol in a certain

143

definite pattern, viz: The production of a twilight state with total amnesia. In this amnesic state the patient may be able to so conduct himself as to escape notice, but often the patient becomes violent and assaults anyone within reach.

Recognizing the seriousness of the matter, Gallagher responded by telling Menzies that he should take his case right to the top, above his own immediate superior, the deputy minister, and directly to the federal justice minister. At the time, that was Louis St Laurent K.C. who was six years away from becoming prime minister of Canada.

Again, Menzies moved in the recommended direction, but he sent much more than a memorandum to St Laurent. He sent a lengthy summation containing his medical evaluation, along with a critique of the evidence presented at the trial, and copies of the letters from Tom's colleagues who had seen his peculiar behaviour both before and after his arrival in Canada.

Perhaps realizing a man trained in the law might not see pathological intoxication as a genuine affliction, Menzies opened his letter to St Laurent by pointing out that, 'This condition is now recognized and classified by the American Psychiatric Association as one of the conditions to which an unsound mind is subject, and it has the following classification number, to wit: 002–332.

He then offered the APA definition:

002–332

PATHOLOGICAL INTOXICATION

Under this heading belong those cases which show as a result of small or large amounts of alcohol sudden excitation or twilight states, often with a mistaking of the situation and also with illusions and hallucinations and marked emotional reactions, particularly of anxiety or rage. Such an attack may last a few minutes or a number of hours and usually there is complete amnesia for the attack. In making such a classification epileptic conditions precipitated by small amounts of alcohol, or catatonic excitation in dementia praecox or manic depressive reactions or general paresis or arterial sclerotic episodes are to be ruled out.

It was Dr Menzies' contention that whatever else might have happened on the night of 5 June and whatever speculation might have arisen around the events, there was one certainty: Tom Hutchings suffered an attack of pathological intoxication. While it is not uncommon for pathological intoxication to be accompanied by violence, the perpetrator is not considered responsible for his actions and remembers nothing.

It was therefore possible that Tom had killed Bernice. But no one would ever know with certainty. There were no witnesses and Tom had no memory of the event. A more likely scenario, as far as Dr Menzies was concerned, was that Tom had nothing to do with Bernice's death.

In his letter to St Laurent, Menzies first spoke of his personal experience with those afflicted by pathological intoxication, then went on to reveal Tom's account of the proceedings on 5 June – information that had not been revealed in court or in Tom's interviews with the RCMP.

'It will be seen that the basis of this mental disease consists in the susceptibility of the patient to enter a dream state when under the influence of alcohol,' Menzies began. 'The amount of alcohol may be very small. I have seen cases in which it was produced by one glass of beer. While in this dream state, the patient may, and often does, become very violent. The violence is always unconscious in character and there is a total amnesia for it. I have seen cases in which friends and relatives of the patient were violently assaulted, the patient having absolutely no recollection of what he did and only being convinced that he had done so by the subsequent statements of his relatives and friends.

'I suspected that this boy was subject to this condition, as a result of my first interview with him, but in the absence of the confirmatory statements which have since come to light, I did not feel that I had enough material on which to go before a court. I was, however, morally certain from almost my first visit that the boy was subject to pathological intoxication. There was a very evident confusion in the boy's recollection of an incident that took place in Yarmouth, Nova Scotia, a month previously, just after this boy had arrived in Canada from England. The story, as I have it from reliable sources, is that the boy was down by the shore with a young woman. The young woman was afterwards found walking along a road, clad only in Hutchings' uniform coat. She had a 'black eye.' Hutchings himself turned up at the barracks without his coat. Hutchings' statement to me was that the woman, after a drink or so, wished to go swimming and he was totally at a loss to tell me how she had got his coat or how she had obtained a 'black eye.' He also could not tell me how he sustained a cut on his head. The point I want to make here is that Hutchings did not suspect that he had a memory lapse. He did not seem to realize that quite an interval of time had elapsed between his being with the girl and his arrival back at camp.

'In other words, his story presented an exact clinical parallel to the stories of other victims of this disease. His story of events on the night of the murder is precisely similar. He had been drinking but not dancing. He went out on the road to have a drink and was accosted by a girl whom he did not know, who asked him for a drink. He gave her one, came back to the door of the hall but did not enter, instead going to an outhouse to urinate. He came back, looked in the hall for only a minute, and then went back to the road to finish the small drink of rum that was in the bottle. (I might say that the previous evidence showed that Hutchings had not drunk nearly all the rum that was in the bottle, but had shared it with several other members of the Air Force.) When on the road he was again accosted by a girl, whether the same one or not he does not know, who asked him for a drink. He shared with her what he had left in the bottle, and then went into the bushes by the side of the road, where he again urinated, dropped the bottle, and came back to the road. The girl, in the meantime, had disappeared. He did not feel very well and sat down on the bumper of a car for a few minutes. One of the Air Force men came up and told him he had blood on his face.

'Throughout my interviews with him, Hutchings insists that this is all that took place and that the times as brought out in the preliminary examination were wrong. A period of amnesia would, of course, account for the difference.'

Menzies was clearly concerned about a miscarriage of justice. As he had shown during his years as head of the psychiatric hospital, he was deeply committed to improving the lives of the mentally afflicted and as far as he was concerned, Tom fell into that category. He told St Laurent that he had formed a 'moral judgment' based on two other considerations.

'First, Hutchings is not, to the best of my belief, a degenerate,' he wrote. 'If he is, then whatever experience I may have in dealing with degenerates of all kinds for the last twenty years is at fault. He went into the Air Force in April 1939 and his commanding officer tells me there is not a blot on his record during that time. He went through active service in England, being in both the London and Coventry 'blitzes', was promoted to full sergeancy, and was working for his commission. He was one of the men picked to be sent out here as an instructor to train Canadians for actual war conditions in London. His brother is a wing commander who has received the DFC and the boy himself was very anxious that the brother should not know of the trouble he was in, saying, "He has enough to think about on his flights over Germany." He did, however, write freely to his father, who is a retired captain of artillery, and to his wife, whom he had married in England the year before. If I am any judge of character, I believe that he is sincerely in love with his wife and devoted to their young child.

'Second, it is a matter of common knowledge that he did not need to assault this girl in order to have sexual intercourse with her. The allegation of rape as brought up at the trial was distinctly not fair, and could not be combatted by the defence counsel for obvious reasons. I may say that I have talked this matter over thoroughly with Dr Branch, the pathologist who made the examination of the body, and he tells me that he cannot say that this girl had been raped. In view of the man's previous record, my own estimation of his personality, and also in view of the fact there was no necessity to assault this girl, I was forced to conclude that there had to be some other reason for the crime, and pathological drunkenness seemed to me to be a very logical answer to the problem.'

Dr Menzies went on to detail Tom's medical history, paying particular attention to his Sydenham's chorea. 'I think I will be supported by all neurologists and psychiatrists,' he wrote, 'when I say that people subject to Sydenham's chorea have always an unstable nervous organization.' He forged a link to pathological intoxication saying that its sufferers invariably also have an 'unstable nervous system.'

To confirm his diagnosis, Menzies contacted Wing Commander Christopher Mann, a former lecturer in psychology at the University of Manchester. He wrote that, 'The commander told me bluntly that he regarded Hutchings as unstable, and that he was sure that he would within twenty years show much more marked evidence than he does now of his underlying mental defect.'

Dr Menzies' submission offered three more points of corroborating evidence: Sergeant Huggett's recollections of Hutchings' 'queer' actions and his period of insensibility; Leading Aircraftman Protheroe testifying that Tom had appeared dazed but not drunk; and the fact that Tom did not know there was blood on his face.

Menzies also was unable to resist an implicit criticism of the justice system.

> I would like to point out that this boy has had absolutely no means with which to conduct his defence. He was ordered into solitary confinement after his preliminary trial. He had absolutely no money himself and his father was prevented by exchange regulations from sending him any. Mr Guss was left alone to conduct his defence without any surety that even

his ordinary expenses would be paid. I would have been very much interested in what might have been elicited had money been found to hire private detectives to unearth what actually went on at the dance that night or to obtain expert medical evidence to support my own conclusions.

By 16 October, ten days after the guilty verdict, Menzies felt comfortable with the package of evidence he had compiled and was ready to travel to Ottawa to make his case.

Knowing that a request for a hearing with the justice minister was liable to be accorded a low priority, he sent a telegram asking for help from a friend and colleague in the medical field, Dr J. D. S. Cathcart, the chief neuropsychiatrist of the federal Department of Pensions and National Health:

CAN I TROUBLE YOU TO MAKE APPOINTMENT NEXT THURSDAY OR FRIDAY WITH MINISTER OF JUSTICE RE AIRMAN CONVICTED OF MURDER VERY INTERESTING CASE WOULD LIKE YOU TO SEE FILE WIRE COLLECT AS TO DATE OF APPOINTMENT E C MENZIES MD

Cathcart forwarded the telegram 'regarding some airman' to Gallagher to submit to St Laurent. His covering letter said, 'Dr Menzies is a longstanding acquaintance of mine in the field of psychiatry.' He listed some of Menzies' qualifications and added, 'He is quite reliable and top notch in the field of psychiatry. Would you be good enough to acknowledge his telegram and make whatever arrangements are permissible?'

On 17 October, St Laurent added a handwritten notation across the bottom of the page: 'As I have to be absent I suggest he see Mr Gallagher. LSL'

Sheriff Mallory had been making arrangements too. His letter to Camille Branchaud, the hangman, had been sent on 7 October:

The jury brought in a verdict of GUILTY with a recommendation for mercy. Date October 6 1942.

Judge Richards sentenced him to be hanged on December 16 1942.

I hereby engage your services for that date at prices quoted in your letter of September 28 1942.

Please let me hear from you at once.

Chapter Thirty-two

The death sentence precipitated a flurry of correspondence, some of it bureaucratic, some of it regulatory and some of it compassionate.

There was also one piece of correspondence that was supposed to be informative but failed miserably.

That was the official RCMP report of the Tom Roland Hutchings case, prepared by none other than Detective Staff Sergeant Frank W. Davis, the man who had decided within hours of viewing Bernice's body that he had identified the guilty party.

Had Davis been asked to merely prepare a report that the RCMP could keep for posterity as a reference, no harm would have been done. But that was not the case. Davis's report, filed on 8 October, two days after the verdict came down, provided the basis for the judge's report to the Ministry of Justice, and together, the two documents were to influence a series of decisions made by bureaucrats as to whether the sentence should be commuted, or the law should take its course.

It is only human nature to justify one's own work. And it is understandable that someone whose whole being is focused on law enforcement would hold a strongly subjective view of a criminal case, especially if he happened to be the person in charge of investigating that case. But the report was loaded with a number of statements that were presented as certainties yet were far from it – including the all-important RCMP Big Lie. Some of these areas of contention have already been discussed. But because they appeared again in Davis's report, they must be revisited. Italicized items are direct quotes from the report:

- *Positive identification* of Tom and Bernice walking away from the dance hall was established when they passed Mildred Justason and Sergeant Edwards. This *positive identification* of Tom was allegedly provided by Edwards, a man who had drunk a bottle of whisky and had

149

just seen bicycles where there were none. He heard a passing remark, so brief and innocuous that he couldn't remember its content, from a man who was such a casual acquaintance that he didn't know his first name. He couldn't see a face, and when pressed by Guss, admitted that he might be wrong about the voice. This was crucial evidence because it is the only testimony that places Tom with Bernice heading away from the dance hall. The whole case rests on this, yet Davis's report presents Edwards as an indisputably reliable witness providing incontrovertible evidence, rather than a man who was drunk, saw things that didn't exist and was unfamiliar with the voice he said he recognized.

- Using this shaky identification as a premise, Davis says a group of boys saw, *the prisoner and deceased.* No evidence at all was presented to support that point. None of the boys identified Tom. In fact, in the preliminary hearing, one says Bernice called her companion Mr White. The other says she called him Whitey. Tom was always known as Roy, not Whitey or Mr White

- Tom is said to have returned to the dance hall with *a lot of blood* on his face. Evidence to support that allegation is scanty at best. There was blood, but some of it was dry which would indicate that it was thinly spread.

- The report says the time of Tom's return to the dance hall, *has been set at approximately 12.30 a.m. by numerous witnesses.* This is not at all true. This is the RCMP Big Lie. No witnesses at all were produced to set Tom's return at 12.30. There were those who saw him there at 12.30, but only two who testified to having seen him return – Leading Aircraftman Protheroe and Leading Aircraftman Christie. Protheroe could not place the time. Christie was adamant that it was 12.15 or very close to it. Vincent Bradford doesn't give an exact time, but implies Christie's estimate was accurate. Two other airmen who gave statements that they saw Tom at 12.15 were not called as witnesses.

- *Then we have the evidence of Gerald Humphrey of the RAF taking a walk along the Deadman's Harbour Road at approximately midnight…in the close proximity to where the body was found.* The man, whose name was in fact Humphries, testified that after the intermission began, he had a coffee before leaving the hall. Intermission began at 11.50 p.m. and even if Humphries was first in line, which is unlikely since he had been dancing, he would still have been drinking his coffee at midnight, and would not have been 500 yards away, near the body.

- Humphries was with his companion Sylvia Gaudet and, *they ... saw a partly nude female ... with a man wearing an Airman's uniform lying on top of her.* No they didn't. Humphries said he saw that, but Gaudet saw no such thing. What she did see was 'a person crawling or moving.' She said she 'saw something white that appeared to be a person unclothed.' When asked by Hughes, 'Did you notice any clothed person at the time?' her answer was direct and concise. 'No,' she said.

- Humphries took Gaudet back to the hall, then returned with Leading Aircraftman Robert Moore. They at the time thought the couple were having sexual intercourse, but still did wonder somewhat owing to the fact there was no sound from the girl. Humphries testified that it was too dark to see the faces of the pair, or even any sign of rank on what he took to be an RAF uniform. The girl, therefore, would not have been able to see who was on the road. It could have been one of her close friends. Or two. Would she want to call out and identify herself under such circumstances?

- *There is evidence to show that human blood was found in the vicinity of this place.* Indeed there was. But whose blood was it? Surely Bernice's. But was there any of Tom's? Or any from a third party? Davis did not mention that these questions remained unanswered because he had delayed so long in sending the blood for testing that forensic scientists could not form a conclusion.

- *The victim had lost a lot of blood.* That was the testimony of Dr Branch but his statement was unsubstantiated. At no time did he give a reasonable explanation of there being 'a lot of blood'. The most grievous wound was a 2-inch cut under Bernice's chin and there was no internal hemorrhaging.

- *Medical testimony proved that the deceased had been criminally attacked.* This was extremely misleading. 'Criminal attack' is a legal euphemism for rape. In fact, Dr Branch himself testified that he could not say that Bernice had been raped, only that she had had sex within days of the dance.

- Regarding his Monday interview with Tom, Davis said, *He endeavoured to make out an alibi by stating that he was not out of the dance hall all evening.* That was Davis's interpretation, not a fact. Dr Branch had conceded the possibility of pathological intoxication which would mean that Tom wasn't trying to create an alibi, he was telling the truth as he knew it.

151

- *Evidence showed that human blood was found in a number of places on the tunic belt and trousers.* Yes, but whose blood was it? Again, Davis avoids mentioning his transgression with regard to the testing.
- *It is in evidence that there were six sergeants attended [sic] the dance (and) the movements of five were fully accounted for.* Black's Harbour was not a gated community. It had bus and taxi service. There was nothing to prevent another sergeant being in town but not attending the dance.

Davis's report illustrates a major failing in the justice system as it existed in 1942. The transcript of the trial should have been used as the foundation for any subsequent evaluation of the case. Instead, Davis's heavily biased and frequently erroneous report was used.

That report was first forwarded to the commanding officer of the RCMP's J Division, the serious-crimes unit. From there, it was forwarded without revision to the RCMP Commissioner in Ottawa, then forwarded even further up the judicial chain to the federal Minister of Justice. It was also forwarded to the attorney general of New Brunswick, J.B. McNair, who was also the province's premier at the time.

It was a monstrously one-sided piece of reportage, not only full of half-truths but also loaded with inaccuracies and misdirected innuendo. Furthermore, it blithely omitted evidence that had been given under oath but did not support Davis's unassailable conviction that Tom was guilty.

Davis appeared determined to live up to the motto of his force. The Mounties always get their man. A more accurate motto might have been: The Mounties always get a man.

Chapter Thirty-three

Dr Menzies was not the only one who had spurred himself to immediate action when Judge Richards pronounced Tom's death sentence. The man with whom Menzies was corresponding in Ottawa, M. F. Gallagher, did the same.

Gallagher was the assistant under-secretary in the Ministry of Justice, the government department responsible for judiciously carrying out the execution. But at the same time, he was also the head of the remissions branch, which endeavoured to make sure that any execution was delayed or commuted, should circumstances warrant it. As a result, Gallagher immediately found himself in the centre of the maelstrom.

An execution was not a common occurrence, even in 1942, and when one was mandated, it required a series of responses from the ministry. Accordingly on 7 October, only hours after Tom had been sentenced to hang, Gallagher, being the dedicated functionary that he was, sent a memo to his boss, Justice Minister Louis St Laurent. In it, he urged him to request a report on the proceedings from Judge Richards, and thoughtfully provided a sample. He explained that it was St Laurent's duty to make a preliminary survey of that report as soon as it was received.

The judge was reminded that his duty, under section 1063 of the Criminal Code of Canada, was to forward his report as soon as possible, 'in order that the Minister of Justice may have time to investigate … direct investigations by experts to determine mental impairment when advisable … call meeting of Council to consider case … submit to His Excellency the Governor General etc. etc. etc.'

It was also St Laurent's responsibility to read the transcript and the judge's charge and evaluate the proceedings. Once all that was done, he would be expected to explain the case to the other members of the Cabinet (all the government's ministers, collectively known also as the Privy Council) and read the judge's charge in its entirety.

As Gallagher pointed out: 'The task is a tremendous one.' In fact, it appears that it was too tremendous to deal with in its entirety as far as St Laurent was concerned. There is no evidence that he followed Gallagher's advice with regard to most of the designated protocol and he almost certainly did not read the transcript, even though it was his sworn duty as justice minister to do so.

Judge Richards didn't seem overly concerned about protocol either. Even though the need for haste had been mentioned to him, it was not until 22 October that his report arrived in Ottawa. And, as was the case with the submission from Staff Sergeant Davis, it was much more of a justification than a report.

He began by saying that 'upon request and with my approval, Mr Benjamin R. Guss was assigned and represented the accused at the trial.'

Having given himself credit for providing a defence counsel, it was not surprising that he went on to say: 'In my opinion, Mr Guss conducted the case for the accused admirably and did all that could reasonably have been expected for the accused.' With the possible exception of calling even a single witness, perhaps.

Judge Richards then went on to review the evidence and said that Bernice 'was at the dance about 11.30 when she was seen going out a road known as Deadman's Harbour Road away from the Community Hall with a man in an Air Force uniform. This is the last time she was seen alive.'

Except for the sightings by Sylvia Gaudet, Sergeant Thomas Edwards, Mildred Justason, Leading Aircraftman Humphries, Alonzo Hall, Gilbert Eldridge, Donald Adams and Foster Eldridge. And except for the fact that Harry Watson testified he saw her at the dance at 11.45.

In listing the injuries to Bernice, he referred to 'a large open cut under the chin'. The pathologist said the cut was 2 inches long. Like Davis, he referred to the finding of 'human blood'. Like Davis, he didn't mention that it had never undergone suitable testing because of Davis's incompetence.

Perhaps the most disgraceful part of the judge's report came when he said, 'In my opinion, the evidence was conclusive that the injuries were inflicted, by someone, in furtherance of the commission of rape, that there was in fact a rape, and that death resulted from the injuries.'

Like everyone else, the judge was entitled to an opinion. But that opinion did not belong in a report on a capital case. He should have stated the facts, not his opinion.

And the facts are: the Crown's own pathologist would not say there had been a rape; not a single Crown witness confirmed a rape; there was not the slightest evidence of rape, just evidence of sex in the not-too-distant past; and even if there had been sexual congress, the injuries could have been inflicted afterwards and therefore not 'in furtherance of the commission of rape'.

Like Davis, the judge accepted the testimony of Leading Aircraftman Humphries regarding the couple at the side of the road, but ignores the conflicting testimony of Sylvia Gaudet who was standing beside him and, as a 15-year-old, more likely to be sober.

He did, however, accept the testimony of Gaudet, a Black's Harbour girl, that one of the couple spoke with an English accent, even though Humphries, who was English, could not confirm that. He mentioned that Humphries saw the amorous couple twice between approximately 12.10 and 12.45 a.m. even though Leading Aircraftman Christie was cleaning blood off Tom's face in the range of 12.15–12.30.

Since this contradiction didn't suit the judge's decision that Tom was guilty, he simply decided Christie's testimony was wrong although at no point was any evidence introduced to substantiate that view.

He also mirrored Davis's report (probably no coincidence) when he pointed out that six sergeants were at the dance and five could account for their whereabouts. And like, Davis, he made the assumption that no other sergeant could have arrived in Black's Harbour and stayed away from the dance.

There was another ominous similarity to Davis's report. It was distributed to the people who were going to decide whether Tom should hang or have the death sentence commuted.

Unlike Judge Richards, Camille Branchaud had not delayed when asked for a response. He wrote a letter to Sheriff Mallory:

Re Tom Rolland [*sic*] Hutchings
Dear Sir,

I have your letter of the 7 instant with regards to the above who has been sentenced to hang on December 16, 1942.

Also your hiring my services for that date at prices quoted in my letter of September 28, 1942.

Therefore, I am reserving the said date of December 16, 1942 on my list as per your engagement. So you can count on me.

Kindly advise in the near future, the date I am to arrive in St Andrews in order to erect the scaffold [*sic*] if you are having it built by carpenters under my supervision.

Yours truly,
Camille Branchaud
Official Hangman for the Province of Quebec.

Chapter Thirty-four

Despite the fact that Dr Menzies had sent a meticulously detailed report to the federal justice ministry and stressed the need for prompt action, it was not until two weeks later, at the end of October, that he was granted his audience in Ottawa. Even then, he didn't get the meeting with Justice Minister Louis St Laurent that his friend Dr Cathcart had requested. Instead, he had to make his case to Gallagher, the assistant under-secretary.

By 5 November, Gallagher still had not bothered to accord the matter any degree of urgency and sent a letter entitled, 'Re: Tom Roland Hutchings' to J. B. McNair, the premier of New Brunswick who also acted as the province's attorney general:

> Doctor E.C. Menzies was here last week and submitted his views in favour of commutation of the sentence of the above-named. Doctor Menzies was not at the trial but he subsequently visited the prisoner on several occasions, and has now submitted his belief that the prisoner suffered from pathological intoxication, was unable to know the nature and quality of his deed, and was not responsible for his act.
>
> At this stage, I have not yet studied the case, but I did mention to Doctor Menzies – although his theory did strike me as somewhat unusual – that I would endeavour to ascertain your views, and would gladly receive any information which you might consider helpful in the disposition of the appeal for commutation of the sentence.
>
> Execution is at present set for December 16, but I would be glad to hear from you at your convenience, before having to study the transcript of evidence and the material now before this department.

Gallagher was clearly taking a cavalier approach to the proceedings. He was wrong when he said that Menzies' visits to Tom were subsequent to the trial. They had taken place during his stay in Saint John, long before Tom was transferred back to St Andrews for the trial.

Gallagher also admitted that a full month after the verdict, he 'had not yet studied the case'.

His assertion that he saw Menzies' theory as 'somewhat unusual' was a bureaucrat's way of saying, 'I think it has no merit.'

And probably, when he said that he wanted McNair's opinion before he began his study, he was suggesting that he would make sure he selected evidence that would allow his evaluation to conform to McNair's.

But Dr Menzies was not the only voice trying to make Tom's case heard inside the governmental fortress.

On 20 October, Reverend Alban F. Bate, the rector of St Paul's Church in Saint John, had written to St Laurent, but his letter wound up in Gallagher's in-tray. The rector said he had visited Tom regularly during the summer and concluded that 'After seeing him and talking with him, it is difficult to believe that he is guilty.'

He cited the difficulties facing a soldier in a foreign land and said, 'May I very respectfully urge that his sentence be commuted to life imprisonment.'

Three days later, Gallagher sent a response assuring him that his 'earnest pleas for commutation will receive careful consideration by the Minister'.

In England, Hutchings' distraught family were also getting increasingly concerned. Although Dr Menzies was in constant communication with Tom Hutchings Sr, neither of them could see any movement on the part of Canada's justice ministry.

Unable to remain silent any longer, on 6 November, Tom Sr sent the following telegram to Louis St Laurent:

GOD GRANT YOUR MERCIFUL VIEW REGARDING MY
SON=CAPTAIN HUTCHINGS

On 7 November, Tom's sister Doreen, a school headmistress, also sent a telegram:

I HUMBLY APPEAL FOR YOUR MERCIFUL DECISION
REGARDING MY BROTHERS LIFE LIFELONG
GRATITUDE TO YOU FROM HEARTBROKEN
FAMILY=DOREEN HUTCHINGS

On 10 November, a brief telegram under St Laurent's name (although almost certainly sent by Gallagher) was transmitted to Tom Sr:

YOUR APPEALS WILL RECEIVE MOST CAREFUL
CONSIDERATION.

On that same day, a Stirling bomber took off on a training flight from Mildenhall Aerodrome in England.

The Stirling, Britain's first heavy bomber of the Second World War, had experienced connecting-rod breaks causing engine fires in the past, and crews had been instructed to immediately abandon the aircraft under such circumstances.

But on this occasion, with the plane having reached an altitude of only 200 feet, bailing out was not feasible. Instead, the experienced pilot, who had logged more than 1,300 flying hours in a Stirling, tried to turn the plane around in order to land back at Mildenhall. As he did so, the fire spread into the fuselage. The plane went into a nose dive and crashed. The entire crew of seven was killed. Squadron Leader Bill Hutchings DFC, Tom's older brother, was dead. His remains were taken to Golders Green Crematorium in London and cremated.

He had given his life for his country, and although he had not been as explicit as his 21-year-old wireless operator, James A. Clough, he probably shared his views. Three months earlier, Clough had prepared a letter for his parents that he marked 'To be opened in the event of my death.'

It read as follows

> I have no regrets dying for my country. It is a grand country and any man who calls himself an Englishman should be proud to die in the struggle for freedom. Give this message to my friends and yours, and to the people of England if it is possible: Let every Englishman fight to the last drop of blood in his body. Let him keep the golden fields and busy streets clean and fresh, and let him keep the air he breathes free from the stench of Nazism.

Meanwhile, in Canada, McNair had not yet responded to Gallagher's 5 November letter. He had decided that he wanted to talk to St Laurent about Tom's case, so no progress could be made until that conference had taken place.

CHAPTER THIRTY-FOUR

Finally, on 16 November, with the execution date now only one month away, McNair met with St Laurent. In an internal memo documenting the occasion, Gallagher said that McNair 'does not share Doctor Menzies' views – says the expert became the advocate.

'He spoke to the Judge, the Crown Prosecutor, and Commanding Officer. No one apparently suggests an exercise of clemency.'

It is not clear why an expert becoming an advocate is considered by McNair to be such a repellant turn of events. After all, an expert on a subject is much more likely to have a full understanding of the situation than a dabbling politician. Surely, if that expert becomes an advocate, it is just a further assertion that he feels so strongly about his evaluation that he cannot, in all good conscience, allow a miscarriage of justice.

Nevertheless, Gallagher had added a handwritten notation to his memorandum: 'and McNair suggests the case be dealt with according to usual practice.'

So three lawyers, none of whom had any medical experience, had effectively told a doctor who was a highly renowned authority in his field that they knew more about medicine than he did.

In St Andrews, Sheriff Mallory was proceeding in his usual efficient fashion, unaffected by the bureaucrats at the higher level. On 20 October, he had sent a letter to the executioner Camille Branchaud:

re Tom Roland Hutchings

Regarding your letter of Oct 9 I would be very glad if you would come several days previous to Dec 16 the date set for the hanging of the above prisoner.

Kindly instruct me as to the sort of any kind of materials you will require so that I shall have them ready.

Chapter Thirty-five

As the execution date drew ever closer, it became increasingly apparent that Tom Hutchings was likely to be hanged.

At the time the death sentence was announced, there may have been a sense of satisfaction in the hearts of some. For most, the sentence came as a surprise, and there was a degree of astonishment.

But even at that point, sentiments, whichever way they leaned, had generally been tempered by a vague expectation that at some time before 16 December, a means would be found to prevent the hanging.

An execution had not been the intention of the jury, and it had not been the expectation of the majority of people in Charlotte County, even those who lived in Black's Harbour. As Carman Eldridge, who had grown up there and had been there in 1942, said in his 2016 interview, the clear consensus was that Tom had killed Bernice but hadn't intended to do so and shouldn't be hanged for it.

For the most part, the county was populated by unpretentious men and women who lived off the land and the sea. Their formal education was limited, and their lives were not easy. They did not condone crime, but at the same time, they knew only too well that sometimes people make mistakes. They believed in punishment, but they also believed in a degree of mercy and saw no need to be vindictive. And after three years of war, there had already been too many deaths. They didn't see any reason for the government to add an ally to the total.

But governments are not known for their willingness to admit to error. In the federal capital of Ottawa and in the provincial capital of Fredericton, there was a determination to carry out the sentence and thereby uphold the reputations of the court systems and police departments. After all, the RCMP had decided Tom Hutchings was guilty and a senior judge had concurred, then decreed that he must die. Any change would be an implicit admission that both had failed in their duties.

160

CHAPTER THIRTY-FIVE

Nevertheless, the support for commutation grew as the execution date neared.

> EARNESTLY BEG AND PRAY YOU WILL GRANT
> MERCIFUL PLEA FOR MY DEAR HUSBAND FROM
> BABY AND HEARTBROKEN WIFE.

This was the telegram from Joyce Hutchings but her surname had been misspelled as Hutchins.

A telegram was sent back to 'MRS JOYCE HUTCHINS' above the name of Louis St Laurent but actually sent by Gallagher:

> REST ASSURED YOUR PLEA WILL BE CAREFULLY
> CONSIDERED

As the end of November neared, the distraught Tom Sr sent another appeal to St Laurent:

> EARNESTLY APPEAL FOR YOUR MERCY REGARDING
> MY SON I SERVED THROUGHOUT LAST WAR JUST
> LOST ELDER SON IN THIS WAR FEEL GREATLY
> DISTRESSED

Gallagher's reply, again above the name of St Laurent, was something less than sympathetic:

> RENEWED APPEAL RECEIVED

Captain Hutchings sent the same cable to Judge Richards, who did not feel the need to respond but did, however, send a letter to St Laurent informing him of its content and its receipt. It was passed along to Gallagher who found the time to send a return letter to the judge, letting him know that St Laurent had received his notification and thanking him for forwarding the message. In a closing salutation that was more than three times longer than his entire telegram to Captain Hutchings, he assured the judge that 'I have the honour to be, Sir, your obedient servant.'

There were no televisions in New Brunswick in 1942, and even radios were uncommon. But there were conversations – many more than there are in this era of widespread telecommunication – and as a result, there was no doubt that the populace was not in favour of the hanging.

THE WRONGLY EXECUTED AIRMAN

Even Benjamin Guss joined those who tried to make the bureaucracy aware of this. On 20 November, he sent a letter to St Laurent:

RE: Sergeant Tom Roland Hutchings, RAF

I am writing you on an errand of mercy.

The above airman was found guilty of murder, October 6, 1942, and the jury recommended mercy. Dr E.C. Menzies, Superintendent of the Psychiatric Hospital and a leading psychiatrist, is convinced that the boy should be over in his institution and I understand he has been in Ottawa to see what could be done to save this boy from the gallows. The jury being the body of men charged with deciding on the facts, has seen fit to recommend mercy. I am asking you to implement this recommendation in view of your having coupled with it the stand taken by Dr Menzies.

There is another aspect of the matter which strikes me because I happened to have a brother overseas, and all of us who have brothers or sons in the armed forces may have to come face to face with actions by our kin when away from home that seem strange to us. For instance, my own brother, who was a model son, got into a jam in England and he ended up in a neurological hospital. Thank heavens he is out now and on active service again. But these are abnormal times and it would seem that justice should be tempered with mercy ...

I know that you are busy and I should perhaps not trouble you about this matter but this boy's family has been writing me and cabling me, and the thought of his going to the gallows haunts me day and night. You will understand that I did not seek this case; on the contrary, I tried to get out of it, but the New Brunswick Bar Association counsel designated me and the Judge assigned the case to me. I gave up a month of my time, gratis. I was certainly money out-of-pocket on expenses alone. I mention these things to indicate that perhaps I have some right in pressing for the implementation of the jury's recommendation for mercy.

There is one thing more. I quote from a cable sent me by Captain Hutchings, the father of the prisoner:

CHAPTER THIRTY-FIVE

'TRUST APPEAL WILL BE SUCCESSFUL PLEASE CONVEY THANKS TO ALL INTERESTED REGRET LOST ELDER SON ON ACTIVE SERVICE ON THE TENTH USE OWN DISCRETION ABOUT INFORMING ROY CAPTAIN HUTCHINGS'

By 'appeal" he means the appeal to you for mercy. This elder son had earned his DFC with the RAF, and was a squadron leader.

Surely this old captain, the father, ought not to have such a terrible Christmas. I hope you will listen to Dr Menzies and myself and to the plea which is contained in this cable.

Please.

Guss's letter was passed along to Gallagher who assured him that it would 'receive careful consideration by the Minister', and would be attached to the record.

On 30 November, Guss renewed his plea and sent a letter to Gallagher:

Thank you very much indeed for your letter of November 25. I trust that the plea for mercy may be implemented.

I just this morning received a letter from a reporter in St Stephen who had been speaking to members of the jury and had asked them how they felt about it. I will quote from her letter:

'In the course of our conversation, he (a juryman) told me that the jury had planned on manslaughter ... they did not want the death penalty ... Then when the judge told them it must be murder or acquittal they did not know what to do. They did not want to have him hang ... They felt that with the recommendation for mercy ... he would not go to the gallows.'

The name of the lady who wrote me this is Dr Maud Vesey of Saint Stephen. I thought I ought to write you this so that if you wish to check my statement you can do so.

Gallagher acknowledged Guss's letter and said he would show it to St Laurent upon his return to Ottawa – 'within the next few days'.

On that occasion, St Laurent attached a handwritten note reminding Gallagher that the judge 'instructed the jury on drunkenness and its bearing upon reduction of murder to manslaughter'.

While this was true, it completely missed the point made by the juryman. The judge's instructions were so steeped in legalese, so meandering, so lengthy, so late in the day, and so obtuse that a jury composed of common Charlotte County men had no chance of comprehending his message – as the letter had said.

Further confirmation of that point was evident in another letter sent to St Laurent on 30 November. This one came from W.W. Quartermain, who was no doubt selected as jury foreman because he was considered to be the best educated and most erudite of the twelve. It is quoted here verbatim, not with any intention to ridicule, but to substantiate the fact that the level of sophistication that existed among the jurors left them in the dark when trying to comprehend Judge Richards' verbosity.

Hon. Louis ST.Laurent
Minister of Justice
Ottawa.

Honourable Sir:

Re case of Tom Rolland Hutchings convicted of the Murder, Miss Bernice Connors, and sentenced to Hanged at ST.Andrews N.B. on Dec. 16 next. Whereas the decision is for you to make as to whether or not the sentnce will be carried out or commuted.

As one who acted as spokesman for the Jury at this Trial, I am taking the priveledge of stating to you that the Jury was very strong of the opinion that their reccomendation would be accepted , and that some degree of mercy be shown at the convicted person.

As one whose work makes it necessary that I travel about the County , naturally my being on the jury people were very anxious to discuss the proceedings , I learned that almost I00per cent were of the opinion that Hutchings was guilty of the crime, and were also of the opinion that the sentence would be commuted, while in the District recently where the Crime was committed , I asked of several Men, as to their opinion, What per centage of the people would favour the carrying out of the Sentence ? their reply in each case was: 'The number would be very small, and that almost I00per cent would feel that the sentence should be commuted'.

164

As Minister of Justice the resopsibility of this Office is great, and in only the humblest manner do I write the above, I felt it my duty wherein so many persons have spoken so strongly to me, as I have tried to out line in a few brief words.

Sincerely,
W.W.Quartermain
ST.Stephen N.B.
November 30 1942.

St Laurent suggested that Gallagher answer the letter. As a result, Quartermain received this response, with a little bit of Latin thrown in for his edification:

I have, by direction, to acknowledge receipt of your letter of the 30 ultimo ...

In response I am to state that the Minister has specially noted your observations, and will give to them, as well as to all relevant facts and circumstances pertaining to this case, his most careful consideration.

Thinking that Premier McNair might be interested in the views of his New Brunswick constituents, Gallagher sent him a copy of Quartermain's letter. McNair, the man who had been annoyed because Dr Menzies had become an advocate, quickly made it clear that Gallagher could keep future correspondence to himself.

I am constrained to say that I have no ready means of obtaining an independent appraisal of the sentiment in Charlotte County on the matter in question; nor do I feel in a position to suggest the degree of relevancy that should attach.

Responding to pleas for mercy was not Gallagher's only responsibility at this time. As he had explained to St Laurent as soon as the death sentence was rendered, an extensive protocol was in place detailing the responsibilities of the justice minister.

St Laurent was supposed to, among other duties, 'analyze evidence'. It fell to Gallagher to collect that evidence for St Laurent's perusal. He compiled a lengthy document – thirteen typewritten, single-spaced, legal-size pages – but really, it was little more than a recital of Judge Richards' report. As a result, it was also a recitation of the judge's mistakes such as the reference to the 'large open cut' that was in fact 2 inches long, and the 'identification' of Hutchings by Edwards.

The rejection of Christie's evidence for no other reason than the judge disagreed with it was included, thereby accepting as accurate the RCMP Big Lie. Also included was his assumption that any RAF sergeant in Black's Harbour must have been at the dance. But the most shameful part of Gallagher's report was his parroting of the judge's opinion that Tom had perpetrated a brutal rape when, in fact, no evidence whatsoever was presented to support that claim.

The only original part of the 'analysis' provided by Gallagher to the minister was the fact that McNair, the judge and the Crown had discounted the medical evaluation of Dr Menzies.

Apparently, he felt that this somehow fulfilled the requirement for the justice minister to 'direct examinations by experts to determine mental impairment'. Menzies was indisputably an expert in that field, as were the psychiatrists whose opinions he quoted, but the lawyers over-ruled them, and no one saw the need to get a further medical opinion.

Gallagher submitted his report on 26 November and just above his signature, he offered his chilling opinion: 'Considering the facts and circumstances of the case, the undersigned is of the opinion that the law may well be allowed to take its course.'

Chapter Thirty-six

In accordance with the protocol laid down for cases of capital punishment, the federal Privy Council met in Ottawa on 27 November.

In attendance was the governor general, Major General the Earl of Athlone. Canada was a dominion at the time, a semi-autonomous nation within the British Empire, and it was the governor general's responsibility to represent the British monarch. In this case, the Earl of Athlone, being the uncle of King George VI, was well suited to do so. He had been born Prince Alexander in 1874 but became the Earl of Athlone in 1917.

More importantly, as far as Tom Hutchings was concerned, the governor general, like the Privy Council, had the right to commute a death sentence. There was never any doubt that the Privy Council would follow the dictates of the prime minister. But the governor general was accorded independent thought.

The basis of the group's deliberations was M. F. Gallagher's submission to the prime minister, a document which did little more than give those who had brought about the death sentence – the RCMP and the courts – the opportunity to support their stance and once again utilize the RCMP Big Lie. There was no submission from the defence. Nor was there any independent medical evaluation. Some of the pleas for mercy were attached but there was also the judge's assertion that 'the crime was of a brutal and revolting character'.

The judge also wrote that he could find no reason to support the jury's recommendation of mercy and was 'unable to see in the whole case any ameliorating circumstances'.

After the meeting, the clerk of the Privy Council filed an internal report detailing its conclusion: 'The Governor General is unable to order any interference with the sentence of the Court.' In accordance with Privy Council policy, no public announcement was made.

As a result, the government continued to receive representations from those seeking commutation.

On 1 December, the Bishop of Fredericton sent a letter to St Laurent, not only following his own conscience, he said, but also because of 'repeated requests from many reputable people in this province'.

It was of 'infinite concern' to him, he added, that an execution would be contrary to the wishes of Dr Menzies, 'who is considered to be one of the best, if not the best, of the mental experts in eastern Canada.'

The bishop pointed out that Dr Menzies was convinced that 'the condemned man is a mental case, and that he is decidedly a subject for treatment in a mental institution and not a subject for the gallows.'

Having heard from 'most reliable' sources, the bishop believed that the 'recommendation to mercy by the jury was not an empty form but was made with the very greatest sincerity'.

St Laurent forwarded the letter to Gallagher with a handwritten note conceding that 'His Lordship seems to be rather well informed regarding certain features of the case.'

Nevertheless, St Laurent continued to slavishly follow the ill-founded opinions of Judge Richards. 'The trial judge, you will recall,' he reminded Gallagher, 'found himself unable to support jury's recommendation to mercy.'

This is an astonishing statement, implying as it does, that Canada's justice minister knew so little about the law that he did not realize that the judge had no option, and was unable to support a recommendation of mercy, whether he wanted to or not.

Even at that late date, commutation by Prime Minister Mackenzie King was still possible. Although the public was not aware of his proclivities, those close to him knew that he was a devout Christian and such a firm believer in spirits that he talked to them on a regular basis, especially those of family members. Accordingly, even within the government, the matter of Tom's execution was not considered closed after the Privy Council meeting.

In a last-minute memo to King dated 14 December, Gallagher said that he had contacted British authorities about the case, even though there had been no reciprocal representations. 'I learned that there had been just one case since the war,' he wrote 'of a Canadian soldier being sentenced to death for murder by a United Kingdom court. On that case the sentence was commuted to life imprisonment.'

On the advice of St Laurent, Gallagher also passed along the information to New Brunswick Premier McNair, who as head of the province in which the Supreme Court had handed down the verdict, also had the authority to commute.

However, Gallagher told King, McNair 'felt that local feeling over the case was so strong that commutation of sentence would be hard to defend.' He did not ask how McNair could have arrived at that conclusion. Only about a week earlier, McNair had told Gallagher he had 'no ready means of obtaining an independent appraisal of the sentiment in Charlotte County.'

The prime minister was not moved by the charity shown to the Canadian soldier in England, but like the Privy Council, he made no announcement of his decision. In fact, it was not until 5.45 p.m. on 14 December, with the execution scheduled to take place the following night – about 2 a.m. on December 16 – that Sheriff Mallory received a telegram from E. H. Coleman, the under-secretary of state.

> I AM COMMANDED TO INFORM YOU THAT HIS EXCELLENCY THE GOVERNOR GENERAL IN COUNCIL IS UNABLE TO ORDER ANY INTERFERENCE WITH THE SENTENCE OF COURT IN CAPITAL CASE OF TOM ROLAND HUTCHING'S [sic] SENTENCED TO DEATH BY THE HONOURABLE MR JUSTICE RICHARD'S [sic] STOP REPEAT BACK THIS TELEGRAM WITHOUT FAIL IMMEDIATELY AFTER IT'S [sic] RECEIPT LETTER WILL FOLLOW IN DUE COURSE.

Being the conscientious man that he was, Mallory replied immediately, sending a telegram to Coleman confirming receipt of his message and repeating its contents verbatim, including the misuse of apostrophes.

The following afternoon, Coleman confirmed receipt of the confirmation.

> YOUR TELEGRAM REPEATING MINE OF YESTERDAY RECEIVED I HERBY [sic] CONFIRM THAT LAW WILL TAKE IT'S [sic] COURSE IN CAPITAL CASE OF TOM ROLAND HUTCHING'S [sic].

Since it was to be the first execution in St Andrews since 1879, Mallory was sailing in uncharted waters. He had read the handbook issued by the secretary of state, *Capital Cases Procedure*, but not all his questions had been answered. The need to confirm and re-confirm the absence of commutation, which was already the existing state, was only the most recent obstacle he had encountered.

Accordingly, on 1 December, he had sought help from McNair, detailing some of the matters which were troubling him.

One was Rule 4, which required the prison bell – or the parish church bell if the prison wasn't suitably equipped – to be tolled for fifteen minutes before and after the execution.

'In a small community like this where it is desired to have the matter attended to with as little publicity as possible,' Mallory explained, 'I am writing to ask if this cannot be omitted.'

There was also the matter of the disposition of Tom's body. 'Under Section 1071 of the Criminal Code, the body is supposed to be buried within the walls of the prison,' Mallory wrote.

'That cannot be conveniently done here for the reason that the ground is practically all ledge.' Mallory therefore suggested burial in the rural cemetery of St Andrews – 'unless the body is to be claimed by relatives and that is a point that I would like your guidance and counsel.'

Mallory, being fully aware of local sentiment and its volatile nature, was also concerned about the possibility of vigilante action. Shortly after Bernice Connors' body had been found, there had been mutterings about a lynching to save the sheriff the trouble. But after the recommendation for mercy, sentiment had shifted and now few people wanted to have Tom hanged.

'I presume that the headquarters of the RCMP will arrange to have their men in this district here that night,' Mallory wrote, 'as the local force is limited to a Town Marshall and we will require every assistance.'

But it wasn't only the local residents who concerned Mallory. Anti-hanging sentiment was very strong at the 34 OTU base where RAF personnel, having come to Canada to help train men for the war effort, did not feel that one of their number should be executed in a foreign country.

'I trust also,' Mallory wrote, 'that on that particular night there will not be any leave to St Andrews of men from the Pennfield Air Port, and I would be obliged if you would take that matter under consideration.'

Mallory closed with a blanket plea for assistance.

'Every regulation that I know of is being carefully carried out, but if there is anything special that your department think is being overlooked, I would be very grateful if you would advise.'

CHAPTER THIRTY-SIX

Mallory had also started to attend to one other matter that was raised in his letter to McNair. In late November, he had received another response from Camille Branchaud:

> In reply to your letter of the 20 inst., I am giving you below a rough idea of the wood required for the creation of the scaffold. The other small things needed, such and hinges etc., I will attend to upon my arrival.
>
> WOOD REQUIRED
> 1 only 8x8 12 feet long
> 2 only 8x6 20 feet long
> 40 only 3x4 12 feet long
> 1¼-inch thick for a floor of 10 by 10
>
> The scaffold will be at 12 feet from the ground. So, a flight of stairs towards the floor will be necessary. I shall arrive in St Andrews on the 10 of December, at night, so I presume that sufficient time will be available within the next days to erect the scaffold properly.
>
> Hoping these informations [*sic*] will be satisfactory, I remain
>
> Yours very truly
> Camille Branchaud
> Official Hangman for the Province of QUEBEC

A week before Branchaud's scheduled arrival, Mallory sent a letter explaining that no train from Montreal arrived in St Andrews at night. Accordingly, he would meet him off the noon train on the appointed day.

The acquisition of Branchaud's wood did not present a problem. The acquisition of workmen willing to assemble a scaffold was another matter altogether.

As Mallory wrote in his letter to McNair: 'I have contacted the carpenters of the town and none of them will take on the job of assisting in erecting same. I am endeavouring to get this assistance from other sections of the County, and trust will be successful.'

He wasn't. The distaste for the hanging was too widespread.

He tried the nearby communities of St Stephen and St George, and was turned down. Thinking that surely carpenters from Bernice's home town of Black's Harbour would cooperate, he went there. He was turned down again.

As a result, the scaffold had to be erected by Norman Johnson, the town marshal who had made the trip to Saint John with Mallory when they took loaded guns into Tom's cell; George Goodeill, the jailer; and one of the local residents who was serving time in the jail.

The construction was not without incident. As Goodeill revealed later, 'We started on a Thursday morning and finished it Saturday night.' The execution was scheduled for the wee hours of Wednesday morning.

Said Goodeill, 'Well Sheriff said, "We'd better cover this up for the night because we don't want anyone around on Sunday looking at it."'

The sheriff, before he became sheriff, used to run a gift shop ... and in those days they had the awnings that rolled down in the summer time.

'Well he put this awning up, put it over the top of the scaffold, so we moved on, never thought much about it.

'The next day, we look at it, and out next to the street was the sign: 'Gift Shop'.

Chapter Thirty-seven

When Sheriff Mallory's letter reached Premier McNair's office in the first week of December, it commanded immediate attention. McNair wanted the whole matter dispensed with as efficiently and effectively as possible.

No matter what he claimed, he was almost certainly aware that in Charlotte County and its surrounding areas, his constituents were strongly opposed to the execution. Therefore, as far as he was concerned, the sooner it was in the past and forgotten, the better. Accordingly, he passed along Mallory's letter to his capable deputy, J. Bacon Dickson.

Dickson promptly dealt with Mallory's concerns point by point, and sent a return letter as soon as he had finished doing so.

The matter of the bell tolling, he said, was not within his jurisdiction. It was a federal matter, and he suggested that Mallory approach Under-Secretary of State E. H. Coleman in Ottawa with his request for dispensation. Dickson said he expected that the request would be granted.

He did not anticipate that anyone would claim Tom's body, and he had therefore made arrangements for an order-in-council to be passed by the New Brunswick legislature to authorize burial in the St Andrews rural cemetery. 'If a claim for the body should be made, I would ask that you report the same promptly to me,' he wrote.

He acknowledged the arrangements Mallory had made with the hangman and moved on to the matter of police support. 'I am instructing the RCMP to have a number of men on hand in St Andrews on the night of the execution.'

He assured Mallory he would also request that the commanding officer of the Pennfield base 'take such steps as may be necessary to keep his men from St Andrews on the night of the execution'.

Furthermore, he had already telephoned Sheriff Mallory's counterpart in Saint John, 'and he has kindly offered to give you any assistance within his power.'

If it were not for the gravity of the situation, the concern over the tolling of the bell would be laughable. After all, it is hard to see how the proceedings would be affected by the absence – or presence – of bell ringing. It is not as if there were any way to negate the effects of the execution on a point of procedure if the bell-ringing rules had not been met. Nevertheless, Mallory wanted to conform to the dictates required for the occasion.

He therefore followed Dickson's advice and wrote to the under-secretary of state, explaining, as he had in his letter to McNair, that he did not feel that bell tolling in St Andrews was a good idea.

He received a quick and typically bureaucratic response from one of Coleman's minions. He was referred to the booklet *Rules Respecting Executions* that had been issued by the federal government on 6 January 1870. He was then reminded of Paragraph One on Page 11 which stipulated 'that preparations are under Provincial control'. Those words were underlined in red.

The final paragraph read as follows: 'The close application of the rules above-mentioned has apparently not been observed in every case, and, for the reason mentioned in your communication, it would appear that, in the event of the execution taking place on December 16, 1942, the tolling of the bell could be dispensed with.'

Translation: Nobody bothers with that rule any more.

But there was nothing humorous about this obsession with petty detail in what was on the verge of becoming a monstrous miscarriage of justice. The federal government had rules about bell ringing, but not about keeping the family apprised of developments in what was literally a matter of life or death.

No one had bothered to keep the RAF informed either, even though it had a liaison office within the government-office building in Ottawa. Mallory had been informed of the decision made by the governor general on 27 November, but by 14 December, that decision had still not been made public.

Finally, with fewer than thirty-six hours remaining before the execution was scheduled to take place, an RAF representative called the secretary of state's office seeking information.

P.H. Thibault, who worked in the under-secretary's office, had been the staffer who responded to Mallory's query regarding bell ringing. The RAF message landed on his desk, and he was ordered to 'Phone him – of decision and write also if he asks.'

Thibault's memorandum was subsequently placed in the Hutchings file:

After despatching the usual telegrams in this case, I tried to get in touch with Flight Lieutenant Jamieson, at local 2834, in order to advise him of the No Interference decision as requested. He was attending a meeting and could not easily be reached before the end of the afternoon. I made it clear to the gentleman who answered the phone that the matter was urgent and left my name, Department, and phone number.

Flight Lieutenant Alexander called this office a few minutes later and offered to take the official message for Flight Lieutenant Jamieson. I, therefore told him that the law would take its course in the case of HUTCHINGS, and that the official notification had been sent out. Upon inquiring whether the RAF would signal England, and inform the family, I was told by Flight Lieutenant Alexander that the RAF would do so. This telephone conversation took place between half past three and four o'clock this day.

The 'usual telegrams' to which Thibault referred had gone to Guss, Mallory, Judge Richards and Dickson. They went out over the signature of E.H. Coleman, the under-secretary of state and announced that 'the law will take its course'.

Barring any last-minute intervention, Tom Roland Hutchings had thirty-three hours to live.

Chapter Thirty-eight

Even though Mallory had been told to proceed with the execution, and the order had been confirmed, there was still a faint hope that Prime Minister Mackenzie King could intervene.

Guss had not given up hope. He had been away for Chanukah, which in 1942 began on 3 December and ended on 11 December, a Friday. When he returned to work on Monday, 14 December, he found M. F. Gallagher's brief note acknowledging the letter he had sent on 30 November stressing the jury's intention to exclude capital punishment from Tom's sentence.

He immediately sent a further plea to Gallagher:

> I have just returned to the office after an absence, to find your letter on my desk. I have been receiving a number of anonymous letters, one of them signed 'A Mother', appealing to me to do all I can to save Hutchings from the gallows. Although I have been out of the office for ten days and people must realize that I am terribly busy, I had two callers today and three phone calls from different people asking me what I was doing about saving Hutchings from the gallows.
>
> With Christmas so near, I do hope that something will be done to spare the boy's father, if no one else.

By this time, Tom was finally showing signs of agitation. Throughout his detention, and even throughout the trial, observers had marvelled at his composure.

Ever since the initial interview with Staff Sergeant Davis on 8 June, he had always cooperated fully with the authorities and had been consistently forthcoming. He had been polite and amenable with Mounties and jailers alike, always conforming to whatever they imposed upon him without complaint.

He had put forth no questions at his preliminary hearing, simply saying clearly and firmly, 'No, your honour', when asked at the end of each witness's testimony if he wished to do so.

According to newspaper reports, he had even appeared unconcerned during most of the trial. Presumably, the fact that he saw himself as innocent had a lot to do with this.

After all, the evidence is overwhelming that even if he was guilty of murder, which is all but impossible, he had no knowledge of it whatsoever. Given his staunch English upbringing and therefore intrinsic faith in the vaunted English legal system, he probably felt certain that as an innocent man, he had nothing to worry about.

Even when the death sentence was handed down by the judge, he had remained stoic. But by that time, it was a brave façade. The Mountie who accompanied him on the short walk from the courthouse to his cell in the adjacent jail was William Chahley. In a 1994 interview with researcher Dick Blatchford, Chahley said that Tom made the walk in total silence and seemed fully composed. But once he entered his cell he began to show signs of stress, wringing his hands and walking around his tiny confines in an agitated fashion.

It was Chahley's first murder case and he had been involved from beginning to end. He was the first Mountie on the scene on 7 June and was one of the group that had discovered the body of Bernice Connors. Furthermore, he had been assigned to sit next to Tom throughout the trial.

'He was a gentleman at all times,' recalled Chahley, who left the RCMP in 1947 to start a contracting business in Saint John. 'He was never flip, always polite. He was as cool as a cucumber. He was not a murderer.'

But by 14 December, after listening for three days to the sounds of a scaffold being built outside his jail cell and hearing the creaking, groaning and thumping of a 200lb bag of sand repeatedly being hauled up the thirteen steps and dropped through the hatch, he was genuinely depressed.

Ever since 24 September, when he had been brought back from Saint John County Jail, Tom had been held in his tiny St Andrews cell in solitary confinement. He was not allowed to interact with the other prisoners – if there were any, which wasn't always the case – but after the sentencing, Sheriff Mallory had developed an exercise plan for Tom during which he would be allowed into the corridor in the company of at least one guard for one hour a day. When the sheriff announced his plan, Tom simply nodded in acquiescence and conformed to it for the remainder of his stay.

Early in the evening of 15 December, with the execution scheduled to take place shortly before 2 a.m., only a few hours away, jailer George Goodeill, visited Tom in his cell.

Goodeill, who had succeeded his father as town jailer, had occasionally acted as a guard for the exercise regimen imposed by Mallory and lived in the back part of the building. His wife prepared all the meals, which Tom usually ate heartily.

He was a deeply religious man, and over the course of Tom's incarceration in St Andrews, the two had spent many hours talking. Partly because Tom frequently sat in his cell reading his Bible, they got along well and, as much as was possible under such constrained circumstances, became good friends.

There had never been lighting in any of the men's cells since the jail's construction in 1832, but Goodeill had found a way to run a wire down from the second storey, attach a socket and give Tom a bare bulb to read by.

He later said, 'Hutchings was the finest man you would ever want to talk to.'

That evening visit on 15 December was a long one, lasting by all reports until the execution party assembled. Goodeill always said that he would leave a record of the conversation, but as far as is known, he never did. Oral accounts from hints that Goodeill had passed along vary, but it seems likely that Tom gave Goodeill the same account that he had given Dr Menzies. As far as he was aware, he had not been involved in a murder.

That would fit with another unconfirmed report. In that one, George H. I. Cockburn, Clerk of the Circuit Court in St Stephen, was assigned the task of ascertaining Tom's wishes with regard to the disposition of his effects. Tom, as always, was polite and accommodating, so on his way out, Cockburn reportedly asked, 'Did you do it?'

Tom's reported answer was, 'I don't know sir, but a jury of my peers said I did, so I'll have to respect that decision.'

Goodeill had also seen indications that Tom accepted his fate. During one of their discussions around the time that summer was turning into autumn, Goodeill had warned Tom that the chill would get worse and that a St Andrews January tended to be very cold.

Tom's simple response was, 'I think I will miss that, old chap.'

Unless some hidden memoirs of Goodeill surface, no one will ever know what was said during his lengthy conversation with Tom on the night of 15 December. But it is clear that they talked almost until 1 a.m., when Tom received a group of visitors from 34 OTU at Pennfield. There was a chaplain, a doctor and RAF Squadron Leaders Mann and Stewart.

Sheriff Mallory's request had been met and all RAF leaves from Pennfield had been cancelled, but this quartet had been allowed to pass the roadblock that the RCMP had set up on the only road into St Andrews. As extra security, an RCMP cruiser constantly circled the block on which the courthouse and jail were situated and warned off any would-be spectators.

Shortly after meeting with his four OTU visitors, Tom walked unaided out of his cell. Newspaper reports of the day say that near the doorway, he stopped, turned, and went back in to his cell to turn out the light. This may be apocryphal, because there was no light switch to turn off. But he may have unscrewed the bulb, thereby attaining the same effect.

He walked back out of the jail door and rejoined the official execution party – Goodeill, Mallory, Squadron Leader Stewart, Dr Hugh Pius O'Neill, Dr R. A. Massie and Camille Branchaud.

Earlier, Mallory had wondered aloud as to the procedure if Tom should balk. Branchaud had assured all those in attendance that he intended to bring up the rear in the procession and if Tom were to hesitate, he would quickly and forcibly move him along.

But Tom did not falter. He resolutely mounted the thirteen steps and stood on the trapdoor while Branchaud covered his head with a hood and placed the noose around his neck.

If a hanging is done properly – with a pre-stretched rope of suitable length to produce the proper amount of drop, and the knot placed so that the head snaps sideways and the prisoner's neck breaks – it is a reasonably humane method of execution. Death is virtually instantaneous.

In 1961, testifying before the Royal Commission during the debate on capital punishment in Great Britain, Albert Pierrepoint, who hanged more than 400 people during his tenure as the government's official hangman from 1932 to 1956, explained the correct procedure.

'The knot is the secret of it,' he said. 'We have to put it on the left lower jaw. When he falls, it finishes underneath the chin and throws the chin back. But if the knot is on the right-hand side it will finish up behind his neck and throw his neck forward, which would be strangulation. He might live on the rope for a quarter of an hour then.'

In Tom's case, despite all of Branchaud's bravado and his assertion to Sheriff Mallory that 'You can count on me', he did a terrible job.

Either his calculations or his rope placement – or both – were incorrect and Tom's neck did not break. Instead, he strangled slowly, twisting on the end of Branchaud's rope for twelve full minutes as his life slowly and excruciatingly ebbed away.

THE WRONGLY EXECUTED AIRMAN

According to the official report filed by Dr O'Neill, the lever releasing the trap door was pulled at 1.50 a.m. 16 December. Tom died at 2.02 a.m. Later that day, in Ottawa, a letter was composed:

Dear Mr Guss:

Your letter of the 14 instant duly reached my office this morning together with a clipping from the press announcing the execution of Tom Roland Hutchings.

Yours very truly
M.F. Gallagher

Chapter Thirty-nine

Once Dr O'Neill declared Tom dead, the body was quickly cut down from the gallows. The winter wind was starting to pick up, and with it came the chill of an advancing front.

The St Andrews men in the execution party knew from experience what that meant. A blizzard was heading their way. They also knew they would have to return in the morning to carry out a series of mandated duties, and they wanted to spend what was left of the night in the warmth of their homes.

In that era, the standard procedure in Canadian executions would have required the body to be taken back inside the jail. But the St Andrews Gaol was tiny and had another occupant at that time. Also, George Goodeill lived there with his wife.

So instead, Tom's body was taken to spend the night inside the adjacent courthouse, back into the very courtroom in which he had heard Judge Richards sentence him to death some ten weeks earlier.

As had been the case ever since Tom had been charged, Mallory meticulously followed the designated procedures, and to that end, he had already made arrangements for the requisite Coroner's Inquest. By 10 a.m., all those who were to be part of the proceedings had come to the courthouse. Like all Canadians, they knew of necessity how to cope with snow.

Mallory had arranged for seven 'good and lawful men', of Charlotte County – six regular jurors and the foreman, J.R. Wren, who had taken time off from his duties as St Andrews harbourmaster.

Before the oral proceedings began, Mallory, Dr O'Neill, Coroner Dr Vance Maxwell and the seven jurors viewed the body as required. Then, responding to the set of customary questions from the coroner, Mallory testified that he was indeed the sheriff, that Tom had been in his custody, and that he had helped carry out the execution. He also confirmed that 'Tom Roland Hutchings was taken to the gallows when alive.'

Similarly, questions were put to Dr O'Neill in order to provide official confirmation that the state had executed the right man. Goodeill was also questioned and added further confirmation.

The jury then retired and quickly came back with the verdict that the man whose body they had seen was that of Tom Hutchings and that he had indeed been executed.

The coroner and seven jurors signed an attestation to that effect, and the county seal was affixed. Now it was official. It had taken an hour, but the mandatory government paperwork now asserted that Tom was dead.

However, Mallory's responsibilities were not finished.

He prepared a letter for the under-secretary of state in Ottawa. For the reference heading 'Tom Roland Hutchings' he used red capital letters. Underneath, he confirmed that 'The execution of the above took place in the vicinity of the hour of 2 o'clock a.m.'

He also said that, as required by Section 1072 of the Criminal Code of Canada, he was enclosing Form 71 signed by Dr O'Neill and Form 72 signed by himself and others.

Form 71 was O'Neill's confirmation that Tom was dead. Form 72 was Mallory's confirmation that Tom had been executed.

To put the under-secretary's mind at ease, Mallory added, 'A copy of the coroner's inquest proceedings will follow as they are at present in the form of being made up.'

After the inquest, Tom's body was moved downstairs in the courthouse to a spot directly below the judge's chambers. The intention was that it would be a brief stay because Mallory had made arrangements to have the body claimed by RAF personnel. Perhaps the RAF finally intended to do right by one of its servicemen and take Tom's body back to England to his grieving family. But if there was such a plan, the specifics of the arrangement have since been lost.

As it happened, even three days after the execution, the roads were still blocked. Heavy snows and high winds had created drifts that were impassable. With a great deal of perseverance, RAF trucks might have been able to get from Pennfield to St Andrews, but the personnel in those vehicles would have suffered. Truck heaters were barely functional in those days, and temperatures had dropped to -20 F.

It was almost understandable, therefore, that no one from Pennfield showed up to claim Tom's body.

Mallory responded by doing what he had done throughout the affair. He took charge and handled the matter as well as he could. He first arranged for the local undertaker to provide a casket for Tom. Then he and his brother, with Goodeill and Town Marshall Norman Johnson, took the body to the rural cemetery that provincial authorities had given them permission to use. As well as they could, given the fact that none of them had been ordained, they conducted a brief graveside service.

As far away from the cemetery's main path as possible, right against the fence, Tom's body was interred. An unmarked wrought-iron cross about 2 feet high was stuck into the ground.

That marker deteriorated over the years and was replaced by another white cross composed of two iron slats screwed together and painted white. This was more likely to have been done to prevent the area being dug up for another interment rather than to show any respect for the presence of Tom's body.

In the cemetery register, no name is written to record the name of the occupant of that plot. The notation simply reads: 'Occupation: murderer'. Even though there had been a strong sentiment against the hanging, Tom was still seen as Bernice's murderer and as a result, a good deal of animosity remained.

But people like Mallory and Goodeill who saw Tom on a daily basis knew that he was not the vicious, cold-blooded murderer who existed in the public perception.

They knew that understandably, fully aware that he was to be sent to the gallows for a crime he had no memory of committing, Tom was already distraught. There wasn't much they could do to exhibit their sympathy for his plight, but they did what they could.

They saw to it that Tom died not knowing that the brother he loved and admired had been killed in November.

Chapter Forty

Today, the grave of Tom Hutchings is not as isolated as it was in 1942. Some surrounding plots have come into use.

The white cross is still there, still unmarked. An even smaller white cross, its provenance unknown, is adjacent.

The military veterans in the cemetery are honoured by small crosses, designated as 'Placed by the Royal Canadian Legion', which are placed beside their headstones. Tom was not accorded one of those, even though he served his country for three years, most of it in wartime. The grave next to Tom's belongs to Bessie Clinch, a United States Army nurse in the First World War. She got a Canadian Legion cross.

But at some point, someone has made a rough facsimile of the Legion cross for Tom and put it next to his marker. It is the same size but made of wood and unmarked, except for the faded and now almost unreadable, handwritten 'RIP', on the left arm of the cross and 'GB 642564', Tom's regimental number, on the right arm.

For decades, Tom's grave was ignored, but recently, because St Andrews is a tourist town and reputed to be haunted in a number of locations, ghost tours have become one of the summer attractions. Tom's ghost, which has been said to be seen in the courthouse and the jail, figures prominently in those tours, and now, a bouquet of artificial flowers occasionally can be found on the grave that was shunned for so long.

Perhaps the St Andrews Legionnaires cannot be blamed for their assumption that Tom murdered Bernice Connors and their subsequent refusal to treat him with basic human decency, even in death.

Their approach reflected one that was far from uncommon in Charlotte County and it stands to reason that since Tom had received very little basic human empathy there while he was alive, the attitude wasn't likely to change when he was dead.

With only the rarest of exceptions, every person and every organization involved with Tom's case assumed from first exposure that he was guilty and subsequently acted accordingly.

Even the RAF, the body responsible for his presence in Canada, treated him in a remarkably shoddy fashion. Desertion is a serious crime in the RAF; but the RAF saw nothing wrong in deserting one of its number when he was charged with a crime in a foreign land.

He was left to fend for himself with no legal help from the RAF, no financial help and no guidance. The RAF didn't even bother to claim his body.

Recent research done by local historian Jason Gaudet – only a distant relation of the Gaudet family which figures in Tom's story – has determined that seventy RAF airmen stationed at Pennfield lost their lives during the war years. Most of those men were buried in Canada but some bodies were returned to England. Tom's was the only one that was disowned.

The New Brunswick Bar Association acted in an equally disgraceful fashion. Lawyers love to talk about the honour and ethics of their profession, but where was the honour in dragooning a defence lawyer who was young and inexperienced and refusing him all financial compensation when a man's life was at stake?

The prosecution had at its disposal all the resources the taxpayers could offer. Mounties from no fewer than four detachments were assigned to the case. Forensic experts were put to work. Even the sniffer dog was brought in to perform his specialty. The prosecution was given all the staff it needed. But the defence had nothing – in fact, less than nothing. Benjamin Guss even had to pay his own expenses and close down his office while he acted on Tom's behalf.

No wonder he didn't call any witnesses, even though Dr E.C. Menzies was so knowledgeable and highly respected that he alone could probably have swung the opinion of the jury. And he told Guss he was eager to testify. No wonder there was no independent investigation of the events of 5 June, no alternative theory put forward, no authoritative contradiction of the superannuated pathologist who found himself forced to decide on shock as the cause of death because he didn't notice the real cause.

The Royal Canadian Mounted Police keep their files secret as much as possible. Federal legislation enacted in 1983 opened some of the doors but even today, the Mounties are not known for willingly sharing their knowledge.

This is not surprising.

It is clear from the information that became available when the Hutchings file was finally accessed that the force routinely ignored information that didn't fit its theory and worked not towards justice but towards conviction of the person it deemed responsible, with or without justification.

Similarly, those in the judicial system should be ashamed of what happened to Tom. The judge appointed to handle the case was part of the New Brunswick ruling elite, a former premier of the province who was given a spot on the Supreme Court bench as a reward for a failed political career. He repeatedly sided with the prosecution which was represented by another leading light in the New Brunswick old boys' club, Peter J. Hughes KC.

Judge Richards had no problem allowing Hughes to make a travesty of courtroom decorum, procedure and precedent. As a King's Counsel, Hughes represented the best the legal profession had to offer, but he appears to have seen nothing wrong with joining the Mounties in paying off a witness. There are conveniently no RCMP files available to support this fact; there are only the repeated statements of the person who was paid.

Then, when it came time to review Tom's death sentence, this learned judge, who should have been the very model of impartiality, chose not to present the facts of the case from both sides, but instead to provide what he saw as a justification of his sentence, complete with incorrect testimony and illogical conclusions not supported by the evidence.

After it was all over, the transcript of the trial was sealed for fifty years and word was spread that the moratorium was 100 years, not fifty. This was presumably done to prevent anyone finding out what a travesty the whole proceeding had been, at least until after all the major players were dead.

The New Brunswick government, headed by John B. McNair who had awarded himself the post of attorney general, saw Tom as a nuisance whose presence stirred unrest. McNair's attitude seemed to be that the sooner Tom could be eliminated, the better.

Tom Hutchings was, by all reports a kind, gracious man. He was technically adept and highly regarded in his profession, the best in his unit according to his commanding officer.

He was not perfect. That can not be said. He was married but, while he was in the service at least, sought the company of other women.

Still, in his defence, it has to be conceded that it was wartime and he was away from home for extended periods. He was a 21-year-old male with normal urges. Many psychiatrists now believe that in time of war, people tend to drink more, have sex more, and be more aggressive.

CHAPTER FORTY

Tom's approach may not have been morally right, but infidelity was not a capital crime, and according to Dr Menzies, who seemed to be the only man in Canada who genuinely cared about Tom's plight, he truly loved his wife.

Tom had been in London and Coventry when the Luftwaffe was staging its blitz attacks and probably assumed a justifiable attitude of *carpe diem* because like all servicemen, he knew that any day might be his last.

And on 16 December, 1942, he was proved right, but that final day came at the hands of his alleged allies, the Canadians, and not the Nazis, whose onslaughts he had survived.

PART TWO

Chapter One

So what really did happen on the night of 5 June 1942? If Tom Hutchings didn't murder Bernice Connors, then who did?

There are a number of possibilities; but first, one crucial point must be stressed. While it is intriguing to hypothesize about those events three-quarters of a century later, it was never the responsibility of Tom or his defence counsel to do so at the time. They were under no obligation to provide an optional set of circumstances to counter those presented by the Crown.

The law was very clear on that point. Tom was to be considered innocent unless, based only on the evidence presented at the trial, his guilt could be proved beyond a reasonable doubt. But that is not what happened. He was found guilty despite mountains of reasonable doubt.

How could Tom possibly be considered *beyond reasonable doubt* to be guilty of rape based on the evidence, when no evidence of rape was ever introduced? And if there was no rape, there was no need for a capital sentence, so how did he deserve *beyond reasonable doubt* to be sentenced to death for a crime that was never shown to have been committed?

How could Tom possibly be considered guilty of murder *beyond reasonable doubt* when at least four witnesses (six counting the two who were not called to testify), including the one most likely to have been specific about the time, placed him 500 yards away from the location the Crown identified as the scene of the crime – at the time that crime appeared to have been perpetrated?

To be understood best, the events of 5 June 1942 should be broken down into two parts and considered separately. One part concerns what happened to Tom; the other concerns what happened to Bernice.

Start with Tom. Using the testimony available, it is known that at one point, he left the dance with Bernice. It is also known that he and Bernice were seen walking back towards the dance hall.

That much is known with certainty. Now for the speculation. Let's assume that the following events occurred.

Perhaps, a few moments after that sighting, a bout of pathological intoxication started to affect Tom and he began acting strangely, almost in a trance perhaps.

Dr Menzies stated the facts as plainly as he could, given the mores of the era. He said that Bernice was not new to sexual liaisons and was rarely lacking for a male companion. Carman Eldridge, who grew up with Bernice, made the same point. It therefore seems likely that if the escort of the moment started to show signs of abnormality, she would surely waste no time moving on to another.

Leading Aircraftman Albert Dungey, who had paid her admission to the dance, testified that she had made it clear to him that she did not consider herself to be his date for the evening. So perhaps once Tom began to behave in a bizarre fashion, she left him to fend for himself.

Tom, who had been known to walk into a lake fully clothed, this time started to wander off into the wooded area at the side of the road. But it had rained much of the day; the ground was slippery and he fell into the roadside ditch or one of the small ponds that tend to form in that type of topography.

In the process, he opened the cuts on his hands that he had suffered earlier that afternoon when he was working on the packing crates. When he put out his hand to break his fall, the water in the ditch splashed up and some got onto his face, so he naturally tried to wipe it off. In doing so, he transferred blood from the open cuts on his hands to his face.

It is also possible that he suffered a nosebleed. Even though Leading Aircraftman Protheroe, one of the men who wiped blood off Tom's face, said he saw no sign of a nosebleed, that point was never amplified. If Tom's nose had bled and he had wiped it off with his sleeve, what could Protheroe be expected to see? He was not a doctor. The light in the area was limited. The fact that he testified to seeing no sign of a nosebleed doesn't mean there hadn't been one.

By the time Tom staggered out of the ditch or pond, the arm of his tunic and the lower legs of his trousers near the cuffs were wet. Eddie Hutchings testified to the damp sleeve; Vincent Bradford spoke of the dampness on the trousers – much lower than the knee, he said.

In the first report he submitted to his superiors about Tom, Staff Sergeant Davis wrote, 'Three pieces of moss were found adhering to one of his socks, even after washing.' That report was not introduced at the trial and since Bernice was covered in moss, Davis no doubt saw it as an indictment of Tom. But the moss was common in the Black's Harbour area and could further support the theory that Tom walked into a wet area.

There is another option. There were a number of houses near the dance hall. Perhaps Tom stumbled up to one, was seen as an intruder, and got into a fight with the occupant, whose blood ended up on Tom. Also, it was not uncommon at the time for the police to be called because a serviceman from the Pennfield base was trespassing – or even sleeping – on private property. Perhaps Tom encountered such a person and a fight ensued.

After all, as Superintendent R.E. Mercer of the RCMP's J Division noted in a memo, 'the accused is quite a strong man.'

Whatever the case, Tom returned to the dance hall where he was spotted by Protheroe who told him that he couldn't go into the dance with blood on his face. Protheroe testified that Tom did not appear to be drunk but was in a dazed condition – as he would be when under the effects of pathological intoxication. Furthermore, he made no response of any sort when Protheroe asked him where the blood came from.

Because the amnesia that occurs during that condition prevented Tom from remembering that Protheroe had attended to him, it was only a few moments later when he asked Leading Aircraftman David Christie if there was blood on his face. Christie, who had arrived at the dance later than any of the other airmen who testified, and was therefore most likely to be precise about the time, is certain that it was very close to 12.15 a.m. when this incident occurred.

That was the approximate time that Leading Aircraftman 'Jeff' Humphries saw what he believed to be a copulating couple 500 yards away. After that sighting, he came back to the dance, grabbed his friend Leading Aircraftman Robert Moore and went back to the scene. The couple was still there. By now, it had to be close to 12.30 and if Tom hadn't been at the hall at 12.15, despite what Christie asserted, he was definitely there at 12.30.

Even the official RCMP Summary of Evidence submitted by Staff Sergeant Davis concedes that Tom was 'seen at 12.30 a.m. by numerous witnesses'.

Not a single item of sworn testimony contradicts a hypothetical scenario which sees Tom wandering off by himself and returning to the dance. There are even other aspects of the testimony that could be seen to support it.

For instance, the Crown made much of the fact that on Saturday, back at Pennfield, when Tom was cleaning his uniform, he pointed out to his roommate Eddie Hutchings a peculiar brownish tinge that could be seen on the cloth he was using when ironing the sleeve of his tunic. The Crown implied it was blood. But if that were the case and Tom knew that he had murdered Bernice, would he bring this discoloration to Eddie's attention? A ditch in a forested area like Black's Harbour is likely to contain tannin-stained water. If his arm had gone into the ditch when he fell, a tannin-stained sleeve is not an unlikely outcome.

Also, if Tom knew he had murdered Bernice, wouldn't he make sure that he had removed the blood from his face before going back to the dance rather than wait for two people to wipe it off? And why would he knowingly draw attention to it by asking Christie if there was blood on his face?

Put together, do not these very reasonable possible explanations of the events constitute reasonable doubt, as seen in the eyes of the law?

Now, look at the other half of the picture and consider what might have happened to Bernice. As far as the legal determination of Tom's guilt is concerned, that aspect is irrelevant. Tom was the one on trial and if the evidence wasn't sufficient to convict him, then he should have been acquitted.

But for the sake of interest, a chain of events that fits the testimony can also be constructed for Bernice.

Assume that when Tom started to wander off and fell in the ditch, she left him and started walking back to the hall. As she drew close, she was spotted by an airman who had just arrived from Pennfield, and was heading for the hall from the taxi rank. He had come to meet single women and here was one walking towards him, so he bypassed the hall, went directly to Bernice, and suggested a stroll down the road. Off they went.

Perhaps she already knew him. Perhaps she didn't. But when they got to the area where the four boys were lounging, she made the introductions. Alonzo Hall testified that she called her friend Whitey; Foster Eldridge said it was Mr White. This testimony was given during the preliminary hearing, but not all of it was repeated at the trial, even though it was available to Guss.

Either way, Bernice did not introduce the man as Tom or Roy or Mr Hutchings.

In the preliminary, another one of the boys, Donald Adams, said he heard the man say, 'Foster Eldridge'. This may just have been part of the introduction, but on the other hand, it may have been a sign of recognition. Perhaps 'Whitey' had met Foster Eldridge before, in which case, Bernice's companion could not have been Tom.

The couple left the boys, and when they got to the unlit section of the road, encountered Sergeant Tom Edwards and Mildred Justason. Edwards had no real idea who Bernice's companion might be. It was too dark and he was drunk. But he knew that Bernice had been with Tom earlier, so from the brief comment 'Whitey' made, he assumed that he had just encountered Tom, a person he hardly knew. When called upon to testify four months later, he said he identified Tom from his voice. In his original interview at Pennfield the day after Bernice's body had been found, Tom said he didn't know the man who had given him a drink of whisky. It turned out to be Sergeant Tom Edwards.

As Bernice and 'Whitey' continued down the road, they agreed to find a suitable location to have sex. Seeing a spot that was a little higher than the others, Bernice kicked off her shoes and they walked off the road.

By this time, Bernice was feeling the effects of Tom's bootleg liquor – which was almost certainly methyl alcohol. Perhaps 'Whitey' had given her more liquor. He too might have visited the bootlegger or brought legal alcohol with him.

The bootleg rum was of such a repulsive nature that seasoned drinkers like Leading Aircraftman Samuel Blakely and Sergeant Eddie Hutchings wanted nothing to do with it. Blakely said it 'tasted like methylated spirits', and burned his tongue. Eddie said he couldn't drink it because it was 'just too strong'.

As a result, Bernice began to feel sick and wanted to change her mind about the sex, but because 'Whitey' was insistent, she took off most of her clothes. Drunk and ill, she was lethargic, a fact which infuriated Whitey. He punched her in the face repeatedly, either in retaliation or in the hope of making her more active, and completed the sex act.

Bernice lapsed into unconsciousness and 'Whitey' panicked. He knew he hadn't hit her hard enough to kill her, but she was clearly unconscious.

After that, only the killer can explain the events. Since there were no signs that any attempt had been made to strangle Bernice, why was the knotted brassiere at her neck? Why were her other clothes neatly arranged? Why were her hands crossed and her legs placed together to make her look demure? Why was her body covered in moss?

These are curiosities, but as far as the outcome of the case is concerned, they don't really matter, other than they make the likelihood of Tom being the murderer even more remote.

Would he have had time to do the arranging? In a pitch-black field, wouldn't it take a long time to find enough moss to cover her body?

How long would it take him to drag her from the side of the road where the two were accosted by Humphries and Moore to the spot where the body was found?

It is reasonable to assume that after having sex, Bernice was still alive. But as Dr Branch conceded in his testimony, injuries inflicted upon a drunken person can do much more harm than they would if the recipient were sober.

Added to that was the amount of methyl alcohol Bernice had consumed. As Dr Branch discovered four years later when he did a report on the subject for the New Brunswick government, even one drink of methyl alcohol could be fatal.

In this case, judging by the discolouration in her face and tongue, Bernice almost certainly died of methyl-alcohol poisoning.

There is an explanation for the shoes as well. It is now known that some boys out playing on their bikes found them on Saturday morning. A 7-year-old picked one up and carried it for a while as they rode off. Further up the road, the group stopped and he dropped off the shoe. Perhaps at that point, one of the bikes fell over or perhaps the boys began playing and made marks in the gravel that were later identified as signs of a scuffle. The shoe was left there until Sunday. At no time did Guptill or any of the RCMP investigators try to fit the shoe heel to the indentations in the gravel to help confirm their theory.

Again, much of this scenario regarding the fate of Bernice is speculative. But as was the case with the hypothetical scenario explaining Tom's actions, nothing in it contradicts any testimony given at the trial or preliminary hearing – except for one point. The Crown, and apparently the jury, accepted Edwards' highly suspect recognition of Tom's voice. However, RCMP documents, not introduced at the trial, show that he had consumed most of a 26-ounce bottle of Scotch whisky. Tom had been given one drink from that bottle but Edwards had taken a drink of Tom's rum in return. Mildred had drunk a little.

But after the first meeting with Tom and Bernice, Edwards had carried on down the road with Mildred and had finished the rest – which he said was 'about 1½ inches' – before throwing the bottle away and walking back to the point where he identified Tom by his voice.

Even without knowledge of that fact, there is 'reasonable doubt' about Edwards' testimony, despite the opinions of both Staff Sergeant Davis and Judge Richards that it served as 'positive identification' of Tom. That was their evaluation, not a fact.

Most people given the job of assessing Edwards' testimony would see it as open to considerable interpretation.

Whatever the case, the scenarios presented above, while hypothetical, are eminently reasonable. There are other options that could explain the events of 5 June 1942, but these alone certainly provide what, in the eyes of the law, passes for reasonable doubt.

Chapter Two

Another optional scenario is based on the possibility that Sergeant Tom Edwards was the murderer.

In this case, the premise continues to be that Tom Hutchings suffered an attack of pathological intoxication, but the specifics of his absence aren't really relevant. The only assumption that needs to be made is that for one reason or another, he and Bernice parted ways after they were seen walking back towards the dance hall.

As any experienced criminal lawyer will attest, it is not uncommon for the chief investigator of a crime to decide early in the proceedings that he has identified the perpetrator. He might call it a hunch. He might call it a gut feeling. But whatever it is, it clouds his thinking and after that, his focus is less on solving the crime than on proving himself right and collecting evidence that supports his theory.

It is quite possible that this is what happened in the case of Tom Roland Hutchings.

RCMP Staff Sergeant Davis made no secret of the fact that as soon as he saw the body of Bernice Connors, 'I knew we were dealing with a sexual predator of the most violent type.'

Within minutes, he spoke to local residents and easily learned that Mildred Justason had been on Deadman's Harbour Road on the fateful night walking with Edwards. He also learned that Bernice had been on the same road at the same time in the company of an unidentified man.

In his report to J Division, the serious-crime section, Davis explained, 'It was absolutely necessary to discover the whereabouts of Sergeant Pilot Edwards as soon as possible to obtain the identity of the man seen walking with Bernice Connors.'

That's not an unreasonable approach. But no consideration ever seems to have been given to the possibility that the man seen with Bernice Connors at that point in the evening was not necessarily the man who murdered her.

CHAPTER TWO

It was the wee hours of Monday morning, less than three hours after his arrival on the scene and already, Davis was nearly certain that he had identified the killer.

He went directly to the Pennfield base and learned that Edwards had not returned from a 48-hour leave that began at midnight Friday and terminated at midnight Sunday. He had, however, notified his superiors that he would be on the overnight bus from St Stephen, where he had apparently gone on Saturday, and since he would arrive before 5 a.m., would not be considered AWOL.

Getting impatient, Davis left the camp, drove towards St Stephen and intercepted the bus. Having previously received approval from the RAF officers in charge at Pennfield, he took Edwards off the bus and drove him to the hotel in Black's Harbour where the Mounties had set up an incident room, their crime-scene headquarters.

Edwards, of course, identified Tom, who in Davis's report describing the events of that morning is twice referred to in one sentence as 'a most likely suspect'.

Davis immediately returned to Pennfield, was shown the RAF service record mentioning the alleged attempted rape in Nova Scotia and at 9 a.m., interviewed Tom. By this time, his mind was almost made up. As soon as Tom denied he had been on the road with Bernice, Davis was no longer in doubt. He had his murderer.

* * *

To this stage of the proceedings, there can be little dispute. The facts are clear. But now the murkiness begins.

Because Davis was so focused on Tom, the investigation into the activities of the other RAF men was cursory at best. Davis was told that Edwards and Mildred went back to her house after seeing Bernice for the final time, stayed for about half an hour, then returned to the hall and stayed there until the dance ended. This was confirmed to Davis by Mildred's mother.

Said Edwards, 'I asked a taxi to call for me, but he didn't call and I remained in Miss Justason's home all night, and caught the 7 a.m. bus to Pennfield the next morning.'

Mildred's statement was that she and Edwards 'went to my home and waited for the taxi, but it didn't come, and Tom stayed at our house overnight and returned to Pennfield air station at 7 a.m. the next morning.'

It would all seem to be conclusive if weren't for the fact that all three of them were shown to be notoriously unreliable.

Start with Mildred's mother. On 15 June, ten days after the dance, Davis's report stated that she had told him that Mildred had come in at midnight. She made no mention of Edwards being present.

But on 17 June, Mrs Justason gave a statement to Davis that read: 'My daughter and Sergeant-Pilot Edwards of the RAF came home from the dance. It was about 11.20 p.m. About 12.30 a.m. Mildred and Sergeant Edwards went back to the dance hall to get their coats. They stayed in the house from 11.20 until 12.30 a.m.'

Edwards told Davis, 'Mildred and I ran down to the hall to get our coats and when we arrived, we found it was only intermission.'

Mildred said, 'Tom and I ran to the dance hall for our coats before it closed but when we got there, it was only intermission. This would be about midnight.'

Since the intermission ended at 12.10 a.m., it is clear, therefore that Mrs Justason's recollections have to be treated with scepticism.

As for Mildred, her testimony concerning the group of boys and seeing bicycles where none existed has already been mentioned. But that was not the only inconsistency that emerged when she was on the stand.

'There was a group of boys standing just on the end of the pavement,' she testified. 'I did not recognize any of them.'

When Guss cross-examined her, he wasted no time pointing out that in the preliminary hearing, Mildred had said that the boys 'were going towards the dance hall and we were going the other way.'

Now she was saying they were standing. Mildred tried to argue her way out of it. 'I don't know that I said they were walking towards the dance hall,' she said. But Guss had a transcript of the preliminary hearing and read it to her. He was right. She was wrong.

Next there was the matter of her being unable to recognize any of the four boys. But one by one, Guss got her to concede that she knew Foster Eldridge, Alonzo Hall and Donald Adams, three of the four. And if she knew Foster Eldridge, she almost certainly knew Gilbert Eldridge. She still insisted she didn't recognize them.

She also said that she didn't see them drinking, although both of the boys available to testify said that they were drinking beer.

Her entire testimony has to be regarded with suspicion. She was interviewed by Davis the night Bernice's body was found and was asked about the discussion when she and Edwards crossed paths with Bernice and her companion for the second time. 'I don't recall what they said,' she told Davis.

But by the time she testified at the trial four months later, she had come to remember a conversation in which Bernice joked that, 'We don't know these people. We wouldn't even bother speaking to them.'

Mrs Justason says that Edwards left the house at 7 a.m. but it is only Mildred who confirms' Edwards' alibi that he was there all night. The reality is that Mildred's mother was probably in her own room and had no idea where Edwards was.

And did Mildred really know? Did Edwards and Mildred sleep together? Given the standards of morality that existed in 1942, even in Black's Harbour, it is more likely that he was supposed to be sleeping on a couch in another room.

Throughout the proceedings, it seems clear that Mildred would say whatever Edwards told her to say. She had obviously parroted his testimony during the trial, and now, her statements regarding their actions on the night of 5 June sound remarkably similar to his. Granted, if they were both accurate, that is to be expected. But on the other hand, they are so alike that they give the impression that they were rehearsed.

Mildred's story to Davis was that Edwards had tried to arrange a taxi after the dance and told her it would arrive at 2 a.m. At 1 a.m., they returned to her house to wait. At no point does Mildred testify that she saw Edwards again before the morning. She probably went to bed while he stayed up and knows only about there being no taxi because that's what Edwards told her.

Without Mildred, Edwards has no alibi and even with Mildred, he's on shaky ground at best. She admitted that she had been drinking and had helped Edwards kill a 26-ounce bottle of Scotch. And no mention was ever made of how much the two drank during their three hours together in Mildred's house prior to the dance.

The inconsistencies in her testimony during the trial show that she cannot be considered reliable. A number of other airmen testified that there were cabs after 1 a.m. that night. Tom and Eddie Hutchings both went home by taxi as did at least nine others.

Given that set of circumstances, is it possible that after Mildred went to sleep, Edwards went back on to Deadman's Harbour Road? Is it also possible that he met Bernice Connors coming back from a long walk, or perhaps from a consensual sexual encounter, or even from a brief spell when she had passed out, and raped and murdered her?

In this scenario, he would have had plenty of time to arrange the body and cover it with moss. It would have been easy for him to keep the knife that cut Bernice until he was ready to dump it at his leisure.

Did all this happen? No one knows. And if there were no further developments, it might appear to be nothing more than a wild, unfounded supposition.

But there were further developments.

* * *

On the afternoon of 9 December, only a week before Tom was scheduled to hang, a commercial traveller named John E. Wilson was passing time in the lobby of the Park Hotel in St Stephen where he was staying, having a chat with the wife of the proprietor, Mrs Guy Mann, and two others.

According to Wilson, when the subject of the impending execution arose, Mrs Mann said that 'One of the fliers was there the day after the murder and passed the remark that he had been at the dance in Black's Harbour the night before, there had been a fracas and there would be the devil or hell to pay.'

This airman, she said, 'was muddied and mussed'.

Wilson expressed his alarm and was told that the story came from Mrs Mann's daughter, Ruth, who got it from the chambermaid.

Wilson pointed out that an innocent man might be facing the noose and urged Mrs Mann to go through her records and find the name of the man who rented the room on 6 June.

Mrs Mann accordingly dug out a shoebox full of registration cards and enlisted her husband to help in the search. Eventually, they came up with the name.

RAF Sergeant Tom Edwards.

Ruth was summoned and confirmed her mother's version of the story. Had Ruth Mann been capricious or unreliable, Wilson might have thought no more of it. But in his subsequent statement to the RCMP, he said, 'I have known Ruth Mann since she was a little girl and she seems to me to be bright and intelligent.'

By the next day, Wilson's travels had taken him to Saint John. He had read that Benjamin Guss had been Tom Hutchings' defence attorney, so with the intention of passing along the story he had heard, he went to Guss's office. But Guss was away for Chanukah so Wilson spoke to another lawyer,

Ralph J. Broderick, and showed him the registration card from Edwards' stay in St Stephen.

Broderick took a statement from Wilson and sent a memorandum to the RCMP.

That memorandum got to Inspector S. Bullard, the head of the Fredericton detachment who described his actions in a memo to Inspector Fred W. Allen, the head of J Division.

'Upon receipt of this information, I discussed it with D/Staff Sergeant Davis who summed it up at once as idle gossip. I too am quite content that this is a case of someone talking for the sake of talking when we all know that the movement of the witnesses, particularly the witness Sergeant Tom Edwards, were gone into in detail during the investigation.'

This response is nothing short of mind-boggling. The report was immediately labelled as 'idle gossip' even though neither of the men had looked into it. The suggestion that Edwards' movements were examined in detail is particularly ludicrous. No one examined his movements at all. Mildred provided him with a shaky alibi and it was immediately accepted as gospel – as was his assertion that he had recognized Tom by his voice when he passed someone he couldn't see on the road.

By 10 December, the chambermaid had been identified as Audrey Jonah. Despite his announced scepticism, Bullard conceded that 'she should be interviewed, however, and a statement taken from her for what it may be worth.'

It appears that a statement was indeed taken. But for some reason, it does not appear in the package of RCMP files that is required to be released in order to conform to Canadian freedom-of-information legislation. Some reports on the Tom Hutchings file appear again and again, as often as four times. But this one is missing.

There is, however, a statement from Audrey Jonah given to the RCMP on 14 December. In it she said, 'I recall giving a statement to the Mounted Police on Dec. 10, 1942. I wish to add to this statement.'

By 'add to', she clearly meant 'recant'.

She admitted to having been the chambermaid on duty in Edwards' room and agreed that in her earlier statement she had said, 'around the first week in June 1942, I was talking with an airman called Tom and he was mentioning about the murder at Black's Harbour.'

In her 'addition' to the statement, she denied this. She denied that the airman's uniform was muddy. She denied there was any mention of a murder at Black's Harbour or anywhere else. She denied having told the story that

Ruth Mann said she heard. She denied that the airman said anything about a fracas. She denied that anyone even used the word 'murder'. She denied the airman said there would be hell to pay.

The clear implication was that she had said all these things in the now-missing statement she made four days earlier, but was somehow encouraged by the Mounties to change her mind.

Had she not recanted with such fervour, surely the execution could have been delayed – and eventually cancelled – in the face of this startling new evidence. If the airman she encountered knew about the murder on Saturday night, then he was the murderer. The body wasn't found until Sunday.

Could the Mounties have coerced her into changing her story? Could they have been so concerned about the possible embarrassment of having their body of evidence refuted that they would not bother to examine evidence to the contrary?

They certainly could, especially since it would necessitate a new trial with all the costs and political fallout that would entail.

For what it's worth – which probably isn't much but it should be considered – in her gossip-riddled and often inaccurate letter, Dot Denyea of St Stephen said, 'The one who took her out down there is said to have been up here Saturday night with another girl.'

The Mounties were probably justified in not giving that allegation much weight but was their approach to Audrey Jonah's statement also justified?

Policing was not as open in 1942 as it is now and it has already been shown that the Mounties bribed Vincent Bradford and told him what to say under oath. Staff Sergeant Davis was committed to proving himself right and he had long ago decided that Tom Hutchings was guilty.

Now, with Jonah's 180-degree swing in her allegations a mere four days after her first statement, the Mounties were not only back on solid ground, they were even given 'proof' that they were right all along and that Edwards could not have been the murderer.

A letter was sent to the New Brunswick deputy attorney general by Inspector Allen, the officer commanding J Division, the RCMP's serious-crime specialists. It contained the explanation that when Audrey said she had been told of a murder taking place the night before, 'it is obvious that she is in error since F/Sergeant Edwards and the general public were not then aware that a murder had occurred at that time.'

It may also be worth noting that in the course of their investigation, the Mounties examined Tom Hutchings' service file. They examined police records in England. They seized his clothes and examined them. They minutely examined his movements before and after the body was found.

Edwards, however, was merely taken at his word.

But in every murder case, the last person known to see the victim alive immediately becomes a prime suspect.

The last person known to see Bernice Connors alive was Pilot Sergeant Tom Edwards. Not only was his alibi accepted without verification, he was allowed to provide the only 'identification' of the murderer.

Chapter Three

Any fan of crime dramas knows that while the truth might seem readily apparent in the early stages of an investigation, the culprit often turns out to be someone who originally appeared to be innocent. Furthermore, the circumstances tend to be much more convoluted than anyone had suspected.

But in the case of the death of Bernice Connors, the investigation never really progressed past those early stages. Staff Sergeant Davis made up his mind that Tom Hutchings was the killer and looked at no one else. In fact, once he had interviewed Tom in Pennfield the morning after the body was found, he never interviewed him again.

He didn't go back, as is customary in a properly conducted investigation, and ask him to clarify discrepancies or further explain his actions on the night of 5 June.

He had asked once; Tom had denied he had been on the road with Bernice Connors although witnesses said he had; case closed.

But if asked to further explain his actions, Tom would probably have told Davis what he told Dr Menzies: He didn't remember being with Bernice and he threw away his rum bottle near the dance hall.

Davis did not hear this story because as soon as Tom was arrested, he was put in solitary confinement in St Andrews while Davis worked in Black's Harbour or Fredericton.

But had his view of the proceedings not been so blinkered, Davis could have searched the brush near the dance hall and tried to find the bottle. If he were successful, he could have checked the bottle for fingerprints. If Tom's were indeed all over it, then he certainly did not kill Bernice Connors.

When Bernice was last seen walking away from the dance hall, she first encountered the group of four boys, then Sergeant Tom Edwards with his girlfriend Mildred Justason.

When they were with the boys, Bernice's escort proffered a bottle of rum.

Therefore, if Tom had already thrown away his bottle, he couldn't have been the man with Bernice. It had already been determined, from the evidence of the other airmen, that he had only one bottle. If he hadn't thrown it away near the dance hall as he told Menzies, then where was it? Where did he discard it?

It certainly wasn't anywhere near the mound of moss where the body was found. According to the testimony of Constable Prime, who was asked on the stand about a search of the crime scene, 'the ground was very thoroughly gone over by five or six policemen. They spent two days going over it.'

The Mounties also searched both sides of the road, but apparently not for bottles that looked to be recently discarded. They searched for blood-stained rocks and said they found some – about 300 yards from the dance hall and 200 yards from the body. Obviously, therefore, they had the personnel available to do a careful search. But as was the case with Tom's clothing, they didn't bother to send the rocks for testing until it was too late to determine blood type.

There is no evidence that when Tom was seen by Leading Aircraftman Protheroe coming back to the dance, he had a bottle with him.

So if the Mounties had bothered to search the bushes near the dance hall and found the bottle where Tom said it was dropped, it would go a long way towards proving his innocence. It wouldn't be indisputable proof. The prosecution would still be able to contend that Tom had committed the murder, snuck back to the area of the dance hall, crept unnoticed into the bushes, dropped his bottle, and then emerged to meet Protheroe. But it would not be easy for a jury to accept such a convoluted turn of events.

All this was moot, however, because the Mounties had no interest in proving Tom's innocence, only his guilt.

Apparently, no investigation into the toxicity of the illicit rum was undertaken either. There was no doubt about the source of the bootleg liquor, and a statement was taken from the man who provided it, Earl Watson, corroborating Tom's story regarding its purchase. But there is no mention in the RCMP files of any subsequent charges being laid or of the rum being subjected to analysis to determine its potency.

If it were shown to have a high alcohol content, Guss would have been able to construct a defence based on drunkenness, as the judge pointed out.

But that aspect aside, there was another factor related to the rum that should have been considered.

It was such a foul substance that later in the evening, Tom vomited behind the dance hall while he and Eddie were waiting for a taxi.

When Leading Aircraftman 'Jeff' Humphries and Sylvia Gaudet first became aware of the couple they encountered – having sex as Humphries testified in so many words – it was the sound of vomiting that alerted them to someone's presence.

Was any attempt made to compare the two residues? Apparently not, even though, had they been shown to be similar, it would have given the Mounties the evidence they so badly sought of Tom's having been present at the scene.

The vomit near the crime scene could have been crucial to Tom's defence. Had the Mounties found some, it could have been compared to the contents of Bernice's stomach because some small amounts of similar undigested material would have remained there.

And if that were the case, then she was clearly awake and capable of letting Humphries and Gaudet know if she felt she was being raped.

Even without the vomit, it seems fairly clear from the testimony that it was Bernice who was ill. Dr Branch testified that her stomach was empty, so the obvious conclusion can still be drawn. She was vomiting and had she wanted to complain about her circumstances, she could certainly have done so.

But there were plenty of inconsistencies in this case, one of the most notable having to do with the amount of blood. Even though there is repeated testimony regarding 'lots of blood', and, 'excessive bleeding', there was never any satisfactory explanation as to the source of this blood. Bernice had a 2-inch cut under her chin, a ¾-inch cut on her scalp and some minor cuts in her mouth. There was no internal bleeding. Yet somehow, Dr Branch saw his way clear to say she lost so much blood that she entered into a state of shock that killed her.

It seems simply incomprehensible that his decision regarding the cause of death was allowed to stand. Blood can't just materialize. It has to have a source and a 2-inch cut doesn't provide one unless it's along an artery or a vein. This cut wasn't.

Perhaps Bernice had a nosebleed, even though Branch said there was matted blood in only one nostril and it was 'of no significance'. That could have been the source of a small portion of the 'excessive bleeding'. But even if that concession is made, nosebleeds are not generally recognized as a cause of death.

Scalp wounds do tend to produce an inordinate amount of blood but when they're as small as the one Bernice suffered, they're still no more than a minor wound, certainly not fatal.

CHAPTER THREE

The tangible evidence presented in court included what Dr Branch called Bernice's 'blood-stained' blouse. But Tom's only cuts were those on his hands that he got from opening packing crates. They could have produced some blood, but not enough to provide the amount that subsequent testimony suggested was in evidence.

So either the pathologist was wrong in his estimation of blood loss or the blood came from the murderer.

If it is the former, then how many other mistakes did he make? If the latter, Tom was innocent.

In either case, it is clear that the pathologist left a lot to be desired. He himself admitted that he designated shock as the cause of death only because he couldn't find any definitive reason and considered shock to be a catch-all. He found alcohol in Bernice's stomach but did no test for methyl alcohol. He noted that her hair was 'matted in front and wet in the back' but didn't test to see whether the water in Bernice's hair was salt or fresh – despite the fact that he said she had seaweed adhering to her body.

Long after the trial, the wet hair and the seaweed gave rise to some local speculation that perhaps Bernice had not been killed on Friday night.

That theory, even though highly speculative, could be supported by some of the facts.

Bernice lived not far from the dance hall but in the opposite direction from the spot where her body was found. To get home, she had to skirt a small salt-water inlet. The theory was that she had decided to go home, rather than back to the dance, and had been accosted along the way. At some point there was a struggle, during which Bernice's head went into the water. She was subsequently killed and her body was put in a nearby shed overnight.

She was left there all day Saturday, then at night, her body was taken down Deadman's Harbour Road to the location in which she was found on Sunday evening. The killer took the time to arrange her hands and feet in what Davis called 'a normal fashion', and cover her body with moss.

But the killer wanted it to be believed that someone who had been at the dance had killed her. As a result, her body had to be discovered fairly soon so that the time of death could be readily established.

To make sure that happened, the killer left a trail of clues. He dropped her necklace in the middle of Deadman's Harbour Road. He hung her panties on a bush. Surely if those items had been in those places on Saturday, they would have been spotted.

The flaw in this theory is that a shoe was found near the body and its mate was found up the road. The second one, according to a later revelation, was moved on Saturday. Panties can easily be moved by passers-by as well. And if Bernice was walking home on Friday night, she wasn't likely to have left her shoes at a spot 500 yards in the other direction.

The best way to explain the apparent anomaly about the hair and the seaweed is the simplest one. Dr Branch was an Englishman who lived in Saint John, and the local moss was peculiar to Black's Harbour and unfamiliar to him. He mis-identified it as seaweed. Bernice's hair was wet because there had been rain on Friday and when she was put on the ground, her head came to rest in a small puddle.

Over the years, other theories surfaced. In most cases, they could be considered plausible to some degree, but their problem was that they lacked supporting evidence.

It was suggested, for instance, that one of the owners of Connors Brothers Ltd. was the culprit and because he was also a federal senator, was able to exert enough clout to get the Mounties to frame Tom Hutchings.

There was even a story that with food being at such a premium on the other side of the Atlantic, a corporate raider wanting to take control of the sardine company had kidnapped Bernice with the idea of trading her for ownership. Something went amiss and she died in captivity. That variation was the least plausible. Bernice's family no longer had any financial interest in the company and if you're making ransom demands, you don't kill your captive on the first day. Nevertheless, it was a story that circulated.

One that made much more sense, even though there was no proof of it and it was never investigated by the RCMP, was that Bernice was wandering down Deadman's Harbour Road by herself when she met a man coming in the other direction.

Deadman's Harbour Road ends 4 miles from the dance hall at Beaver Harbour, which was a flourishing port in that era and as such, attracted a number of disreputable characters, especially on ships coming from Europe. It was suggested that she was attacked by such a person who then walked back to Beaver Harbour and left with his ship before the body was discovered.

But none of these hypotheses, from the sensible to the highly improbable, was investigated by the RCMP. They were sure they already had their man.

Chapter Four

After all the evidence had been heard, after all the theories had been shared, after all the inconsistencies had been considered, was it clear that Tom Roland Hutchings murdered Bernice Connors?

The Crown made the case that it was, and presented enough corroboration for that stance to convince the jurors.

But what happens if the question is approached from the other direction? Instead of having the prosecutors show evidence to support their contention that Tom was guilty, and challenging the defence to prove them wrong, let's do it the other way. Start with a defence contention that Tom did not kill Bernice Connors and challenge the Crown to prove it wrong.

Under that scenario, the defence would begin its case by attacking one of the major weaknesses in the Crown's case.

'Tom says he was never at the so-called scene of the crime – which, by the way, was never proved to be the scene of the crime. What evidence do you have to show he was ever there?'

The Crown would have none.

'Tom says that any blood on his clothing was his own. What evidence do you have to show that any of it belonged to Bernice Connors?'

The Crown would have none.

'Tom says that Bernice Connors exhibited all the symptoms of methyl-alcohol poisoning and that was the cause of her death. What evidence do you have to show that he is wrong?'

The Crown would have none.

'Tom says that in the past, he has suffered from pathological intoxication and that on the night of 5 June, he had another attack. What evidence do you have to prove him wrong?'

The Crown would have none.

'Tom says that at least six witnesses place him at the dance hall shortly after the intermission ended at 12.10 and certainly no later than 12.30. Even the official report of Staff Sergeant Davis concedes that he was seen 'by numerous witnesses' at 12.30. The testimony of Leading Aircraftman 'Jeff' Humphries is that he twice saw a copulating couple 500 yards from the dance hall. The first time, Humphries was in the company of Sylvia Gaudet; the second time in the company of Leading Aircraftman Robert Moore. He walked back with Gaudet and arrived at 12.20. When he walked back with Moore, he arrived between 12.40 and 12.45. Can you give an explanation for this discrepancy?'

The Crown would have to take the same stance as the judge – that all the others were wrong about the time.

And really, after all the discussions regarding cause of death, sources of blood, identification of escorts, and the various other peripheral aspects, this is where the Crown's case has to rise or fall.

Either that was Tom down the road in a compromising situation, or it was someone else and Tom was near the dance hall in the clear view of Leading Aircraftman William Protheroe, Leading Aircraftman David Christie, Eddie Hutchings, Vincent Bradford, Corporal Harold Walker and Corporal Cyril Griffiths.

Those six people – all in an illuminated area – said they saw Tom. That is the defence's stance.

To accept the Crown's repudiation of that point, you have to believe that Moore, Humphries and Sylvia Gaudet saw Tom Hutchings 500 yards away. Two of them said it was so dark they wouldn't have known anyone was there had they not heard the sound of vomiting. All three admitted it was too dark to see anyone's face or even badges of rank. They say they were no more than 5 feet from the couple. Yet the Crown said those three must be right and the five in a well-lit area were wrong.

It is sometimes hard for city dwellers to comprehend how dark it can be on a cloudy night in a rural area. There are no streetlights, no passing cars, no illuminated buildings. It is relentlessly black and neither the stars nor the moon can provide enough light to penetrate the clouds. In such circumstances, the mind can play tricks. A waving weed can look like an animal. A cat can look like a porcupine. Even Gaudet and Humphries, standing side by side, couldn't agree upon what they saw.

So does the testimony of these three repudiate that of the defence that Tom was not at the scene?

If it does, a dubious proposition at best, what does the Crown contend happened next? Every witness asked about the point says that Tom was at the dance hall at 12.45 a.m. But if that was Tom down the road, then Moore and Humphries were at most five minutes ahead of him when they returned.

CHAPTER FOUR

In those five minutes, Tom had to take the body of Bernice Connors and drag it 20 feet or so. Then in pitch-black surroundings, he had to make her appear as demure as possible. He had to fold some of her clothes and lay them across her body; he had to fold her arms and partly clasp her hands. He had to place her legs a few inches apart. He had to wipe her face because according to Dr Branch, someone had done that. He had to gather moss and make a neat pile of it over the length of her body.

Then he had to dash back to the dance hall to have blood wiped off his face by both Protheroe and Christie, be seen by three others, and have all of them be completely wrong about the time.

But astonishingly, that is the scenario that the Crown got the jurors to believe.

Those men can't be blamed. They gave every indication of being well-meaning local citizens who were guided towards a questionable conclusion by an unscrupulous lawyer and a politically oriented judge And they were given no reason to doubt that conclusion because the defence lawyer was either incompetent or uninterested or both.

It is also certain that the judge's meandering verbosity led them to agree to a verdict that carried implications they did not understand.

The bureaucrats in Ottawa who were supposed to examine the trial transcript and undertake independent medical evaluation before confirming the death sentence did neither. They simply read the self-justifying reports of the people who had brought about the death sentence in the first place and shrugged their collective shoulders.

The governor general, a man sent from England to represent his nephew, King George VI, joined the parade. In his job, he had little to do but deal with the minutiae of the post and could very well have undertaken a proper examination of the verdict. He didn't. He decided that 'the law will take its course'.

The RAF, for reasons that were never made clear, stayed as far away from the proceedings as possible, facilitating nothing more than regular visits by a chaplain.

Tom Roland Hutchings was in Canada trying to help with the war effort. He was an ally who fully intended to return to his loving wife, his year-old daughter and his devoted father.

But the Canadian judicial establishment put him to death primarily because he was a sick man whose affliction prevented him from providing an alibi for himself. They ignored the protests of the jury that the death sentence was never their intention. They ignored the inescapable fact

211

that they were inflicting capital punishment on the basis of evidence that was totally circumstantial. They ignored the diagnosis provided by Dr E.C. Menzies, one of the country's most respected and benevolent medical authorities. They even ignored the heart-breaking plea from a grieving father:

EARNESTLY APPEAL FOR YOUR MERCY REGARDING MY SON I SERVED THROUGHOUT LAST WAR JUST LOST ELDER SON IN THIS WAR FEEL GREATLY DISTRESSED.

They were unmoved. They hanged Tom Hutchings slowly for crimes he did not commit.

And they wouldn't even put his name on his grave marker.

Sources

The King vs Tom Roland Hutchings before R. A. Nason Esq., Police and Stipendiary Magistrate for the Parish of Pennfield, County of Charlotte. Black's Harbour N.B., 2 & 3 July 1942.

The King vs Tom Roland Hutchings before Rt. Hon. Charles Dow Edwards, Supreme Court of New Brunswick, King's Bench Division, Charlotte County Circuit the Court House, St Andrews N.B., Sept. 29 – Oct. 6, 1942.

Walsh, David A., *Occupation Murderer*, (2002) St Andrews, N.B., Black Swan Publishing Inc., ISBN 1–894312–02–3.

Index

INDEX